S0-BJS-477

*The
Logic of
Markedness*

The
Logic of
Markedness

EDWIN L. BATTISTELLA

New York   Oxford
OXFORD UNIVERSITY PRESS
1996

Oxford University Press

Oxford   New York
Athens   Auckland   Bangkok   Bogota   Bombay
Buenos Aires   Calcutta   Cape Town   Dar es Salaam
Delhi   Florence   Hong Kong   Istanbul   Karachi
Kuala Lumpur   Madras   Madrid   Melbourne
Mexico City   Nairobi   Paris   Singapore
Taipei   Tokyo   Toronto

and associated companies in
Berlin   Ibadan

Copyright © 1996 by Edwin L. Battistella

Published by Oxford University Press, Inc.
198 Madison Avenue, New York, New York 10016

Oxford is a registered trademark of Oxford University Press, Inc.

All rights reserved. No part of this publication may be reproduced,
stored in a retrieval system, or transmitted, in any form or by any means,
electronic, mechanical, photocopying, recording or otherwise,
without the prior permission of Oxford University Press.

Library of Congress Cataloging-in-Publication Data

Battistella, Edwin L.
The logic of markedness / Edwin L. Battistella.
   p.   cm.
Includes bibliographical references and index.
ISBN 0-19-510394-7
1. Markedness (Linguistics).   2. Chomsky, Noam—Contributions in
markedness.   3. Jakobson, Roman, 1896– —Contributions in
markedness.   I. Title.
P299.M35B37   1996
415—dc20   96-18869

9 8 7 6 5 4 3 2 1

Printed in the United States of America
on acid-free paper

Acknowledgments

I am indebted to the National Endowment for the Humanities for providing me with a Fellowship for College Teachers, which enabled me to complete the research and writing of this book. An Instructional Improvement Grant from Wayne State College also provided valuable resources for this project at a crucial stage.

Some of the research here was presented in very preliminary form at the Vilém Mathesius Workshop on Linguistics held in the Czech Republic in April of 1993 (funded by the Soros Foundation), and I benefited from the feedback of the other participants. Preliminary versions of some of the ideas presented here appeared as an article titled "Jakobson and Chomsky on Markedness" in the *Travaux du Cercle Linguistique de Prague* (Battistella 1995). Catherine Chvany and Michael Shapiro provided helpful comments on an earlier draft, and I thank them as well.

I gratefully acknowledge the Roman Jakobson Trust for permission to cite materials from Jakobson's *Russian and Slavic Grammar Studies 1931–1981*, edited by Linda R. Waugh and Morris Halle (Berlin: Mouton de Gruyter, 1984), and *The Framework of Language* (Ann Arbor: Michigan Studies in the Humanities, 1980); and from Jakobson and Pomorska's *Dialogues with Krystyna Pomorska* (Cambridge: MIT Press, 1983).

Contents

The
Logic of
Markedness

Introduction

Twentieth-century linguistic theories have developed the idea of hierarchy within language structure largely in terms of the concept of *markedness*, a concept that entails certain aspects of language being *marked* while others are *unmarked*. The marked versus unmarked distinction is shared by both Chomskyan generative grammar and Jakobsonian structuralism, though each intellectual tradition treats the idea differently.

In the Jakobsonian view, markedness ranges over the synchronic and diachronic oppositions of a language's structure and function, and the marked or unmarked character of elements is determined by examining the language as a system of oppositions that reflect conceptual and perceptual properties, some of which are universals. In the Chomskyan view, universals are both more central and more abstract: markedness is part of a metatheoretical Universal Grammar that is drawn upon in language acquisition. Learning is likened to the fixing of innate parameters, some of which are unmarked (existing as default hypotheses), others of which are marked (and thus require additional evidence to deduce).

Markedness has often been recreated and reconceptualized even within a single linguistic framework. Jakobson's work on the topic spanned more than fifty years and dealt with not only grammar, meaning, and sound structure but also with aesthetic and social categories. And within generative linguistics, markedness has been treated at various times as an economy metric, as a set of defaults, and as a classificatory scheme for data. In continually refocusing markedness, Jakobson, Chomsky, and their associates have produced a web of overlapping and related concepts that need interpretation and reconciliation.

The Logic of Markedness is a study of the development of this concept in the structuralism of Roman Jakobson and his intellectual descendants, its importation into generative linguistics, and its subsequent development within Noam Chomsky's Principles and Parameters framework.

3

The book traces how both structuralist and generative theories have expanded markedness as a way of characterizing linguistic constructs and as part of a theory of language. The purpose of the book is not to propose a new theory of markedness, but rather to clarify the evolution of the concept and its treatment in two different, but related, frameworks.

In my 1990 book, *Markedness: The Evaluative Superstructure of Language*, I attempted to illustrate a present-day incarnation of Prague School markedness by analyzing structuralist criteria for determining marked and unmarked oppositions, applying markedness to English syntax and phonology and to language change and discussing the role of patterning and asymmetry in language. The present project, by contrast, aims at uncovering the historical parallels and divergences in the way markedness has been developed by Jakobson, Chomsky, and their respective followers. I focus here mainly on grammar and semantics, and the ultimate goal is to discern whether there is a common core to Jakobson's and Chomsky's views of markedness.

In a sense, this book is my own reaction to my earlier work. When I originally began thinking seriously about markedness, my first goal was to both treat its historical development and illustrate its current status. I quickly abandoned the idea of doing that in a single book and settled into the task of organizing and illustrating a contemporary view of structuralist markedness, drawing on Jakobson's early ideas and on additional criteria that emerged in the 1960s, 1970s and 1980s. As markedness became increasingly important in generative syntax, and as I delved more deeply into some of the historical issues, the plan for the present book took shape.

Areas of overlap between the two books have been kept to a minimum by treating a number of new topics here in *The Logic of Markedness*, including Jakobson's views on aphasia and some structuralist approaches not discussed in the first book. In addition, a major portion of this book deals with markedness in generative grammar and in Principles and Parameters syntax, topics that did not fit into the exposition of the earlier work.

I have also tried to structure this book in such a way that it doesn't presuppose having read the first one, not just by eliminating overlapping content but by developing the main theme historically rather than conceptually. I of course would be happy for people to read, and even enjoy, both books, but readers should know that the first work was intended for those interested in an explication and illustration of structuralist markedness. This book, by contrast, is intended for those who are interested in markedness in generative grammar and for those who are interested in the intellectual history of markedness and the connections between generative and Praguean approaches.

The first half of this book focuses on treatments of markedness in Jakobson's work and in the work of his structuralist and functionalist heirs. The second half is about the generative tradition, beginning with Chomsky's work, continuing with other generative work on markedness, and treating the relation of markedness to core grammar, to parameterization, and to issues of learnability. Chapter 1 introduces the concept of markedness and presents the main issues that the book addresses. Chapter 2 is a historical survey of Jakobson's views on markedness, beginning with his earliest work in the 1920s and 1930s and continuing through to his final synthesis in the late 1970s. Chapter 3 discusses the work of linguists who have taken up various leading ideas in Jakobson's treatment of markedness, focusing on the iconism of value, the advocacy of invariance of meaning and its relation to neutralization and markedness reversal, approaches to language universals, and functional explanations for linguistic asymmetries. Chapter 3 also provides some further examples and synthesis of the structuralist approach, exemplifying markedness with data from naming conventions and English punctuation. Chapter 4 parallels chapter 2, providing a historical survey of Chomsky's views on markedness, beginning with the notion of the evaluation metric and the incorporation of markedness in Chomsky and Halle's *The Sound Pattern of English* and moving on to the "Conditions on Transformations" approach, the core grammar approach, and Principles and Parameters theory. Chapter 5 discusses theoretical work in syntax that develops the generative conception of markedness, expanding on themes introduced in chapter 4 and covering work by van Riemsdijk, Koster, Hyams, Kean, Lasnik, Pinker, Bikerton, Manzini and Wexler, and Lightfoot. To conclude, Chapter 6 summarizes the key aspects of the evolution of markedness and contrasts some of the overarching themes in the work of Jakobson and Chomsky, including formalism, universals, and the role of autonomy.

Finally, a few terminological notes: when I use the term *language*, for the most part I mean *language and other sign systems*, though I am attempting to keep things concise by referring to both as *language*. Similarly, the terms *speakers* and *language communities* can be understood as sign users and sign communities, respectively. The term *asymmetry* also requires comment, in that different writers use the term in different ways. I've used it both to indicate the nonequivalence found in language and to designate certain types of feature relations, though the usage at any given point should be clear from context. I have used standard linguistic abbreviations: NP for noun phrase; V and VP for verb and verb phrase; INFL for the Inflection categories of a clause; COMP for the clause-initial complementizer; and S and S' for clauses. Square brackets have been used to denote feature labels. Finally, I've also attempted to follow the usual convention in generative grammar of capitalizing the word *case* when it refers to the abstract grammatical feature associated with the Case theory module of core grammar. Thus it is capitalized in chapters 3 and 4, but not in other places.

ONE

On Markedness

The Greek philosopher Democritus proposed that matter was made up of units he called *atoms*, units he could not see but which he believed explained the properties of matter. Democritus was ridiculed for his ideas, yet today every chemistry student knows that Democritus was right. Of course the concept of the atom that we have as we approach the twenty-first century is quite different from the atom as Democritus conceived it. Examples like this can doubtless be multiplied, since whenever there is progress in a field, the meaning of its technical terms evolves. As a consequence, every discipline develops certain problematic terms that have been expanded beyond their original definitions.

In linguistics there are many such problematic terms: *deep structure, logical form, phoneme, grammar*, even *rule* have all been construed in different ways.[1] The focus of this book is one particular problematic linguistic term: *markedness*, a nominalization referring to the relation between constructions, rules, and features said to be *marked* and others said to be *unmarked*. The marked versus unmarked dichotomy is one of the key concepts in both the theory of generative grammar developed by Noam Chomsky and the theory of structural linguistics advanced by Roman Jakobson.[2] It has been used in areas of linguistics ranging from descriptive and typological to applied, and it has been borrowed into fields as diverse as anthropology, art, music, poetics, and literature.

The concept of markedness, as developed in both Jakobsonian and Chomskyan schools of linguistic thought, has its origins in the analysis of binary oppositions between abstract classificatory features and has been extended in each framework to questions of language acquisition and decay and to linguistic universals. Yet it has developed in very different ways in each of these traditions. Moreover, the meaning of markedness has not remained constant even within a single intellectual framework.

Jakobson's work on markedness spanned more than fifty years, and while his interdisciplinary outlook ultimately led him to view markedness as a property of all signs, his focus at different times on grammar, sound, aesthetics, and culture resulted in a wide range of positions. Within Chomskyan linguistics, which has been concerned with markedness for more than twenty-five years, the concept has also been refocused at various times as part of a simplicity metric for grammars, as a means of categorizing language structures and rules, and most recently as a set of default hypotheses for language acquisition.

The term markedness then presents a special sort of problem—one in which a concept is reflected in a multiplicity of technical notions within a field and within different traditions in a field. The problem has not gone unnoticed, of course, and many have commented pessimistically on the diversity of definitions and approaches to markedness.[3] Others have tried to sort out the diversity, a task that involves looking at both the definition of markedness and its application. We might think of the definitional issue as the logical basis of the principle of markedness together with an examination of its empirical consequences. We might think of the applicational issue as the practical basis of markedness analysis—how we can determine what is marked and what is unmarked. Needless to say, the two issues are intertwined.

The definition of markedness has been plagued by a chicken-and-egg problem: whether markedness is a theoretically primitive property of language or whether it can be reduced to some other independent property or set of properties. Put another way, the problem is this: does markedness explain other linguistic properties, or do other linguistic properties explain markedness? If the latter is the case, one must ask whether there is any need for the term markedness at all.

Both the definition and application of markedness also involve a correlation problem (which is related to the chicken-and-egg problem). Many definitions of markedness entail or imply a set of correlations between marked and unmarked categories and other properties, such as augmentation, frequency, differentiation, and so on. The correlation problem is that of distinguishing correlative properties from defining ones. Which of the possible consequences of marked/unmarked status are definitive and criterial and which are merely options or tendencies?

The application and definition of markedness also involves a consistency problem at several levels. One aspect of the consistency problem concerns whether markedness relations are universals or language-particular asymmetries or both. In other words, do we determine markedness values—what is marked and what is unmarked—by looking at the facts of a single language or at the facts of many? And if markedness is both language-particular *and* universal, are we dealing with two different concepts?

Another aspect of the consistency problem involves the reversal of markedness values—whether markedness is a general property of an opposition in a language or whether values are sometimes reversed in different contexts. If the latter is the case, the problem of determining markedness values extends to delimiting the conditions under which reversal is possible.

The consistency problem extends as well to the issue of what types of entities may be marked or unmarked and to the generality of markedness. It could be that only certain types of linguistic entities may be in a marked/unmarked relation—phonological distinctive features, for example, or parameters of Universal Grammar. Or markedness might range over any category of sound, grammar, meaning, and beyond. The generality of markedness impinges on the question of whether markedness is a property of all sign systems, and therefore to some degree theory-independent, or whether it is tied to a particular type of linguistic theory.

There are, as we shall see, different approaches to these questions. One way to organize them is to begin by surveying some (though certainly not all) of the leading ideas that have arisen as linguists have tried to define what markedness is, themes ranging from a general view of information content to theory-particular hypotheses about language acquisition. We turn to this first. Following that, we look at some of the possible correlations and criteria of markedness that have been proposed. Finally we survey the range of applications of markedness in linguistics. The goal of this introductory section is to provide a sense of the diversity of markedness in contemporary linguistics, and perhaps a hint also of some common themes and concerns.

LEADING IDEAS

Catherine Chvany has identified one of the main themes of markedness in her observation that the "key word uniting all kinds of markedness . . . is *informativeness*" (1985: 248). Much work on markedness takes a semiotic view, being concerned with the information content and information value of an element. Thus, Linda Waugh wrote in a 1976 article in *Language* that for the domain of meaning, marked "refers to the necessary presence of the information given by the feature in all the contexts in all the uses of the particular item" (1976b: 85). On the other hand, unmarked "means the information given by the feature X is not necessarily present in all the contexts where the unmarked form occurs. . . . It

remains neutral, uncommitted" (1976b: 86). In an article in *Semiotica* a
few years later, Waugh glossed markedness more broadly as "the asymmetrical and hierarchical relationship between the two poles of any opposition" (1982: 299), involving elements "endowed with a mark" and "non-
endowed with that same mark." The marked term of a grammatical
opposition shows a "constraining, focusing characteristic" and "necessarily conveys a more narrowly specified and delimited conceptual item
than the unmarked" (301). Waugh's view is one version of a semiotics-
based program that conceives of markedness as a structural principle underlying a system of oppositions. These definitions echo the chord struck
by Nikolai Trubetzkoy's early definition of opposition as involving a relation that "acquires in the linguistic consciousness the form of an opposition between the presence of some feature and its absence,"[4] a definition that stresses both the language-particular nature of the relation and
its connection to the conceptualization that speakers of a language have.
Other recent semiotic approaches emphasize the connection of markedness to conceptualization as well. Henning Andersen (1979:378–9) notes
that markedness in phonology is a property of the relation between the
"two signs of a diacritic paradigm," which is "in part independent of
linguistic substance [i.e., articulation and perception] and should be defined primarily as conceptual." Michael Shapiro takes a similar view,
associating semantic markedness both with reference and with conceptual complexity. He writes that "[t]he marked term of an opposition has
a narrowed referential scope, while the unmarked term is broader in the
scope of its application to the field of reference" (1983: 16), adding that
more narrowly defined means "of greater conceptual complexity" (79).

Some linguists have noted the similarity between marked/unmarked
categories and the notion of figure/ground and have characterized
markedness more prosaically in terms of norms within a language, drawing implicitly on the idea that less informative, less conceptually complex
elements will be the norm and that more informative, more complex
elements will be somehow foregrounded. Aert Kuipers (1975) describes
markedness figuratively as whatever is unusual in a particular context (a
distinguishing typeface or color, for example). James McCawley (1985:
23) equates unmarked with "normal" and marked with "special" or exceptional.[5] George Lakoff (1987: 60) sees markedness as "an asymmetry
in a category, where one member or subcategory is taken to be somehow
more basic than the other (or others)," while John R. Ross (1987: 307),
who equates markedness with the notion of prototype, identifies prototypical elements by combinability and productivity. Related to this, or
perhaps underlying it, is the idea that speakers and language communi-

ties develop a "conceptual rapport" (Moravcsik and Wirth's term, 1986: 1) with certain familiar types of categories that constitute norms.

What accounts for such a conceptual rapport? Bernard Comrie suggests that the broad answer is that markedness reflects "independently verifiable properties of people, the world, or people's conception of the world" (1986: 85), and one aspect of this could be that we develop a conceptual rapport with categories because they are simple and common. Comrie's description of markedness also suggests that the idea of norms and normalcy within a language can be extended to naturalness across languages, based in part on the hypothesis that recurring norms reflect natural properties and that universals of experience will engender recurring asymmetries. Following Jakobson (1968a [1941]), some linguists have attempted to tie the notion of naturalness to properties of communication channels and communication events. The German natural morphologist Willi Mayerthaler, for example, defines unmarked as "in agreement with the typical attributes of the speaker" (1988 [1981]: 8), and others have suggested that unmarked properties are those that are typical of speech situations or which facilitate information flow (incorporating factors ranging from communicative and cognitive ease to cultural and biological preference).

The questions that arise when we consider the shift from norms to naturalness are the extent to which norms must be natural and, more generally, the relation between language-particular and universal asymmetries. If it is the case that cross-linguistic naturalness determines universal marked/unmarked relations, it is still possible that particular languages might have internal norms that differ from the majority tendencies. For example, the unmarked pronominal case in English is objective (see Battistella 1990: Chapter 3), though cross-linguistically the nominative is unmarked in nominative/accusative languages. Similarly, the phenomenon of preposition stranding is the norm in spoken English, but it is marked cross-linguistically. In the domain of cultural oppositions, the difficulty of positing universal markedness values is even sharper. To take a rather commonplace example, consider the wearing of socks. Wearing socks is unmarked in much of Western culture, but it is not inherently natural nor do cross-cultural tendencies seem particularly relevant to determining its markedness value.

The idea that certain linguistic asymmetries can be attributed to universal properties of sound, meaning, or communication raises the possibility of stating markedness relations as implicational universals, that is, as relations in which the presence of a marked option implies the presence of its unmarked counterpart. This opens the way to using the marked/unmarked relation to make predictions about language development and language change.

However, the possibility of universal marked/unmarked relations is attenuated by other factors. One is the observation that asymmetry is often context-sensitive. This makes markedness a local rather than a general phenomenon (see Tiersma 1982) and means that context must always be considered when determining markedness values. It could be, of course, that the contextual aspect of markedness is given universally, but this is by no means easy to show beyond the level of phonology. A related concern about universal implications arises from the fact that many asymmetries can be reversed among different speech communities, time periods, or registers.

Themes of conceptual complexity, norms, naturalness, and universals may be considered theory-independent, since in their broadest use they ultimately rely on little more than the insight that language is a system of relations. In some approaches to markedness, however, these themes are intertwined with further theoretical assumptions about linguistic structure or function. Jakobson's phonological and grammatical theories, for example, are tied to a particular inventory of distinctive and conceptual features, as is van Schooneveld's approach to semantic structure. Shapiro's and Andersen's value-based approaches are embedded in a view of markedness principles that define a notion of goodness-of-fit for a language.

Markedness in generative grammar illustrates the key theme of universals as well, though in a more theory-particular way. Chomsky's work in what has become known as the Principles and Parameters theory links naturalness and implicational universals with an explicit concern for the acquisition problem for grammars, a leading idea being that unmarked aspects of grammar arise naturally in the course of language learning with little or no effort or evidence required, while marked aspects of grammar require more specific evidence and more effort to learn. The Principles and Parameters approach is so named because it involves abstract explanatory constructs of grammar—invariant principles and predetermined parameters—rather than traditional categories or relations between elements. The theory-internal view of naturalness that results cannot therefore be connected transparently to what is natural in communication situations or in ordinary human experience.

Views on markedness in the Principles and Parameters theory have not developed without some variation among themselves as well. Definitions of markedness range from its being "a function which maps linguistic data onto a particular grammar" (Hyams 1986: 156) to a theory "that leads to the preference of one parameter setting over another" (Lightfoot

1991: 186) to simply "the study of how languages can differ from each other" (Williams 1981: 8). Chomsky himself distinguishes three different senses of markedness in his 1986 book *Knowledge of Language*, and as we will see when the details of some current views are considered, there are a number of different ways of implementing a theory of preference in generative grammar.

CORRELATIONS AND CRITERIA

As should be evident by now, the term markedness covers a range of concepts. Some attempts have been made to tease apart the concepts underlying this term and to distinguish between different types of markedness. Jakobson, for example, maintains a distinction between *phonological markedness*, which involves categories whose meaning is mere differentiatedness, and *semantic markedness*, which involves conceptual categories that signal meaning as well as distinctiveness. Catherine Chvany, who has attempted to bring the Jakobsonian and Chomskyan approaches together by foregrounding similarities in their approaches to grammatical features, has distinguished two *levels* of markedness: one for inherent "specification of asymmetric syntactic or semantic features" and another for "markedness values that are relative to context" (1985: 248–9; see also Chvany 1993). The first she sees as part of semiotics, the second as an aspect of information theory. And as noted just above, Chomsky distinguishes three types of markedness: the distinction between an unmarked core grammar and a marked periphery, and preference structures both within the core and within the periphery.

There are other possibilities as well. John Lyons, in his book *Semantics*, distinguishes what he calls three types of lexical markedness: *formal marking* (formal elaboration, as in *lion* vs. *lioness*), *distributional marking* (restriction in range of contexts), and *semantic marking* (specificity of meaning, as in *old* vs. *young*) (1977b: 304–7). Lyons's classification takes the step of treating correlates of markedness (such as formal marking and distributional restriction) as types of markedness themselves. This is perhaps a useful expository technique, but it may be ill-advised in other ways, since it implies that a correlative factor like the presence of an affix is a defining criterion for a type of markedness. Zwicky (1978) distinguishes seven kinds of markedness in morphology: *material markedness* (Lyons's formal marking), *semantic markedness*, *implicational markedness*, *abstract syntactic markedness*,[6] *productive markedness* (productivity), *stylistic markedness*, and *statistical markedness*.

Some approaches to markedness have taken the opposite approach to splitting, treating markedness as a cover term for a number of criteria.

Mufwene (1991: 124), for example, suggests that "[m]arkedness in grammar is determined by a variety of factors, such as syntactic distribution, semantic transparency . . . , generality of meaning, and salience." Witkowski and Brown (1983: 569), though they primarily discuss markedness in terms of longer versus shorter forms, see it as defined by a set of eight criteria "that tend to co-occur in typical marking relationships."

Joseph Greenberg's 1966 *Language Universals* takes this approach in a different direction, surveying various properties of marked and unmarked categories (as described by Jakobson, Trubetzkoy, and Hjelmslev) and ultimately concluding that, while markedness lacks a precise definition, frequency serves as the most useful diagnostic.[7]

Greenberg's work illustrates the tension between the chicken-and-egg problem and the correlation problem. On the one hand, assuming that frequency (or any other single criterion) is the defining one reduces markedness to another concept. On the other hand, assuming that markedness is an open-ended set of properties results is a kind of "and/ or" view in which markedness has no central definition. The "and/or" view is what Moravcsik and Wirth take to be the contemporary core notion, remarking that "[t]he one of the two entities that is consistently more widely distributed and/or simpler and/or more richly elaborated is called 'unmarked' " (1986: 3).

The "and/or" approach draws attention to diagnostics of markedness as either criterial for determining asymmetry or as merely correlative. The criteria or correlations that have been proposed (or assumed) in the literature include those mentioned above: formal marking, syncretization, neutralization, semantic indeterminateness, typological implication, frequency across languages, frequency within a language, breadth of distribution within a language, language change, productivity, combinability, regularity, stability, learnability, and prototypicality. Some of these we have already identified, but others require glossing. Syncretization refers to the lack of subdistinctions in certain categories—for example, the common situation in which the singular shows gender distinctions that the plural does not (cf. *he, she, it* vs. *they*, where gender is syncretized in the plural). Neutralization is an originally phonological criterion that has been extended (not always clearly) to the situation in which some context requires cancellation of the contrast between the members of an opposition.[8] Productivity and combinability are variants of distributional criteria that are most applicable to grammatical oppositions and lexical oppositions. Regularity refers to paradigm shape and the susceptibility of a paradigm to exceptions, while stability has been interpreted as resistance to lexical and pragmatic factors and to dialect variation

(Koster [1978, 571], for example, describes marked constructions as being less stable and showing "differentiation across languages, variation in judgement, and susceptibility to lexical and nongrammatical complexity factors.") Prototypicality refers to a language's norms of feature co-occurrence—what features occur together. Implicational relations refer to cross-linguistic generalizations about features that presuppose other features. And diagnostics involving language acquisition and language change reflect the hypothesis that unmarked categories serve as a foundation for language acquisition and as a target of language change. On occasion, there are special criteria that play a role only in certain domains. Phonology, for example, traditionally has relied on the idea of phonological simplicity as phonetic naturalness (that is, as a correspondence with some neutral articulatory position).[9] And the study of adjectival antonyms has a set of specialized tests (see, for example, Lehrer 1985). To the extent that the criteria and expectations of marked and unmarked categories are mutable, it is difficult to treat any of these criteria as defining.

One possibility is that markedness is simply a cover term for a vague categorial asymmetry in which one element dominates its opposite. Another possibility is that the "and/or" view provides a set of useful heuristics for tacking about in the data to determine markedness values but that certain foundational aspects of markedness should take precedence over ones that are merely correlational.[10] Certainly one goal of the study of markedness must be to distinguish correlational properties from criterial ones, or at minimum, to clarify this relation. Moravcsik and Wirth (1986: 3) see the "core hypothesis of markedness theory" as being that the diagnostics of markedness will have converging results and that the criteria should be logically independent. In this view, the theory of markedness is a theory about correlations.

Work on markedness often goes beyond the minimal task of clarifying the criterion/correlation relation. A number of researchers have suggested specific ways in which markedness plays a role in language description, change, or acquisition. The last chapter of Chomsky and Halle's *The Sound Pattern of English*, for example, suggests that grammars as a whole may be more or less marked to the extent that they make use of preferred options provided by a general linguistic theory defined on the basis of language universals. The idea that markedness plays a role in defining the optimal grammar has other incarnations as well. To take just two examples, Lapointe (1986) proposes that grammars are less marked if they combine simple meanings and simple forms, and Shapiro (1983) suggests that iconic patterns of markedness values among units and contexts define a notion of a grammar's goodness-of-fit. Moreover, diachronic studies in both structuralist and generative frameworks have advanced the hypothesis that the direction of language change involves a reduction of markedness (or a gradual increase of markedness followed by a sudden reduction). And the idea that unmarked elements are somehow easier to learn has been used in studies of both first and second language acquisition as a predictor of the order of language acquisition. So "markedness theory" ranges over correlations, definitions of grammatical preference, and predictions concerning language history and acquisition.

MARKED AND UNMARKED

One issue yet to be raised is the question of what entities can be marked or unmarked. Markedness has been applied to a wide variety of data, with different approaches focusing on different levels of analysis. The earliest applications of markedness analyzed phonological correlations (Trubetzkoy 1931) and grammatical opposites (Jakobson 1932). A number of subsequent studies by Jakobson and others (see Waugh 1982; Shapiro 1983; Battistella 1990; Chvany 1992; Croft 1990; Givón 1990; Mayerthaler 1988 [1981]; Tobin 1993, 1994; van Langendonck 1986) have extended the analysis of grammatical oppositions. Others have extended markedness to connect grammar and discourse categories as well. Givón (1990, Ch. 21), for example, gives the following set of unmarked/marked categories in discourse:

> oral/written
> informal/formal
> conjoined/embedded
> morphologically sparse/morphologically abundant
> flexible word order/rigid order
> high context-dependence/low context-dependence
> human affairs subject matter/academic subject matter
> conversational/narrative
> main clause/subordinate
> declarative/manipulative
> affirmative/negative
> active/passive
> continuative/disruptive
> agent semantic role/other roles
> subject grammatical role/other roles
> continuity of reference/definite reference

In generative linguistics, markedness has been applied to grammatical rules, to rule orderings, to constructions, and to abstract parameters. In addition to proposals about marked and unmarked feature systems, we also find suggestions about the treatment of irregularity (G. Lakoff 1970, R. Lakoff 1968), the application of rules (Taraldsen 1981), and the domain of rule application (Muysken 1981).[11]

It has also been suggested that different linguistic and stylistic processes are markings or unmarkings, that is, that they increase or decrease markedness. Lehmann (1989), for example, proposes that grammaticalization is an unmarking and lexicalization is a marking. Shapiro (1983) has suggested that truncation is generally an unmarking, while augmentation is a marking. Liszka (1989) proposes that euphemism is an unmarking since it attenuates the force of language, while vulgarism is a marking since it augments it. And Jakobson, Waugh, and Shapiro have all suggested that metaphor is the unmarked troping mechanism in poetry while metonymy is unmarked in prose.

In addition, markedness has also been extensively applied to lexical opposites, a possibility first suggested for masculine and feminine nouns by Jakobson (1932). Typical examples of lexical markedness involve adjective pairs like the following:

tall/short
long/short
big/small
old/young
far/close
close/distant
smart/dumb
good/bad
happy/sad

Here the lefthand terms are the unmarked ones, and they represent the enveloping property of height, length, size, age, etc.[12] In general, categories that reflect magnitude appear to dominate in adjectival and adverbial oppositions. It has been suggested that the word *more* is unmarked and the word *less* is marked (see Clark 1970, Donaldson and Wales 1970) and that the *more/less* asymmetry is confirmed by the differential ease of acquisition of these items.

Markedness has also been applied to other lexical fields. In a recent textbook, Finegan and Besnier (1989) illustrate markedness by proposing that the color terms *blue, red, yellow, green, black,* and *purple* are unmarked, while *indigo, saffron, royal blue, aquamarine,* and *bisque* are marked.[13] Waugh (1976a) exemplifies unmarked versus marked with, among other examples, *go* versus *walk* and *in* versus *at* (*go* and *at* being less informative and thus unmarked). Lehmann (1989) suggests that *horse* is unmarked as compared with *mare*, *stallion*, and *colt*, noting that *horse* is the neutral equine term, lacking specification for sex or age. Zwicky's (1978) discussion of stylistic markedness suggests that the "formal or poetic" *dreamt* is marked as opposed to *dreamed*, and that "informal or jocular" *snuck* is marked as opposed to *sneaked*.

Markedness has been vigorously extended to extralinguistic concepts as well. Waugh (1982) suggests that oppositions like male/female, white/black, sighted/blind, hearing/deaf, heterosexual/homosexual, right/left, fertility/barrenness, clothed/nude, and spoken/written, among others, can all be analyzed as cultural oppositions between unmarked and marked categories. Jakobson was also prepared to apply markedness to any "historico-cultural" oppositions, explicitly mentioning the pairs life/death, liberty/bondage, sin/virtue, and holiday/working day. More recently, McCawley (1985) has given an example from religion in American society, suggesting that belief in a certain type of supreme being is culturally unmarked, while other options (atheism, agnosticism, belief in a nonprototypical supreme being) are marked.[14]

As I noted previously, the disparate nature of markedness has been a cause for pessimism in some quarters, and confusion in others. Yet, I believe that recurring themes in the development of markedness will enable us to make sense of it. In what follows I trace aspects of the development of markedness in the work of Jakobson and Chomsky and in that of scholars and researchers influenced by them. One of my purposes is to clarify the similarities and differences among the many versions of markedness. However, I will not necessarily strive to resolve these differences. This work is an attempt not at the optimism of a renovation, merely at the antipessimism of a good housecleaning.

Why should we be concerned with studying the development of markedness? There are two compelling reasons, I think. First and foremost is that its various incarnations are related historically, and a better understanding of the different versions will help us place contemporary research in a broader intellectual context. In addition, the range of uses of markedness in each framework has shifted over the years, and a critical examination of the unfolding of the concept can tie up loose ends and bring to light unargued, outmoded, misguided, or conflicting assumptions.

Ultimately, I hope to determine two things. The first is whether there is a theory of markedness at all. The second is to what extent the concept of markedness in different linguistic traditions is the same concept—in other words, how much of a common core exists between various markednesses?

TWO

The Development of Markedness in Jakobson's Work

The terms *marked* and *unmarked* were developed in the intellectual atmosphere of early twentieth-century, eastern European structuralism. While the basic insight of categorial asymmetry was recognized by a number of earlier scholars, markedness has received its most enduring and expansive treatment in the work of Roman Jakobson, who embraced the concept in the 1930s and developed it throughout his long career.

One of the central tenets of the structuralism pioneered by Jakobson and Nikolai Trubetzkoy was the idea of phonological correlation, defined by Jakobson in the 1928 "Proposition au Premier Congrés International de Linguistes" as "a series of binary oppositions which share a common defining element" (1928: 3). It was in the context of the search for correlations among phonemes that the terms *marked* and *unmarked* were first proposed. Trubetzkoy's *Letters and Notes*, published in 1975 under Jakobson's editorship, are often cited as containing the first use of the terms *marked* and *unmarked*.[1] In a now famous letter of July 31, 1930, Trubetzkoy suggested that a phonological correlation "acquires in linguistic consciousness the form of an opposition between the presence of some feature and its absence." He went on to add parenthetically that the opposition might also be "between the maximum and minimum of some feature" (1975: 162).[2]

As Baltaxe (1978) and others have noted, Trubetzkoy saw marked correlations as connected both with phonological alternation and with the physical nature of sounds, that is, he saw them as having both a logical nature and a phonetic one.[3] The logical nature of the marked/unmarked relation permitted it to vary from language to language, and Trubetzkoy cited instances in which the linguistic consciousness of speakers of different languages characterized features such as voicing or length in different ways.[4] The linguistic consciousness of speakers appears to have been the intuitive feel for simplicity that speakers of a language have, which Trubetzkoy equated with freedom from any secondary articulation (see Trubetzkoy 1931, 1969 [1939]; and Baltaxe 1978: 42). In his work in the mid-1930s, Trubetzkoy associated markedness increasingly with the logical operation of neutralization and restricted it to just those oppositions that could be neutralized.[5] In Trubetzkoy's last work, his 1939 *Principles of Phonology*, neutralization is taken as the defining criterion of unmarked status, and linguistic consciousness is a factor only insofar as it is connected to neutralization. In *Principles*, Trubetzkoy also observed (drawing on the work of George Zipf) that unmarked sounds could be expected to be more frequent because of a connection between neutralization and frequency, a theme later taken up by Joseph Greenberg and others.

Roman Jakobson's most important work on phonological markedness did not appear until more than a decade after Trubetzkoy introduced the terms *marked* and *unmarked*. Instead, Jakobson's early work focused on marked and unmarked correlations in semantic categories. That this should be the case is not surprising in light of Jakobson's November 26, 1930, reply to Trubetzkoy's letter, where he embraces the marked/unmarked correlation as having "significance not only for linguistics but also for ethnology and the history of culture" (Jakobson and Pomorska 1983: 95).

The first published application of the marked/unmarked relation to morphological meaning was in Jakobson's 1932 article "The Structure of the Russian Verb." Here Jakobson, citing Trubetzkoy's 1931 article "Die phonologischen Systeme," treats nonequivalence as an "essential" property of phonological oppositions and notes that it can be applied as well to morphological categories and lexical opposites. Jakobson also briefly alludes to the intellectual background of the concept of asymmetry in the work of such Russian grammarians as Aksakov, Nekrasov, Vostokov, Fortunatov, Šaxmatov, Karcevskij, and Peškovskij.[6]

"Structure of the Russian Verb" provides the first of several definitions of the marked/unmarked relation in Jakobson's writings. Jakobson develops the view of semantic asymmetry as the opposition between the marked "signalization of A and the [unmarked] non-signalization of A" (1932: 12), where by "A" he means some property of "given reality." The crucial aspect of this definition is that the unmarked sign may either indicate the opposite of the marked sign or it may indicate a broader concept that merely "makes no mention of this mark" (12).

In applying markedness to linguistic material, Jakobson attempts to establish morphological correlations in traditional terms, though he adds

a codicil concerning the "inexactness" of such terms. Drawing on traditional descriptions of Russian grammar, Jakobson surveys the verb system and suggests which categories are marked and unmarked on the basis
of their meaning and use. Jakobson also introduces his idea of levels of
meaning, proposing that the unmarked form has both a "general" meaning, which is equated to the nonsignalization of the mark, and a "partial"
(later called "specific") meaning, which is the signalization of the opposite
of the mark (in other words, the signalization of non-A). Thus the general meaning of the nonpast tense is nonspecification of past; its specific
meaning is present tense.

Jakobson concludes the article by discussing the function of marked
and unmarked categories in language, that is, how the meaning difference between marked and unmarked categories is played out in other
aspects of language. "Structure of the Russian Verb" sets the stage for
much of Jakobson's later markedness theory, foreshadowing topics and
themes to which he returns in later works. Citing Karcevskij, Jakobson
suggests that "the asymmetrical structure of the linguistic sign is an essential prerequisite for language change" (1932: 12). He also raises the
issue of the substitutability of the unmarked for the marked, suggesting
that the unmarked category often takes the place of the marked one—as,
for example, with "the replacement of finite forms by the infinitive, the
preterit by the present" (11) and so on.[7] He speculates that unmarked
categories tend to be represented by zero rather than nonzero endings,
and he suggests here for the first time that marked and unmarked grammatical categories play a role in the speech of aphasics, prefiguring a
theme of his 1941 *Child Language, Aphasia and Phonological Universals*.[8]

In the course of his later grammatical studies, Jakobson returns to
markedness often, connecting it in various ways to his broader views of
linguistic and semiotic structure. Of particular interest are his two studies of the Russian case system, (his 1936 "Contributions to the General
Theory of Case" and its 1958 sequel "Morphological Observations on the
Russian Cases"), his follow-up study of the Russian verb ("Shifters, Verbal Categories, and the Russian Verb," published in 1957), and his 1939
paper "Zero Sign."

Before turning to these, I should mention one of the important early
reactions to Jakobson's use of marked and unmarked categories in semantics by Louis Hjelmslev, the Danish founder of the theory of glossemat-
ics. As Henning Andersen (1989: 15–8) notes, Hjelmslev's 1935 *La catégories des cas* associated markedness with the value of a category, rather
than with its meaning.[9] In this and later works, Hjelmslev incorporated
markedness into his theory of "participative relations," which viewed inclusion as fundamental to language. In his view, traditional, exclusive

logical relations such as contradiction and contrariness were special cases of inclusion relations (see Andersen 1989: 18). According to Andersen, Hjelmslev viewed markedness not in terms of an item's meaning—which could vary from language to language—but in terms of its "value" in a language. Hjelmslev's focus on value thus emphasized reference potential and the use of categories rather than their meanings, and it provided a perspective on markedness similar in some respects to that developed by Trubetzkoy for phonology.[10]

In his 1936 piece, "Contributions to the General Theory of Case: General Meanings of the Russian Cases," Jakobson revisits his view of semantic analysis, in part as a reaction to Hjelmslev.[11] Jakobson attempts to determine a unitary general meaning for each Russian case in the context of an overall case system. While his 1932 analysis of the Russian verb had relied on traditional semantic categories, here he treats cases as analogous to phonemes, as bundles of semantic features. Jakobson identifies, for example, the Russian nominative as the unmarked case form and the accusative as marked for a feature of directionality of action, capturing the traditional notion that the object is the goal of the action. In analyzing the case system, Jakobson reiterates and sharpens his previous definition of marked and unmarked as involving a mark of "objective reality" (1936: 70). He also sharpens the definitions of general and specific meaning and their connection to distinct uses of the unmarked term, maintaining that the unmarked term refers to both the nonsignalization of α (its absence or irrelevance) and to the signalization of non-α (the opposite of the mark α). In the course of his analysis of marked and unmarked cases, Jakobson moves beyond the domain of semantic features to examine marked and unmarked uses of grammatical constructions involving case. For example, he remarks that the use of the nominative as subject is "naturally perceived as unmarked," in contrast to uses that suspend the difference between nominative and accusative (70). Thus active constructions are unmarked uses of the nominative, and passive constructions are marked uses. The idea of marked and unmarked uses of a case departs from the mere use of features to describe specification versus nonspecification of meaning, thereby adding a second function to markedness.

Toward the end of "Contributions to the General Theory of Case," Jakobson also raises the issue of case syncretism, which he describes as a "constitutive factor" of language. Syncretism involves the way in which different categories are differentiated into subcategories, and Jakobson argues that marked categories tend to show less differentiation (1936: 97).

One further important observation is that the marked/unmarked case relationships need not be the same in all languages. Jakobson emphasizes that such languages as Basque and Northern Caucasian have markedness relations that are the reverse of those in Russian and other nominative/accusative languages since "in [Basque and Northern Caucasian] the marked case does not imply that the referent is the object of an action, but, to the contrary, that the referent subjects something to an action, while the unmarked case does not have this implication" (1936: 71).

While his 1936 piece was devoted to an in-depth analysis of the case meanings and the relation of meaning to expression, Jakobson takes a different, more expansive and more ambitious, approach in his 1939 article devoted to the "Zero Sign." He begins by noting the importance of Saussure's observation that language exploits the opposition between something and nothing and goes on to draw together the various types of zero signs in morphology, syntax, grammar, and stylistics.

In the course of his exposition, Jakobson explicitly identifies the zero sign with the unmarked member of an opposition and employs it as a general semiotic principle. Noting that phonology "runs parallel to the general system of the language" (1939: 157), Jakobson treats the absence of a sound quality as zero quality, the absence of a phoneme as a zero phoneme, and the absence of an opposition as zero opposition. Zero opposition refers to neutralization, and Jakobson remarks that zero opposition "gives greater relief to that which unifies and that which distinguishes the two terms of the suppressible opposition" (159). Thus, here Jakobson is treating neutralization as unmarked. But note that this apparently departs from his earlier view of the uses of the nominative and accusative.

At the morphological level, Jakobson posits zero desinences and a zero degree of grammatical alternation. He exemplifies the former with the zero ending of the Russian nominative singular. The latter he exemplifies with the Russian genitive singular *rta*, derived from the nominative singular base *rot* ('mouth').[12] In addition, Jakobson suggests a zero morphological function, which he illustrates with Russian declensional paradigms that refer to more than a single grammatical category. In such instances, an ending has a well-defined form but "no functional value" (1939: 152). (An English example of the zero morphological function would be the *-ed* ending for regular verbs, which can signal either a past tense or a past participle use.)

Jakobson also discusses zero meaning, which corresponds to the definition of unmarked given in "Structure of the Russian Verb" and "Contributions to the General Theory of Case." He writes:

> the nominal system and the verbal system can be decomposed into binary oppositions, where one of the terms of the opposition signifies the

presence of a certain quality and the other (the unmarked or undifferen-
tiated term of the opposition, in brief, the zero term) indicates neither
its presence nor absence. (1939: 153)

Jakobson illustrates zero meaning by discussing gender oppositions (masculine having the zero meaning), aspect (the Russian imperfective and
indeterminate being zero aspects), and case. In addition, Jakobson extends the notion of zero to oppositions between partial synonyms, suggesting that *like* is the "zero synonym" with respect to *love*, which "adds
a meaning of strong passion" (1939: 155).

Jakobson also returns to the problem of a marked sign being used in
place of its unmarked counterpart, illustrating with the Russian versions
of the sentences *She is a skilled craftsman* versus *He is a skilled craftswoman*.
The former he treats as an example of the unmarked term (*craftsman*)
being used generally; the latter he treats as a marked use of words
(1939: 155).

Jakobson extends this approach to word order as well, writing that
in Russian "there is a primary word order which is opposed to its various
inversions" (1939: 156). Thus, the subject-verb-object order and
adjective-noun order exemplify "word order with a zero value" (156). He
also distinguishes a zero of expressivity, by which he means a sign that
lacks a stylistic expressive value. In addition, Jakobson expands his view
of syncretization to include the "principle of compensation," that is, the
tendency for the marked category not to undergo further differentiation
(see Brøndal 1943). And Jakobson continues to explore the synchronic
function of markedness in the hierarchy of categories, pointing out, for
example, that Russian verbs do not allow two marked aspects to be expressed in the same form and that in nouns the masculine and neuter are
syncretized in the nonnominative (marked) cases.

Jakobson's essay "Zero Sign" is especially significant in that it reflects
his attempt at a global markedness analysis of various linguistic levels—
from sound to style. In this essay, markedness is treated more as a general value relation between oppositions than as a relation associated with
a particular semantic or phonological feature. "Zero Sign" is noteworthy
too in that it presages the possible complementary relation between the
expression of a category and its meaning. Jakobson points out in one
instance that a zero ending is paired with a positive morphological function for gender while the corresponding nonzero ending is paired with
the zero morphological function. The forms, he notes, show "a clear
chiasmus" between general meaning and morphological function since
the marked meaning is paired with the unmarked morphological function
(1939: 153).

The next major phase of Jakobson's work on grammatical markedness comes nearly twenty years later, with the publication of "Shifters, Verbal Categories, and the Russian Verb" in 1957. Here Jakobson embeds his analysis of the verb in a theory of communication and develops an analysis of verbal elements defined with reference to the speech events as (using Otto Jespersen's terminology) *shifters* and *nonshifters*. In his analysis of the meanings and asymmetries of Russian verbal categories, he draws on his previous definitions of markedness, which he reiterates as follows:

> One of two mutually opposite categories is "marked" while the other is "unmarked". The general meaning of a marked category states the presence of a certain (whether positive or negative) property A; the general meaning of the corresponding unmarked category states nothing about the presence of A, and is used chiefly, but not exclusively, to indicate the absence of A. The unmarked term is always the negative of the marked term, but on the level of general meaning the opposition of the two contradictories may be interpreted as "statement of A" *vs.* "no statement of A," whereas on the level of "narrowed," nuclear meanings, we encounter the opposition "statement of A" *vs.* "statement of non-A". (1957a: 47)

Jakobson modifies some points here, referring to a "property A" rather than a "mark of objective reality." He also delimits the idea of general meaning further by suggesting that the *chief* meaning of the unmarked category is to serve as the opposite of the marked term.

In addition to providing an extensive listing of the marked and unmarked categories in the Russian verbal system (1957a: 48–52), Jakobson analyzes the relation between markedness and the syncretization and combination of features. He also touches on the relation between the value of a category and its expression, reiterating the idea that marked meanings are reflected with augmentation.[13]

Jakobson revisits the theme of expression/content relations in his 1958 "Morphological Observations on Slavic Declension." Here he reanalyzes the Russian case system, stressing the correspondence between semantic features and their phonological expression. He notes, for example, that "a nasal phoneme serves as the mark of the marginal cases, while fricative consonants mark the quantificational cases: -*x*- the prepositional and -*v*- the genitive" (1984: 121). Jakobson's emerging goal is to analyze sound structure by uncovering "the common phonological characteristics" of a case or a case feature (128). Jakobson also continues to express interest in case syncretism, defining a notion of "partial syncretism" to treat instances in which similar cases show "the existence of the same number of phonemes" or by "the common occurrence of one of the phonemes" (128–9). This approach is characteristic of Jakobson's desire to integrate sound and meaning. He sums up his "Morphological Observations" by remarking that "[t]he central theme of this report has been the isomorphism of the relationships between grammatical categories and their sound shapes, examined on the basis of Russian declension" (130).

In his 1966 "Quest for the Essence of Language," Jakobson extends his view that the nature of language is iconic rather than arbitrary, invoking the sign theory of Charles Sanders Peirce. He reiterates the idea that sounds symbolize grammatical features, noting that the phoneme /m/ appears in the endings of Russian instrumental, dative, and locative (the marginal cases) (1966b: 353). Markedness, however, is not central to Jakobson's views on iconism here. Instead he connects aspects of grammatical form directly to putatively isomorphic semantic relations, as when he suggests that the syntactic precedence of conditional clauses and of subjects is related to the "hierarchy of grammatical concepts" (351).

Three short articles on Slavic grammar are also important for understanding the development of Jakobson's views on markedness. Jakobson's 1957 squib on "The Relationship Between Genitive and Plural in the Declension of Russian Nouns" (1957b: 135–40) illustrates how markedness helps make grammar coherent. Pointing out that the genitive and the plural in Russian are both marked categories, Jakobson proposes that zero endings are characteristic of the unmarked nominative singular and of the doubly marked genitive plural, occurring in the least marked and most marked parts of the paradigm. Thus, nouns that have an overt ending (-a or -o) in the marked (feminine or neutral) nominative singular have a zero ending in the genitive plural, while nouns that have an zero ending in the unmarked masculine nominative singular have an overt genitive plural ending (-ov or -ej).[14]

In "The Gender Pattern of Russian," published in 1960 (1960a: 141–3), Jakobson posits a reversal of markedness values of gender in different grammatical categories. He argues that the neuter, which he takes to be generally marked as opposed to the masculine in noun paradigms, is the unmarked category within the verb and adverb paradigm. Jakobson notes the parallel between this and the contextual reversal of phonological features, adding that such shifts are not at all unexpected in language. He writes:

> The neuter, which is a specified, marked category in the case-forms, proves to be the least specified—the unmarked gender—among the caseless forms. Here a "subjective" class is opposed as marked to the unmarked neuter, and the former signals that the verb or short adjective

actually relates to a subject, namely to a more specified, marked feminine or to a less specific and, in this respect, unmarked masculine.
(1960a: 142)

Finally, I should mention Jakobson's 1959 essay "On the Rumanian
Neuter" (1971b: 187–9). Here he posits that Rumanian nouns oppose
feminine to nonfeminine in the singular, but masculine to nonmasculine
in the plural. In other words, he suggests that two distinct features are
involved in the characterization of gender in Rumanian and that shifts
are implemented in terms of a bifurcation of gender into different features.[15]

One additional aspect of Jakobson's later work that should be mentioned is his adoption of aspects of the information theory developed in
the 1940s and 1950s to support his views on binarism and phonemic
representation. Information theory was concerned with representing
mathematically the amount of information contained in a message, and
in information-theoretic terms, the best coding of a message is one that
optimizes a few binary choices. In the course of fitting phonology to
information theory, Jakobson treats phonemic representation as a
redundancy-free level of representation that contains only distinctive information.

Jakobson ties his descriptive practice to the use of pluses and minuses
in feature inventories, generally equating pluses with marked, minuses
with unmarked, and blanks (or zeroes) with predictable features.[16] Jakobson's information-theoretic descriptive practice had an important influence on the redundancy-free notation of early generative phonology and
syntax, a practice aimed at, as Halle (1962: 335) put it, "a mechanical
procedure by means of which preferred alternatives are chosen from
among several alternatives." The basis of preference in Halle's early in-
vestigations was simplicity, with simplicity determined by the number
of symbols in the description. As a consequence, redundancy rules that
saved feature specifications in the lexicon or segment inventory contrib-
uted to the optimization of a grammar, and redundancy-free feature matrices were preferred over redundant ones.

In the descriptive practice of Chomsky and Halle's *The Sound Pattern
of English* and of Paul Postal's *Aspects of Phonological Theory*, the idea that
redundancy-free inventories and lexicons were highly valued was recast
in terms of a notation of *u*'s and *m*'s, representing unmarked and marked
feature choices, where the unmarked specification represented the "normal" state and the marked specification represented the "nonnormal"
state.[17] In this framework, *u*'s did not contribute to the complexity of a
grammar, while *m*'s did. Rules then converted the *u*'s and *m*'s to pluses

and minuses, encoding universal generalizations about preferred distributions of phonological features.

CHILD LANGUAGE, APHASIA, AND UNIVERSALS OF LANGUAGE

While one part of Jakobson's structuralism involved the asymmetry of signs and the iconism of sound and meaning, another important aspect was the priority of one term of an opposition over another on a universal basis. This is developed most extensively in Jakobson's 1941 monograph *Child Language, Aphasia, and Phonological Universals* (1968a [1941]).[18] While *Child Language* does not explicitly use the term markedness, it is clear nevertheless that the concept is implied in the notion of phonological opposition set forth in that work, and later expositions are explicit in connecting these.[19]

Drawing on medical literature, Jakobson examines language acquisition and aphasic speech in light of phonological universals, and he proposes a relationship between a universal hierarchy of features, their acquisition by children, and their loss during aphasia. In his words,

> the phonological acquisition of the child and the sound disturbances of the aphasic are based on the same laws of solidarity as the phonological inventory and the phonological history of all the languages of the world. (1968a [1941]: 92)

The idea that aphasic sound disturbances and child language acquisition were related was not an entirely novel idea. The French investigator T. A. Ribot had proposed this in the late 1800s, and Freud also suggested it in his 1891 monograph *On Aphasia* (1953 [1891]). The idea was adopted as well by such researchers as Kurt Goldstein, Hughlings Jackson, and Henry Head. Jakobson's main contribution was to put the discussion of regression on an empirical basis by providing an account of Ribot's generalization in terms of the universal "laws of solidarity" arising from the distribution of sounds across languages. Jakobson and Trubetzkoy's studies of phonological typology led Jakobson to propose that sound systems are hierarchically organized and that certain phonological oppositions provide the core of every language's sound system. These are the oppositions that define the most prototypical sounds—vowels and consonants that every language will have: cardinal vowels like /a/, /i/ and /u/; the plosive consonants /p/, /t/, and /k/; and the nasals /m/ and /n/. These sounds are found in virtually all of the world's languages.[20]

Jakobson proposes further implicational laws between these sounds and sounds outside of the basic inventory. For example, typological laws predict that no language will have nasal vowels unless it also has oral vowels; no language will have a front rounded vowel unless it also has a front unrounded vowel; no language will have a back unrounded vowel unless it also has a back rounded one; no language will have a smooth dental fricative without a strident dental fricative. Jakobson also notes that certain sounds are very rare in the languages of the world—sounds like clicks, lateral fricatives, and the Czech strident ř, for example—and he proposes that such sounds are furthest from the core and lowest on the hierarchy. Jakobson suggests that the hierarchy of phonological oppositions defined by typology is also found in the development of a child's sound system. Based on diary studies of language acquisition, he confirms that the core sounds are indeed learned first, that more marginal sounds tend to be acquired later and often present more difficulty to children, and that rare sounds seem as a rule to be acquired relatively late and to present the most difficulties in learning.

Jakobson thus sees the structure of language as a biologically driven hierarchy and language acquisition as a predictable unfolding of that hierarchy. Universals reflect hierarchy according to a natural economy: the most optimal sounds biologically will form the basis of every language and will be universal; sounds further down in the hierarchy will have a less wide distribution, occurring in some languages but not in others, and sounds low on the hierarchy will tend to be very rare. In addition, Jakobson extends his theory beyond a ranking of basic, less basic, and rare sounds, suggesting a universal order of acquisition even in the way that children construct their core systems of vowels, stops, and nasals. This order unfolds, he proposes, in oppositions between maximally distinct perceptual categories, categories like vowel and consonant, wide and narrow, and front and back, nasal and oral.[21]

While Jakobson's views on the acquisition of phonology involve more than the theory of unfolding oppositions, it is that which has received the most attention. Contemporary research is skeptical of the particular order of acquisition suggested in *Child Language*. For example, Ferguson and Farwell (1975), while confirming some of Jakobson's generalizations, note such divergences from his ordering as the child's preference for voiced labial and alveolar stops over their voiceless counterparts.[22] More recently, David Ingram (1988), in a detailed reassessment of *Child Language*, has demonstrated that Jakobson's original proposals can be interpreted in various ways depending on how one defines the idea of "acquiring an opposition." The predictions of Jakobson's theory thus depend on the acceptance of a particular view of distinctive features and maximal

oppositions, and Ingram argues that since this cannot be uniquely determined, Jakobson's theory of child language is ultimately indeterminate
as well, and so can be neither accepted nor rejected.

The third aspect of *Child Language* was Jakobson's claim that the
speech of aphasics also conforms to certain "laws of solidarity" and that
aphasic speech disorders are the mirror image of the sequence found in
child language. Jakobson seems to have meant this in two ways. One
was that the errors and substitutions of aphasic speech (such as *ripe* for
write, and so on) generally involve substitutions of more basic sounds for
less basic ones. The other was that the overall dissolution of phonological systems (as, for example, was the case for Broca's famous patient
Lebornge) would be the inverse of phonological acquisition, with the
core sounds being the last to be lost.[23]

Examining the literature on case studies of aphasics from several European countries, Jakobson found example after example in which errors
and substitutions followed his hierarchy: he noted the early disappearance of nasal vowels by French and Polish aphasics, the loss of θ sounds
prior to the loss of *s* by English aphasics, the replacement of velar nasals
with dentals; he found reports of affricates being replaced by fricatives,
of fricatives being replaced by stops, and of velar consonants merging
with dentals and of dentals with labials. From such data, he posited
that the sound replacements of aphasic speech—both sporadic errors and
systematic ones—tend to follow his phonological hierarchy.

In the subsequent literature, there has been both support for and
evidence against Jakobson's version of the regression hypothesis. Sheila
Blumstein, in her 1973 book *A Phonological Investigation of Aphasic Speech*,
reports on her study of seventeen aphasic speakers, which found a tendency for the substitution errors of both Broca's and Wernicke's aphasics
to replace marked features with unmarked (1973: 73).[24] The most thor-
ough review of the regression hypothesis is a collection of studies edited
by Alfonse Caramazza and Edgar Zurif (1978), the proceedings of a 1974
meeting of the Academy of Aphasia specifically devoted to this question.
The consensus was that the regression hypothesis holds in certain types
of language decay (such as segmental speech perception) but not for
aphasic deficits across the board.

In later work, such as his "On Aphasic Disorders from a Linguistic
Angle" (1975), Jakobson also extended the regression hypothesis to other
domains, suggesting that "[m]any syntactical problems faced by the
study of aphasia can be explained with reference to the hierarchy of
linguistic structures, namely to the relation between the derived,
marked, and the primary, unmarked, variety" (1975: 106). Drawing on
work by Harold Goodglass (1968), who noted that aphasics lose the En-

glish -*s* inflection first as agreement inflections, next as possessive markers, and last as plural endings Jakobson points out that this is the opposite of the order posited by Benveniste (1966) for language acquisition. He argues himself that:

> [t]he actual explanation lies in the hierarchy of levels: the plural form, "dreams", is one *word*, which implies no syntactic sequences, whereas the possessive "John's" implies the *phrase* level, where "John's" is a modifier dependent on some headword like "dream", and finally, the third person [verb form], "dreams", requires a *clause* with subject and predicate.
>
> It is completely clear that the more complex syntactic structures are the first to be discarded, and the first to be lost in the case of agrammatism is the relation between subject and predicate. (1975: 101)

Jakobson also treats nouns as less marked than verbs and imperatives as less marked than nonimperatives. And he argues that personal pronouns, as shifters, are "typical marked superstructures in the grammatical system," which "explains their late emergence in children's language and their early disappearance in classical cases of agrammatical aphasia" (1980: 103).[25]

Ultimately the main benefit of *Child Language* and Jakobson's related work was a sharpening of the regression hypothesis. By formulating regression in terms of markedness and hierarchy, Jakobson's approach made it possible to take seriously the idea that child language and aphasia are connected. Today few linguists or aphasiologists adopt Jakobson's position literally, though many view his observations as a useful summary of tendencies, and some, like Stephen Anderson (1985: 129), argue that the broad outline of Jakobson's work continues to be confirmed. It is worth noting too that modified versions of Jakobson's ideas are still being proposed today: aphasiologist Yosef Grodzinsky, for example, has argued in a 1990 book that the regression hypothesis provides an elegant approach to disorders of pronoun reference within the Principles and Parameters theory (see chapter 5).

Jakobson's Later Work

Jakobson's work on phonological relations emphasizes the existence in language of a series of universally ranked oppositions based in part on the intrinsic acoustic and perceptual content of sounds. This contrasts with his work on morphology, which focuses instead on the language-particular meanings of categories.[26] In his 1963 article "Implications of Language Universals for Linguistics," presented at a 1961 Dobbs Ferry,

New York, conference on language universals, Jakobson reiterates the connection between language universals and implicational statements (1963: 265). He also continues to connect marked and unmarked word order to stylistic dominance, restating one of Greenberg's universals as follows: "In declarative sentences with nominal subject and object, *the only or neutral (unmarked)* order is almost always one in which the subject precedes the object" (269).

In addition, Jakobson speculates that iconism is a universal property of language, suggesting that a "zero affix cannot be steadily assigned to the marked category and a 'nonzero' (real) affix to the unmarked category" (1963: 270). Jakobson's comments here highlight an important bifurcation between markedness as stylistic neutrality and markedness as inherent ranking. His practice, as we have seen, ranges over both aspects of this bifurcation.

Jakobson's last major work, *The Sound Shape of Language* (1979), coauthored with Linda Waugh, provides additional clues about his final views on markedness. The book as a whole further elaborates Jakobson's phonological theory, stressing the basis of phonological markedness in acoustic contrasts and setting forth the view that phonological features have more functions than mere distinctiveness. Rather, Jakobson and Waugh argue, the distinctive function of features is supplemented by a number of other types of phonological functions, which yield configurative features, expressive features, redundant features, and physiognomic features.[27] Jakobson and Waugh also develop further the ideas of iconism and sound symbolism, delineating the function of sound in verbal art and verbal play, providing a further connection between the themes of "Quest for the Essence of Language" and Jakobson's phonological studies.

One of the main themes of *Sound Shape* is markedness, and Jakobson and Waugh characterize phonological markedness as a set of contextual relations defined primarily in terms of acoustic and typological properties and as contrasting with semantic markedness. Jakobson and Waugh write that "[t]here is an intrinsic communality between markedness on the level of grammatical categories and markedness on the level of distinctive features" (1979: 94). But they maintain that the different character of the semantic and phonological levels is reflected as well. For semantic features the "constraining, focusing character of the marked term of any grammatical opposition is directed toward a more narrowly specified and delimited conceptual item" (94), while for phonological distinctive features:

> the marked term is opposed to the unmarked one by its closer concentration on a certain, either positive or negative, perceptual sound prop-

erty polar to that of the unmarked term, and is accordingly characterized by a restriction of occurrence to specific sequential or concurrent
contents. (1979: 94)

Thus both the marked and the unmarked term are characterized by a
narrower specification of the relevant pole of an opposition, but in different ways.

Jakobson reiterates the idea of unity in bifurcation in his final retrospective book, the 1983 *Dialogues* with his wife Krystyna Pomorska.
After reviewing the background of markedness, he stresses the context
dependence and system dependence of markedness relations in phonology:

> On the phonological level, the position of the marked term in any given
> opposition is determined by the relation of this opposition to the other
> oppositions of the phonological system—in other words, to the distinc-
> tive features that are either simultaneously or temporally contiguous.
> (1983: 97)

To take just one example, compactness is unmarked for vowels (as in /a/),
while for consonants it is the marked feature. He contrasts phonological
oppositions with semantic oppositions, where

> the distinction between marked and unmarked terms lies in the areas of
> the general meaning of each of the juxtaposed terms. The general mean-
> ing of the marked is characterized by the conveyance of more precise,
> specific, and additional information than the unmarked term provides.
> (1983: 97)

Jakobson exemplifies using the terms *lion* and *lionne*, coming full circle
back to a contrast parallel to his original 1932 examples of *osël* and *oslíca*.
Jakobson's later views may best be summed up in a statement he made
in a 1972 *Scientific American* article titled "Human Communication," published ten years before his death:

> [E]very single constituent of any linguistic system is built on the oppo-
> sition of two logical contradictories [marked and unmarked] . . . the
> entire network of language displays a hierarchical arrangement that
> within each level of the system follows the same dichotomous principle
> of marked terms superposed on the corresponding unmarked terms.
> (1972: 85)

For Jakobson, then, markedness is a relation between features that
characterize some aspect of structure, with a natural bifurcation between
semantic and phonological markedness being a consequence of the different nature of phonological and semantic oppositions. In his practice, the

principle of asymmetry underlying markedness has both universal tendencies (when viewed in its typological aspect) and a relative aspect (especially when extended to domains outside of language structure).

Several interconnected themes emerge in Jakobson's work on
markedness. One is the relation of properties of meaning and sound to
value, the characterization of a meaning or sound as a relation between
a feature A and a feature non-A, which creates a logical and evaluative
asymmetry. Another is the role of asymmetry as a organizing principle
of categorization—markedness ranges over all categories and mediates
their further subdivisions and uses. A third is the potential for isomorphism between the levels of language. A fourth theme is the possibility
of value isomorphism and value-based change—that is, for marked and
unmarked grammatical categories to be implemented by marked and unmarked expressions. A fifth theme is the potential role of markedness in
analyzing the information structure of semiotic, aesthetic, and communicative systems beyond language.

Despite attempts in his retrospective work to present markedness in
a unified way, Jakobson's treatment of markedness is neither fully
worked out nor wholly consistent, but instead is often speculative, fragmented, and overly broad.[28] Because his work and interests have tacked
about among the various themes mentioned above, we are left with an
expansive and eclectic view that is reflected in the diverse ways many of
his intellectual descendants have approached markedness. The resulting
picture is variegated and conflicting, with different approaches focusing
on different facets of markedness. We shall return to Jakobson's views
by way of a synthesis in chapter 6. Now, however, we turn to the work
of some of his intellectual heirs.

THREE

The Heirs of Jakobson

In this chapter we turn to the work of some of Jakobson's intellectual descendants, linguists working in the broad structuralist tradition who use the opposition between marked and unmarked to inform linguistic or semiotic analysis. In looking at approaches that have drawn on themes from Jakobson's work on markedness, I hope to develop a clearer picture of markedness and some associated principles that have to do with the assignment and realization of values and to explore how markedness has been extended to other sign domains.

ICONISM OF VALUES

In a number of works over the last twenty-five years, Henning Andersen and Michael Shapiro have formulated a view of markedness as a means through which the isomorphism of form and content is expressed, fleshing out Jakobson's theme that the form/meaning relation is partly iconic rather than wholly arbitrary.[1] They have argued that patterns of markedness values reflect semiotic universals, the most fundamental of which has to do with iconism of value, but which may also include relationships of reversal (reverse iconism) and sequential complementarity as well.

What is meant by *iconism of value?* In the neostructuralism of Andersen and Shapiro, iconism exists between the markedness values of linguistic units. Rather than positing form/meaning correspondences based directly on the qualities of forms and meanings as Jakobson does in his "Quest for the Essence of Language" (1966b), value iconism posits a correspondence between unmarked forms and unmarked meanings. Extended to syntagms, value iconism implies that unmarked units and unmarked contexts will correspond. There are thus two central aspects to

35

the iconism of value: the pervasiveness of markedness across the levels of language and the existence of universal semiotic tendencies, expressed as principles. Andersen and Shapiro develop the idea of value iconism with three main principles: *markedness assimilation*, *markedness reversal*, and *markedness complementarity*.

Andersen introduced the term markedness assimilation in phonological work in the late 1960s.[2] He first proposed markedness assimilation as a means of specifying redundant features in positions of neutralization, suggesting that in (some) marked contexts neutralization results in the cancellation of an opposition, which leaves the marked feature rather than the unmarked feature. Later, in his *Language* article on "Diphthongization," (1972: 45, note 23), he extended the idea to grammar as well. One of Andersen's grammatical examples involves the English subjunctive, a marked mood. He proposes that tense is neutralized in the subjunctive in favor of the past form rather than the present form, explaining why the expression of the subjunctive mood is *If I were rich*, . . . rather than *If I was rich*, ... Andersen suggests that the use of the past form in this construction is *an assimilation of markedness of form to markedness of the context*. The correctness of this particular example aside,[3] Andersen's larger point is that language might allow assimilation of properties other than simple phonological or morphological ones and that this assimilation can be defined in terms of markedness values. Morphological and grammatical examples are particularly crucial to the testing of this hypothesis, since they are less likely than phonological examples to be open to an analysis based on raw physical assimilation.

To exemplify further, let us consider Shapiro's analysis of stress placement in English substantives. Shapiro proposes that since nouns and adjectives are unmarked, they should favor an unmarked stress placement.[4] He notes that phrases like *rènt a cár* or *lòng beách* undergo stress retraction to the initial syllable when they are nominalized as *rént-a-car* and *Lóng Beach*, a change that he explains as follows:

> This phenomenon is to be explained, just as retraction in verbal/nominal pairs like *permít/pérmit*, *frequént/fréquent*, *rejéct/réject*, *envélop/énvelope*, as a markedness assimilation. Initial stress in English is unmarked, noninitial marked. Correspondingly, the category of nominals (substantives, adjectives) is unmarked relative to verbals, which are marked. (1983: 97)

Shapiro's treatment of compounds exemplifies the assimilation of values across categories, which can be represented schematically as an analogy:

u stress pattern   :   m stress pattern   ::
u part of speech   :   m part of speech

Note that Shapiro's example of markedness assimilation differs from Andersen's in that it is not tied to a specific context such as subjunctive
mood. While Andersen's example treats markedness assimilation as the
result of neutralization of the past and present forms in the subjunctive
context, Shapiro's example of stress retraction is a more general characterization of the alignment of a marked category with a marked context
and an unmarked category with an unmarked context. In recent work,
Andersen (1991) seems to move toward this broader view also.

A second principle developed by Andersen and Shapiro is *markedness
reversal* (or markedness dominance). This term was coined by Andersen
to identify "the reversal of markedness values in oppositions dominated
by a marked context" (1972: 45). Andersen seems to have considered
markedness reversal as a special case of markedness assimilation, characterizing instances in which neutralization yields the marked term.[5] Shapiro (1983), however, extends markedness reversal to describe more
broadly "the phenomenon whereby a marked context reverses the normal
markedness values of the terms of an opposition" (93). In other words,
he assumes that reversal need not be associated with neutralization. The
contexts that can dominate and reverse an opposition can include phonological contexts, morphological categories, and broad stylistic features.

How is markedness defined in this framework? Shapiro sees
markedness as a matter of paradigmatic asymmetry, citing such characteristics as the "more narrowly defined" nature of the marked term,
which is equated with a "conceptual complexity" arising in any opposition (1983: 79).[6] Similarly, Andersen (1989) sees markedness as manifest
in a relation between a less delimited, inclusive unmarked term and a
more delimited, exclusive marked term (see also Andersen 1979: 379).

Such definitions are consonant with Shapiro's and Andersen's view
that markedness assimilation applies to many linguistic and cultural phenomena. Shapiro has applied the ideas of assimilation and reversal to a
wide range of linguistic data, providing examples of their interaction in
phonology, morphophonemics, and semantics. A representative example
is his treatment of truncation, which he suggests is typically a reduction
in marking (that is, an unmarking), as opposed to augmentation, which
is typically an increase in marking (1983: 96). He suggests, however, that
when the opposition between truncation and augmentation occurs in a
marked context, such as the diminutive, truncation increases markedness. Thus (to use the English version of Shapiro's Russian example),
the derivation of the diminutive *Mike* from *Michael* would be a marking
if, in stylistically marked contexts, reduction has the reverse of its usual
effect. Shapiro's example is somewhat sketchy, since he doesn't exemplify the use of augmentation and truncation in unmarked contexts or

the use of augmentation in marked diminutive contexts.[7] But the example nicely illustrates the tricky relationship between markedness assignment and reversal. Is truncation marked simply because it is in the diminutive, or are there independent grounds for this evaluation? Does assimilation to a marked context drive reversal or does reversal characterize a set of phenomena that have independent justification?

Shapiro has also introduced a third principle, markedness complementarity, according to which "oppositely marked stems and desinences attract, [and] identically marked stems and desinences repel," and which he sees as "the cornerstone of a general understanding of word structure" (1983: 146). Shapiro describes complementarity as reversing the primarily assimilatory pattern that holds in phonology, reinforcing the difference in function between phonology and morphophonemics. Patterns of complementarity also illustrate the mutual dependence of markedness assignment and reversal in his framework. To illustrate, we consider another of Shapiro's examples. He posits that in Japanese, stems that end in a vowel are unmarked, while stems that end in a consonant or glide are marked. In addition, endings that begin with a vowel are taken to be unmarked, while those beginning with a consonant are marked. Given this assignment of values, stems and endings are complementary: for unmarked stems such as *tabe*, the nonpreterite ending is the marked *ru*, while for marked stems like *yom*, the ending is the unmarked *u* (Shapiro 1983: 146). Schematically, markedness complementarity predicts a tendency toward the following sort of pattern:

m element + u element   and
u element + m element

Shapiro extends the example to include reversal in the marked context of the preterite, where the underlying form of the past-tense ending is *ta*. After unmarked stems, the marked (consonant-vowel) ending occurs, yielding *tabeta* (parallel with *taberu*). With marked stems, however, the preterite ending remains *ta* (which alternates with *da*), but the ending triggers a phonological unmarking in the stem: *yom* + *ta* → *yonda*, *kaw* + *ta* → *katta*, and so on.[8] Shapiro suggests that complementarity is preserved by unmarking of the stem rather than marking of the ending.

Several questions arise in connection with analyzing language in term of principles of markedness assimilation, reversal, and complementarity. First, we must inquire why such principles should exist: what is their ultimate basis? Shapiro and Andersen see markedness as inherent in the structure of language and as the projection of asymmetry onto the full range of linguistic processes. Assimilation and reversal are based on primary organizational principles of similarity and differentiation, which may be manifest as replication and complementation of values. The medium of replication and complementation is abstract value, and the theory of markedness is thus extended to a theory of sign coherence, its main analytic goal being to understand language in terms of values.

Assuming the desirability of such investigation in principle, questions of detail and technical execution remain. With respect to markedness assimilation, for example, how can we know which feature is relevant for assimilation? Given that a category is made up of many features, there seems to be no a priori way of determining what feature is relevant to an assimilatory pattern. A related question is how to know whether it is assimilation or complementarity that characterizes any particular situation. Given that both patterns are possible and that we cannot be sure which features are relevant, can we know with any certainty which pattern reflects the correct analysis?

When reversal is taken into consideration, the situation becomes even more problematic, especially if the option of reversal exists in virtually any context. Reversal seems to make it possible to analyze any pattern of data as a set of assimilations and complementarities. Shapiro of course recognizes the mutual dependency of markedness assignment and markedness patterns and in fact takes this to be a virtue. He maintains that categories of linguistic analysis "all cohere *as an ensemble* of conditions informing the phenomena in question" (1983: 87) and that mutual dependency among units and contexts and among assimilations and reversals makes the analysis of linguistic value and pattern holistic rather than limited to discrete and independently assigned markedness values.[9] But this holism also places his approach outside of the tradition of linguistic analysis that is grounded in a concern for independent evidence.

Related to the question of grounding in evidence is the problem that patterns of markedness assimilation and reversal are not required in language; rather they are possibilities. Shapiro notes that iconism is not "compulsory," though he maintains that diagrammatization is something which frequently occurs in language (1983: 92). He also emphasizes that it is not possible to know in advance which contexts entail reversal or other diagrammatization. But of course if it is not possible to determine when reversal is motivated, then any reversal is open to the criticism that it is can be posited simply to make patterns of assimilation or complementation work, as Shannon (1986) has noted.

Shapiro sums up the spirit of his approach in the following passage:

> What is theoretically and explanatorily interesting is discovering precisely what sorts of cohesions there are, while relying on a uniform exegetical framework, i.e., one which considers all components of lan-

guage . . . to be isomorphous with each other and to be analyzed using
a unitary set of explanantes. (1983: 216)

Shapiro has refined his view in his 1991 book *The Sense of Change*, where
he argues that the effects of language change and drift are ultimate tests
of the goodness-of-fit of a language—the growth of language, in his view,
provides the best evidence for diagrammatic principles that might appear
arbitrary at the synchronic level (1991: 65–70). He writes:

> [D]rift is explained by a kind of goodness (of fit). . . . We might say
> that each type of language reveals new values, to be fully realized in
> the further drift of that language toward a fuller realization of those
> values. The only overarching value, then, is fuller realization (alias dia-
> grammatization) of the values specific to one's type. (1991: 66)

Both of Shapiro's remarks highlight the strength of his approach: its
ability to draw together different aspects of language under the broad
rubric of semiotic value. The weakness of the approach is the holistic
and nondeterministic way in which values and patterns are determined,
which can result in seemingly ad hoc and arbitrary analyses, which
"make sense" as patterns but stand on uncertain ground. Perhaps by
giving greater weight to justifying of the values units and contexts and
by limiting markedness reversal to clear cases of broad-based value reversal rather than ones driven to fill out patterns, a less speculative sense of
grammar could be realized. The main objections that have been raised,
however, are not objections to the ideas of markedness assimilation, complementarity, or reversal but rather objections to the problems that arise
in identifying value and appropriate context and in the proliferation of
reversals.[10]

Invariance of Meaning

A rather different, but equally interesting, development of markedness
is a version of structuralism developed by Cornelius van Schooneveld,
Edna Andrews, and Rodney Sangster. To appreciate this approach, we
must revisit the idea of the general meaning of a category and bring to
the foreground the notion of *invariance*.

Recall that in his definition of markedness in 1932 (and in its reitera-
tions in later works) Jakobson posited that the broader meaning of the
unmarked term was identified as its "general meaning" (1932: 12). General meanings are abstractions that reflect the system of recurring relations in a language and the semantic commonality of all of the specific
meanings (meanings in context) of an element. They are determined by

analyzing systems of categories into abstract features. In one view, each of these features is an *invariant*, an "abstract, relational quality that remains constant through the various transformations it undergoes as a result of its occurrence in concrete contexts" (Sangster 1982: 18). Invariance has its roots in Jakobson's approach to phonology, where an invariant phonological feature like *grave* has a different phonetic manifestation in different contexts. Likewise, a semantic feature may have different specific meanings in different contexts: the nominative, for example, has different meanings as the subject of an active clause, as the subject of a passive clause, as the subject of a nominative absolute, or as a predicate nominative, though all meanings presumably share a common core. Similarly, a word like *out* may have a different meaning when used as a particle *(look out, hold out)*, when used as a prefix *(outgrow, outdo, outgoing)*, and when used as a preposition, but again all meanings may share a common core. Sangster, in his book *Roman Jakobson and Beyond* (1982), and Andrews, in her *Markedness Theory* (1990), emphasize Jakobson's conviction that because meaning is the function of linguistic units, all formal distinctions carry a meaning and all meaning is analyzed in terms of linguistic form. This idea was concisely put in Jakobson's motto, "There is no *signatum* without a *signum*," which Sangster calls the Principle of Formal Determinism (1982: 48). This principle is one of the main influences on the formulation of a semantic theory based in invariants, with sameness of form providing the material basis for organizing abstract semantic relations.[11]

The most well known semantic invariants are those in Jakobson's analysis of the Russian case system (Jakobson 1932 and 1958) and the verbal features posited in "Shifters" (1957a). Jakobson's case features of *directionality* (indicating the existence of directness), *marginality* (indicating peripheral status) and *quantification* (indicating limited involvement) and his verbal features are grounded in an analysis of the speech situation that takes into account the relations among participants and the relations of participants to the whole speech event.

Van Schooneveld's *Semantic Permutations* (1978) and other works have extended the framework of invariance established by Jakobson. Van Schooneveld's overarching thesis is that all language is organized by a small set of features that can be used to characterize any situation and which can account for the full range of general meanings in language. Central to this approach is the idea that semantic invariants are perceptual features (a parallel with Jakobson's definition of phonological features in acoustic terms) and that they apply across all grammatical and lexical categories. His feature system is comprised of features for *plurality*, *dimensionality*, *distinctness*, *extension*, *restrictedness*, and *objectiveness*, where the last three features roughly correspond to Jakobson's *directionality*, *marginality*, and *quantification*.

Following Andrews's explication (1990: 21–4), these features can be described as follows. Plurality indicates the existence of a plural set; dimensionality indicates that the set created by plurality has a subset; distinctness posits separate subsets that order perceptions; extension indicates a relation between the distinct subsets created; restrictedness cancels the relation established by extension; and objectiveness closes off the relationship by indicating that no further subsets are possible.[12]

This feature system provides a material basis for invariance on the semantic side. One objective of such a feature system is to address a recurring problem of structural semantics: that it is a closed system in which meanings are often elegant but lack verifiable connection with reality. The search for invariants, as Sangster remarks, must aim at a semantics "neither imprisoned within the structure of language nor divorced from it by being defined on objects in the external world" (1982: ix). Ideally, meaning should be grounded both in linguistic form and in the external world—grounded by form in that formal distinctions provide the basis for features and grounded externally by connection to an overarching theory of perception and the speech situation (provided by van Schooneveld's feature framework).

The study of meanings and invariants is grounded in a third way as well: by markedness, which plays a role in semantics via Jakobson's proposals about general meaning. If invariants are identified with unmarked general meanings, then determination of markedness relations is crucial to semantics. The general meanings will be set up by abstracting the common denominator from a set of forms, with markedness being used as a constraint on the meaning relation. A book-length example of the establishment of an invariant (though not in the Jakobson–van Schooneveld feature system) appears in Yishai Tobin's *Aspect in the English Verb* (1993). Tobin analyzes a range of English semantic data as the reflex of an invariant relation between verbs that are unmarked (such as *do*) and verbs that are marked for result (such as *make*). Verbs marked for result consequently imply a sense of completion, goal, or outcome, while their unmarked counterparts are unspecified or neutral in that regard. Thus *do* can be used in either a process-oriented or result-oriented sense—for example, *I already did the laundry* (process) vs. *I already did my term paper* (result). Defining invariant meaning as "composed of a general semantic domain shared by both forms and the postulation of distinctive semantic features that are placed in an asymmetric markedness relation" (1993: 47), Tobin provides textual data from various styles and discourse levels to support a nonresult/result distinction between such verb pairs as *look/see*, *listen/hear*, *say/tell*, *speak/talk*, and others.[13]

As a practical matter, contextual properties of marked and unmarked elements—properties such as substitutability of the unmarked for the marked and the broader distribution of the unmarked—are often used as tests of the general meaning of the unmarked term and of the semantic property itself. But while Sangster is amenable to such contextual criteria in his 1982 book, he takes a more restrictive position in his 1991 article "Two Types of Markedness and Their Implications for the Conceptualization of Grammatical Invariance." There he argues that distribution and other facts about contextual uses of categories should not be connected with markedness directly. Rather, in his view, markedness should be determined solely on the basis of *acontextual* relations arising from the analysis of forms into semantic invariants. Sangster suggests that there has been an unfortunate shift toward treating

> what was originally proposed as a RELATIONAL property of language . . . as a RELATIVE one, and consequently the determination of markedness relations has been shifted out of the realm of general meanings into the domain of contextual meanings. (1991: 141)

The emphasis on contextual and relative meanings rather than general meanings is a misstep, Sangster thinks, in that reliance on context subverts the invariance of the markedness relation between the two poles of a feature.[14] Moreover, reliance on context makes the determination of markedness relations subjective in Sangster's view (though, as we shall see, exactly the same criticism has been made about the approach that determines markedness relations based on invariants). The process of systematizing specific meanings into general ones is thus seen as a process of reducing variant distributional relations into invariant paradigmatic ones that have an asymmetric structure, markedness being removed from the distributional structure of language.

The view that markedness relations are invariant asymmetries has implications for the treatment of neutralization and markedness reversal, phenomena that Sangster and Andrews reject. Regarding neutralization, Sangster argues that although phonemic oppositions can be contextually neutralized, semantic oppositions cannot. He writes:

> When the distinctive function of a phonemic opposition is contextually removed, nothing else remains, and we are correct in saying that the opposition is neutralized. But removing the purely distinctive function of a morphemic opposition still leaves its inherent meaning intact, and we should not speak of neutralization in such a case. (1982: 68)

It is not clear that this conclusion is correct for phonology. Phonological neutralization describes the situation the distinctive function of an opposition is canceled but the remaining archiphoneme is realized as the unmarked feature value of the opposition. One might say that removing the distinctive function of a phonemic opposition still leaves its inherent phonological property intact, since (for example) neutralization of the voiced/nonvoiced opposition in word final consonants leaves the nonvoiced member of the opposition rather than a phoneme with no realization of the feature of voicing.

The motivation for denying semantic neutralization seems to be that it is incompatible with invariance—that if meanings are neutralized then the invariant must be missing from a form, which invalidates the theoretical underpinnings of formal determinism. This does not seem to me to be problem, however, if neutralization is treated as *suppression* of oppositive aspects of meaning rather than *elimination* of meaning.

Exactly what is meant by suppression of a feature's meaning? Consider typical examples of neutralization, as in the use of the present for timelessness or the use of enveloping terms like *old*.

> Yesterday, I *went* (*go) home.
> In the fall, I *teach* (taught) composition.
> Robin is thirty years *old* (young).

In the first example the present tense is suppressed, but it is not reasonable to consider this an example of neutralization, since the adverb *yesterday* is incompatible with the use of the present. In the second example, the contrast between forms is not neutralized, though the present tense form has the general meaning; so here the general meaning of the unmarked term (which can include the future) is opposed to the specific meaning of the marked term. The third example is slightly different because the contrast between *old* and *young* in this context carries a stylistic meaning. If we exclude examples like *Robin is thirty years young* from consideration, this would be a neutralization. However, there is no compelling reason to exclude such examples (other than to simplify the definition of neutralization). What we have instead is an example where in stylistically neutral contexts *old* and *young* are neutralized but where *young* is certainly possible in other stylistic contexts.[15]

Thus while neutralization can be treated as suppression rather than elimination of a specific semantic feature, it is not particularly easy to determine when neutralization occurs.[16] It may be that what is important ultimately is not neutralization of marked and unmarked categories but the distribution of marked and unmarked categories.

Sangster and Andrews also critique the idea of markedness reversal. Andrews argues that markedness reversal should not be possible in a semantic theory that is based on invariance, because reversal is inconsistent with a definition of markedness as *inclusive* asymmetry. Inclusive asymmetry reflects the definition of markedness as the signalization of A versus its nonsignalization, while mere polar opposition refers to the polarity of A versus its opposite B, with no inherent asymmetry and with markedness contextually imposed. Andrews writes that "[m]arkedness theory in morphology cannot retain any consistency as a theoretical approach if it is defined by both asymmetrical and polar oppositional types simultaneously" (1990: 151). In her view, all relations are A versus non-A and such relations cannot be reversed by a simple change in the polarity of the feature, since non-A is by definition unmarked. Reversal of inherent asymmetries requires positing an additional (polar) feature definition, a step that destroys the invariance of the underlying relation. As an example, consider the past/present opposition, characterized as (marked) past versus (unmarked) nonpast. It is not possible to simply reverse these—to say that past is unmarked and nonpast is marked—if markedness is defined as inclusive asymmetry. To reverse markedness requires saying that the relation is (marked) *present* versus (unmarked) *nonpresent*. But this step, if taken, entails that the relation is no longer invariant, since a second feature definition is involved.

Sangster too rejects reversal in his 1991 article, though he embraces it in his 1982 book.[17] Discussing the use of the Russian nominative in situations where a quality is perduring rather than transitory—as, for example in the Russian sentences *Lenin byl revoljucioner* 'Lenin was a revolutionary' (nominative) versus *On byl soldatom* 'He was a soldier' (instrumental)—Sangster notes that the use of the nominative in this context should not be treated as a reversal, since it follows from the unmarked status of that case. In addition, he critiques the approach of designating the perfect as unmarked in the past but marked in the present as telling "nothing about the conceptual properties involved in either the tense or the aspects, since the term unmarked is being used simply to describe relative frequency of occurrence" (1991: 143–4).

Andrews (1990) also critiques several examples of markedness reversal.[18] She argues that Andersen's example of reversal in the subjunctive (discussed earlier) can be reanalyzed in terms of the use of the past tense form to express both subjunctives and conditionals, a use consistent with its ability to express "disjunction with the moment of utterance" (149). In her view, reversal is only apparent and falls under the meaning of the past tense. Andrews extends her reanalysis to suggest that the reversal of number (as in the subjunctive *if I were rich*) also follows from disjunction, her reasoning being that disjunction allows number to be potentially absent (149).

Andrews suggests as well that the apparent reversal of markedness of the Russian perfective/imperfective opposition in the imperative can be explained by the definition of the imperative as producing a result, so that the natural state of affairs is for the positive imperative, which commands a result, to co-occur with the perfective.

Finally, Andrews considers the reversal of gender features in social contexts, exemplified by *male nurse* and similar locutions. She argues that true reversal does not occur in such instances. In her view, the categories "male" and "female" are not true conceptual features but are merely "tags" or pseudofeatures assigned to categories. She comments that "[t]hese extra-linguistically defined 'marks' exemplify polarized oppositional relationships which, not being inclusive, cannot be applicable to asymmetrically defined markedness relationships" (1990: 151), and she adds that using the terminology of markedness "is not particularly relevant" (152). Her objection in this instance is not so much to the fact of reversal (as with the subjunctive and the perfective examples) but to the type of analysis—that is, her critique is centered not on the particular facts but on background assumptions about the types of features available.

The critique of markedness reversal presented by Sangster and Andrews highlights two important points. One is that a clearer delimitation of markedness reversal is needed, one that distinguishes carefully between instances in which marked and unmarked features are reversed and instances in which reversal might be explained in terms of the range of meaning of a particular feature. The second point is that reversal of semantic features must be treated in terms of reversal of asymmetric features rather than mere opposites—that is, it must involve multiplying the set of features if the A versus non-A definition of markedness as inclusive asymmetry is maintained.

The positions developed by Andrews and Sangster, which rely on Jakobson's formal determinism principle and van Schooneveld's semantic invariants, are quite restrictive. By in principle reducing all morphological meanings to a few invariant features, strong constraints are placed on semantics and on markedness. However, their approach has never received wide attention in American linguistics, in part because of its commitment to abstract semantic relations between ineffable general meanings. As Birnbaum remarks in a 1984 review of Sangster's book:

> The abstract *Gesamtbedeutung* [general meaning] suffers from a methodological flaw. It gives the impression of a circular argument: a particular "general meaning" is usually established on the basis of generalizing (abstracting) from a set of ascertaining contextual meanings, which in turn are all claimed to be derivable from precisely that underlying general concept. (1980: 414)[19]

The weakness of the invariance approach is its commitment to abstract semantic features based in a theory of perception. But this is also its strongest appeal, since it is that aspect that presents the possibility of unifying morphological semantics and perception.

Given their underlying assumption of a fixed and minimal set of conceptual features, Andrews's and Sangster's rejection of markedness reversal is a reasonable position to adopt. However, what is not obvious is that the underlying assumption is worth preserving. Newfield and Waugh (1991) provide a Jakobsonian counterpoint to the restrictive view of markedness, arguing that the relational basis of language *is* compatible with contextual variation.[20] They maintain, following Jakobson (1974) and Jakobson and Waugh (1979), that the mark of an opposition is distinct from the feature that characterizes the two poles of the opposition, and they argue further that the mark is a function of context (1991: 228). Newfield and Waugh view either pole of an opposition as marked depending on which "is more narrowly specified and delimited, which in turn is related to *contextual variation*" (1991: 227). They add that

> [e]ach grammatical element of an opposition is endowed with a conceptual invariant (general meaning, *Gesamtbedeutung*) which is defined in terms of the conceptual choice between the two features (e.g., one vs. more-than-one for singular-plural). In addition, there is a privative opposition between presence of a mark and its absence. (1991: 229)

Here markedness is treated as a property that is superposed onto a polar opposite. Newfield and Waugh identify the unmarked term as "the most generic meaning, in which the category as a whole is designated without specific subdivision into negative and positive" (1991: 229). They treat markedness reversals (which they call shifts) between masculine and neuter and between singular and plural as value shifts unconnected to a shift in meaning, though they do not specifically reconcile this with their definition of markedness as an A versus non-A relation (229; see also Waugh 1982).[21]

The question of the definition and reversibility of markedness has also been addressed by Catherine Chvany. Chvany's work on markedness in syntax has consistently attempted to bridge Jakobsonian and Chomskyan approaches, connecting inherent semantic value with the notion of formal cost in syntax. By integrating the Jakobsonian semantic framework with the precision of generative syntactic features (Chvany 1984: 66), her approach treats marked and unmarked syntactic features as having both a substantive definition and an evaluative function in grammar. At the same time, her recognition of multiple levels of markedness allows contextual factors and distributional norms to be taken into account and evaluation to proceed at different level of analysis.

Chvany's 1992 article "Multi-level Markedness in Russian, English and Bulgarian" is particularly helpful in clarifying the issue of reversibility. Here she distinguishes the inherent specification that characterizes an opposition from various types of contextual evaluation of features. Inherent specifications are feature definitions that designate one value of a feature as more complex and more specified. This corresponds to Andrews's inherent asymmetry. Contextual evaluations, on the other hand, are associated with "normative expectations," which may be linguistic, typological, or cultural. This corresponds to the contextual markedness recognized by Newfield and Waugh.

Chvany also emphasizes the need for a set of conventions to distinguish different kinds of markedness and to encode the relationship between inherent specifications and contextual ones. She suggests a notation in which M and U are used for inherent markedness values (signalization of A versus nonsignalization of A), while "M" and "U" (in quotes) are used for contextual markedness values of various types.[22] As she shows, such conventions can be used to assign relative cost to the relation between inherently specified units and variably specified contexts. She has also applied this convention to the iconic relation between units and contexts itself, suggesting that iconism is "U," and to typology as well, suggesting that typologically natural specifications are "U," though they may be inherently M in a particular language. Chvany's notation provides a means for linking cross-linguistic and contextual factors to inherent specifications and for applying markedness across analytic levels. For this reason, it bears further investigation.

More central to the present discussion is the way in which Chvany's approach shows how we can encode and understand markedness reversals as involving a *pair* of inherently asymmetric features.[23] As she notes, contextual shifts may involve a pair of oppositions that yield more than a two-valued analysis. Chvany points out, for example, that verbal aspect may be encoded in two distinct ways—in terms of discreteness versus nondiscreteness (perfectiveness vs. nonperfectiveness, as in Russian) or in terms of continuity versus noncontinuity (as in English), and she suggests that certain Bulgarian aspect forms require both discreteness and continuity. The need for polar features like discreteness and noncontinuity provides evidence for exactly the kind of feature duplication that underlies reversal, since similar semantic features may be marked or unmarked depending on which opposition is relevant to a particular pattern of facts (see Jakobson's discussion in "On the Rumanian Neuter" [1959], mentioned in chapter 2).

Another example is the gender opposition in Russian. Russian has masculine nouns, like *student* and *učenik*, that refer only to males as well as masculine nouns, like *doktor* and *sotrudnik*, that may indicate males or females. *Student* and *učenik* could be analyzed as having the marked feature [masculine] and thus would refer to males. Words like *doktor* and *sotrudnik*, on the other hand, could be analyzed as nonspecified for feminine—that is, as having the unmarked feature [nonfeminine] that allows them to indicate both males and females. For such an analysis to be possible, both sets of features (feminine vs. nonfeminine and masculine vs. nonmasculine) must be available in the gender system of Russian.[24]

The issues of invariance, neutralization, and reversal raised in this section represent a second set of leading ideas that have arisen from Jakobson's work on markedness as a semantic property. They provide a contrast to the value iconism discussed in the first section, which is largely divorced from semantics. However, the approaches to markedness discussed above have their guiding themes in Jakobson's semantic theories of asymmetrical conceptual features and in his views on the relation between form and meaning. Another line of markedness research in grammar and semantics is one that emerged from Jakobson's work on language universals and linguistic typology. This is the view of markedness as a coding of universal hierarchies.

UNIVERSALS

Just as Jakobson treated phonology as entailing a universal hierarchy, it is also possible, and necessary, to treat features of grammar and semantics as showing cross-linguistic, universal rankings. Of course the shift from a language-particular, purely binary relation between features to an essentially scalar ranking of categories cross-linguistically engenders a change in both the scope and the nature of markedness, retaining its evaluative aspect but separating that from the linguistic consciousness of speakers and from grounding in the signalization versus nonsignalization of features.

A key work in developing such a typological view of markedness is Joseph Greenberg's *Language Universals*, published in 1966. In his earlier contribution to the Dobbs Ferry Conference on Language Universals in 1961, Greenberg had defined markedness in terms of neutralization. Essentially following Trubetzkoy, he wrote that "[t]he category which does not appear in the position of neutralization, in this case the plural, may be called the marked category" (1963: 94). However, in his 1966 book, Greenberg approached the topic from a broader perspective, surveying the correlates and diagnostics of markedness proposed by Jakobson, Tru-

betzkoy, Hjelmslev, and others in an attempt to find a unifying characterization of a "notion which tends to take Protean shapes" (1966: 11).
Examining the various ways that markedness had been defined in phonology, grammar, and lexical semantics, Greenberg emphasized the possibility of parallel diagnostic criteria existing across levels of language.

He observed that unmarked grammatical categories in a language
show a number of characteristics—including semantic indeterminacy and
syntactic facultative expression, zero structural expression, inflectional
syncretization and defectivization, neutralization, morphological irregularity, and dominance (1966: 25–31). Many of these in turn correlate to
the greater frequency of a category vis à vis its opposite, and consequently Greenberg took frequency to be the "primary" determining factor of markedness in grammar (65), suggesting that unmarked categories
may be determined by "the frequency of association of things in the real
world" (66). Discussing singular and plural, for example, he remarked
that "[i]t is plausible, insofar as there are constants in the human situation, that . . . everywhere the singular should be more frequent than
the plural" (66).

In part, Greenberg's motivation was the idea that a frequency criterion allows an unlimited application of markedness and that it provides
the option of a scalar interpretation, allowing categories to be ranked as
more or less marked (that is, more or less frequent). In addition, following Jakobson (1939), Greenberg posited an application of frequency in
the idea of emphatic versus normal word order. Greenberg writes (somewhat cryptically) that "[t]he so-called normal order, it would seem, is
necessarily the most frequent. We may refer here to the well-known
story of the boy who cried wolf" (1966: 67). Yet frequency can also be
a protean notion itself. In addition to emphasizing the role of frequency
intralinguistically, Greenberg applied frequency to cross-linguistic
markedness—treating cross-linguistically unmarked categories as those
that have unmarked status in a wide number of languages (32).

While using frequency as a diagnostic is appealing in that it promises
to provide a common yardstick for determining markedness across different levels of language and across languages, the bifurcation of frequency
raises some questions about the unitary nature of markedness. How is
cross-linguistic markedness distinguished from language-particular
markedness? How should we treat phenomena that are infrequent (or
less frequent) cross-linguistically but more frequent in a particular language? A much-used example is preposition stranding in English, which
appears to be marked cross-linguistically but unmarked in English.[25] To
determine the markedness of this phenomenon we need to know not
just its cross-linguistic generality but also its value within the language
being considered.

A second issue concerns whether frequency is in fact an appropriate criterion for intralinguistic definitions of markedness. Is it possible to determine markedness based on raw corpus frequency in a language? Given that categories will have different frequencies in different subdomains, genres, or corpora, frequency must be attenuated by attention to contexts. Certain types of constructions, for example, are more common in written discourse, while others are more common in speech (see Givón 1990); similarly, animate and definite noun phrases are more common in subject position, while inanimate and indefinite ones are more typical of objects. The unmarked category will be that which is more frequent in a given context, even though it might not be the most common in terms of raw number of occurrences across the language. Yet once we make a commitment to examine the frequency of elements contextually, some of the appeal of frequency disappears, and it becomes more compelling and revealing to consider directly the grammatical or phonological properties that are reflected in distribution in context than to merely count occurrences.

A further, related issue is that relying on frequency as a sole or primary criterion changes the definition of markedness. If the definition of markedness is no longer tied to its informational content (either its relational general meaning or its relative conceptual complexity in context) we must ask whether there is value to retaining a notion of markedness at all. Why not simply assert that we are studying frequency?

In his 1966 book, Greenberg seemed to be aware of the problems with frequency, and he wavered about its foundational role in defining markedness. While he indicates in some passages that frequency determines markedness (cf. above), elsewhere he suggests that it does not capture the whole picture:

> [F]requency is itself but a symptom and the consistent relative relations which appear to hold for lexical items and grammatical categories are themselves in need of explanation. Such explanations will not, in all probability, arise from a single principle. (1966: 70)

Greenberg suggested that frequency was symptomatic of implicational relations between categories, the unmarked term being more frequent since it is implied by the marked term (1966: 60). However, while it may be natural for the more basic element to have a higher frequency (both intralinguistically and cross-linguistically), this does not appear to be a necessary connection: the implying term of an opposition could easily be less frequent universally than the implied term within a language.

The view of markedness as reflecting implicational universals rather than frequency also avoids reference to intrinsic phonological or semantic properties in the definition of markedness and replaces discussion of properties with typological generalizations. Nevertheless, the idea of defining markedness in terms of universal implicational relations is still a richer idea than mere frequency, because it opens up the possibility of a universal ranking of categories and features.[26]

Implicational typology has also been taken up, with a somewhat different focus, by Fred Eckman and others working on second language acquisition. Eckman sees what he calls *typological markedness* as a means of accounting for ease or difficulty in second language learning. The definition of typological markedness given by Eckman (1977: 320) is intended to apply cross-linguistically to both phonology and syntax and is framed explicitly in implicational terms:

> A is typologically marked relative to B (and B is typologically unmarked relative to A) if and only if every language that has A also has B but not every language that has B also has A.

Eckman and others have applied this notion of markedness to second language acquisition, investigating the hypothesis that marked structures are more difficult to learn in a second language and that the degree of difficulty in some way corresponds to the degree of markedness. Conversely, aspects of a second language that are less marked than in the first language are expected to be easier to learn. The logic of this view is that of a universal hierarchy of implications such that language learners can access structures higher on the scale with less effort than they can access structures lower on the scale.

Croft, in his survey of the field of typology (1990), takes up the issue of implicational universals and markedness from a somewhat different, more fine-grained perspective. He distinguishes four kinds of typological universals: implicational universals, basic markedness relations, hierarchies, and prototypes. Implicational universals are universals of the form "If P then Q" (in the simplest case), and they reflect generalizations about logically dependent patterns, such as word order types. Basic markedness relations are binary asymmetries such as the relation between singular and plural, declarative and interrogative, or active and passive. Hierarchies are multivalued relations, such as the broader scale of number (singular < plural < dual < trial) and grammatical relations (subject < direct object < indirect object < oblique; see Keenan and Comrie's Accessibility Hierarchy [1976]). Prototypes are unmarked combinations of features that occur together, such as animacy and subjecthood (see Silverstein 1976).

Croft argues that the latter three types of universals can be identified using criteria similar to those delineated by Greenberg, and he reformulates Greenberg's criteria to distinguish structural, behavioral, and frequency criteria. As Croft notes, all of these are defined, in different ways, in terms of relative quantity. Structural criteria have to do with the relative quantity of form used to code a category—with unmarked, less marked, and more prototypical categories tending to have shorter (or zero) forms.[27] Behavioral criteria include both inflectional criteria (the unmarked having a greater quantity of inflectional subdistinctions) and distributional criteria (the unmarked having a wider range of morphological and syntactic environments).[28] Frequency criteria may be textual or cross-linguistic, and Croft explicitly recognizes the need for different texts and styles to be taken into account (1990: 87).

Givón (1990) proposes a similar set of criteria, defining markedness in terms of *formal complexity, frequency distribution,* and *substantive grounds* (1990: 645). The first two sets of criteria are already familiar, and parallel those discussed by Croft. We discuss Givón's substantive grounds in the next section.

In the view in which markedness is part of the theory of universals, markedness is essentially a theory of correlations—a theory of evidence for hierarchy—and the theoretical result is the set of correlations (which serve as diagnostics for hierarchy) and the ensuing set of hierarchies (universals) themselves. Within such an approach, Greenberg, Croft, and others see the main significance of markedness in terms of its applicability across languages and across the levels of language: typological markedness provides a set of criteria that can be applied regardless of whether a category is phonological, semantic, morphological, or syntactic, and regardless of whether different languages have the same categories.[29]

FUNCTIONALISM

A question that arises with respect to implicational relations or broad universal hierarchies is, of course, why they exist. Generally speaking, there are two possibilities: one is that preference structure is based in relatively abstract internal properties of grammar, having their basis in a species-specific learning mechanism (see chapters 4 and 5). The second possibility is that preference structure is based in relatively transparent external properties of linguistic material and communication, properties they have a basis in physical attributes of humans and the nature of communication.

This latter, external view of markedness connects hierarchies of grammatical categories with properties of extralinguistic experience in a fairly direct way to address the question of why basic categories are basic. Recall that Jakobson, in his phonological studies, proposed that the optimal features that are are those that maintain or enhance a perceptual contrast; similarly, van Schooneveld posits a set of features that are connected with perception of situations. In the functionalist view, the connection of preferred properties of languages and basic universal human experiences and capacities is the guiding principle.

This may involve describing markedness relations in terms of prototypical properties of speakers and speech situations, with the underlying principle being that the linguistic properties that reflect prototypical communicative schemas should be preferred. Mayerthaler (1988 [1981]: 8), for example, identifies unmarked grammatical categories as those that are in the Gestalt background of language use, that is, those that are "in agreement with the typical attributes of the speaker." Such attributes include animateness, definiteness, present tense, use of imperfective dynamic verbs, and so on (see van Langendonck [1986] for an extensive listing). This general approach is echoed and extended by Bernard Comrie (1986: 85), who suggests that "one could try to account for markedness in terms of . . . independently verifiable properties of people, the world, or people's conception of the world." Comrie observes that people's conception of the world may vary from language to language, adding a relativistic aspect to the functional definition of markedness. This concern with conceptual rapport is apparent also in the approach to local markedness (markedness reversals) developed by Tiersma (1982), who notes that plurality is unmarked for nouns that generally occur in pairs or groups and who develops the linguistic consequences of reversal for word derivation and paradigm regularization.

It seems quite reasonable that universal situations can provide a basic common experience that serves as a background against which other more idiosyncratic elements or experiences are defined. However, to the extent that different languages can define their background concepts in different ways, prototypicality may be language-particular, and the degree to which prototypical situations can be identified with universals remains an open question.

Attempts have also been made to explain qualitative markedness relations in terms of different kinds of universal economic and iconic motivations. As Croft (1990) notes, asymmetries among linguistic elements may be explicable in terms of adaptation to the exigencies of communication in terms of economy of form. George Zipf's suggestion that "[h]igh frequency is the cause of small magnitude" (Zipf 1935: 29) has been proposed as a way of accounting for the brevity of form of unmarked elements (see also Trubetzkoy 1969 [1939] and Haiman 1985: 147–51). Croft points out that economy may be a plausible motivation for the inflectional diversity and distributional breadth of unmarked categories as well, the idea being that more frequently used categories will support greater differentiation than less common categories (see also Moravcsik and Wirth 1986). However, as Croft emphasizes (1990: 160), explanations in terms of economy and frequency raise the further question of *why* certain categories are more frequent, a question that cannot be answered by appealing to markedness.

Croft also observes, drawing on Haiman (1985), that iconism may be posited as a motivation for markedness, his reasoning being that "[s]ince language is a human faculty, the general assumption on the part of functional linguists has been that the structure of language should be compared to human conceptualization of the world" (Croft 1990: 171). In other words, concepts that are somehow cognitively primitive should be expected to show the diagnostics of the unmarked. But Croft emphasizes that the notion of cognitive primitiveness itself needs further refinement, clarification, and connection to evidence from psychology (1990: 172).[30]

Givón's (1990) "substantive grounds" for determining markedness also fall under the heading of functional criteria for markedness. Givón posits that "[t]he marked category tends to be cognitively more complex—in terms of *attention, mental effort* or *processing time*—than the unmarked one" (1990: 947). But he notes too that definitive conclusions about conceptual complexity in context are not always possible. He suggests that distributional factors must ultimately be explained "by referring to substantive domains such as communication, socio-culture, cognition or biology" (948) and contextual factors such as "social group," "cultural universe," "physical environment," "subject matter," and "shared background information" (956). The result would be a postulated set of basic features taken to be associated with shorter or simpler communicative forms.

The work of the German naturalists (see Mayerthaler 1988; Dressler 1985, 1989, 1995; and Dressler, Mayerthaler, Panagl, and Wurzel 1987), while focusing in part on how extralinguistic principles of perceptibility and psychological efficiency characterize naturalness and natural developments in language, has also examined the role of semiotic efficiency and preference. Thus, as Dressler emphasizes, conflicts of level-specific markedness relations lead to an investigation of what broader interlevel semiotic preferences resolve these conflicts over time (see especially Dressler 1985: chapters 10 and 11). For a case study applying this approach to second language acquisition, see Berretta (1995).

As should be evident, the view of markedness developed in work on universals takes a rather different perspective from the approaches discussed in the previous two sections, putting forward both typological considerations and general functional ones.[31] Work in this vein moves markedness away from a binary, feature-based conception toward a more general picture of hierarchy as a typological preference structure or functional norm. This is the main attraction and strength of the quantitative-typological approach to markedness: it provides a set of diagnostics for cross-linguistic hierarchies that have diachronic and cognitive implications. The approach has its roots in Jakobson's phonological theory, which emphasized cross-linguistic typology much more than his semantic studies did, and the modern typological approach largely eschews the qualitative aspect of Jakobson's semantic studies.

It is perhaps worth a momentary digression to consider the connection between the quantitative side of markedness and its qualitative side (inherent specification as the signalization of A versus the nonsignalization of A). As Andersen (1989: 17) suggests, there seems to be an inverse relationship between the depth of a semantically marked category and the breadth of its use. This suggests an overarching functional principle arising from markedness: that conceptually deeper and more complex categories have fewer subdistinctions and a narrower distribution.[32] Categories that have a relatively focused and specific meaning will tend to be used in narrowly defined ways; conversely, categories that have relatively less focused and more generic meanings will have a wider range of uses and may be more available to be used in new ways, resulting in their broader distribution.

FURTHER ASPECTS OF MARKEDNESS

As we have seen, Jakobson's views on markedness can be, and have been, developed in a number of different directions—from iconism of values to invariance to information structure to universal hierarchies. Though all of these approaches reflect different aspects of the original notion of markedness, each to some degree addresses different issues. Ultimately, however, any discussion of markedness must come to grips with the basic definitional question, and with the possibilities of reversal, value assimilation, and neutralization. Each of these in turn raises other questions having to do with the nature of oppositions; with the correlation of distribution, meaning, and value; and with the projection of values across oppositions.[33]

In my view, the most defensible and productive definition of markedness arises by taking the relation to be one of conceptual complexity imposed on categories in a language. In addition, however, the concepts of reversal, assimilation, and neutralization need to be maintained but also constrained. Together a broad definition of the basic notion of markedness and a more narrow view of its function may allow us to ground markedness in the meaning and distribution of categories. In the remainder of this chapter, I consider definition, reversal, neutralization, and assimilation in turn, then move on to further exemplify of markedness in some quasi-linguistic phenomena.

First, let us consider the definitional issue. My view is that markedness must be grounded in the concrete meaning and the distribution of the elements on which it is defined. To be useful as a means of determining ultimate semantic properties, markedness values must be free from an a priori commitment to any particular set of invariants. Markedness must also be free from an a priori requirement that values be iconic, complementary, or chiastic: the values must make sense with respect to the facts of language, not be tied to self-justifying principles. In addition, markedness must be free of contingent properties of morphological form and of inflectional behavior that may or may not always correlate to conceptual asymmetry. Finally, markedness must be free of the constraints of typology, since the value of a particular feature or construction cannot always be determined on the basis of what categories are *generally* implied and implying. Of course, all these factors enter into the background against which markedness relations are determined, but the justification of any particular asymmetry has to be made on the basis of the information inherent in the opposition and its use in the particular language under consideration.

With this as background, we may define the markedness relation, somewhat similarly to Jakobson and Waugh (1979), as an asymmetry between opposed categories such that one of the categories focuses on and singles out a more narrowly delimited conceptual feature than the other. This asymmetry is logically characterized as an A versus non-A relation, with the unmarked non-A value having the double meaning of both opposition to A and indefiniteness (nonsignalization). By insisting on this last aspect of markedness, the double meaning of A versus non-A, I intend two consequences: the first is to require asymmetry to be tied to some property, some A-ness. This step requires analyses of asymmetry to commit to a particular feature analysis—to a property A (even if that property is not immediately evident). Thus, the analysis of singular as unmarked and plural as marked requires an analysis of plural as [specification of plural] and singular as [nonspecification of plural]; it will not suffice just to say that singular is unmarked and plural is marked.

The second intended consequence is to allow the possibility that a logical asymmetry can be imposed on a material one. In other words, treating markedness as a classificatory logic that is imposed on language creates the possibility of applying the concept to asymmetries that are not inherently represented by predefined phonological or semantic features.

REVERSAL

Now let us turn to the issue of reversal, which remains one of the key connections between extralinguistic reality and the analysis of relations and oppositions. Given the definition of markedness adopted here, there is no reason, other than economy of features, to assume that reversals are not possible. But there is also no reason to assume that they are so pervasive that constancy is impossible.

The definition of markedness suggested here ties reversal to equipollence of features. Since an asymmetry is characterized as A versus non-A, to characterize reversal we need to posit a marked feature B, defined as the polar opposite of A, together with its corresponding unmarked partner non-B. A and B are then an equipollent opposition, and the polar opposition between them defines four features: [34]

    A   vs.   non-A
    non-B   vs.   B

Reversal is the situation in which a category is sometimes characterized as A and sometimes as non-B (or, equivalently, sometimes as B and sometimes as non-A).

To illustrate, we can use the familiar masculine/feminine opposition. The traditional Jakobsonian analysis of gender maintains that masculine is the unmarked nominal gender and feminine is marked, this evaluation being based largely on distributional factors such as the more common use of the masculine as a generic (see Jakobson 1932, Greenberg 1966, Lyons 1977b). The feature analysis for a marked feminine and unmarked masculine then involves [specification of feminine] versus [nonspecification of feminine], where the latter feature would in principle refer either generically (as in *Anyone who thinks he can succeed probably will*) or specifically (as in *John believed that he would win*). [35] The question that arises is whether there are contexts in which the masculine occurs as marked and feminine as unmarked, that is, contexts that require analysis in terms of [specification of masculine] versus [nonspecification of masculine].

Treichler and Frank, in the introductory essay to their *Language, Gender and Professional Writing* (1989: 162–6.), suggest that a generic *she* is used in "special circumstances," and they give as examples the following:

> The turn-of-the-century Mount Holyoke student knew she wanted an education.

> The professional female athlete of today assumes she will be treated professionally.

In these examples, however, it is unclear whether the occurrences of *she* are better analyzed as [nonspecification of masculine], in which case masculine is marked, or as [specification of feminine], which is predictable in context. It could be argued that, to an audience that adheres to a view of a masculine norm, *she* is still the marked specification but that the immediate context (of Mount Holyoke and female professional athletics) leads one to expect the marked case. By contrast, consider the context of a work specifically written with women as the likely audience, say, a handbook for women in academe. Here the typical audience might be assumed to be female and, moreover, the topic of the material is about women. Thus a typical reader of this work would expect that such noun phrases as *a professor, every new faculty member, an academic, anyone, everyone*, and so on, would generally refer to women. Such an expectation—that in some context the prototypical person is female— seems crucial to distinguishing actual cases of reversal from pseudo-reversals.[36] Exactly what that context is remains an open question. In their discussion of pronouns of solidarity (1989: 183), Treichler and Frank provide some additional evidence regarding the creation of context in discourse. They note that feminist writing must choose between such pronouns as *we* and *they* when writing about women. Thus, contrast the sentence "Women, especially, need to understand the tenure process before *we* go through it" with the sentence "Women, especially, need to understand the tenure process before *they* go through it," where the examples entail different assumptions about the prototypical reader and the writer.

Considering context allows us to speculate about when reversal might occur. But we still need to develop a picture of how (or why) it happens. What we have are two pairs of features—[specification of feminine] versus [nonspecification of feminine] and [nonspecification of masculine] versus [specification of masculine]—whose use is connected to assumptions about male and female norms. Traditionally, many (probably most) cultural contexts have been normed to an assumption that the prototypical person is masculine, and we can schematize this as a situation in which a norm dominates and provides a context for the opposition.

    assumption of masculine norm
          /   \
    specification   nonspecification
    of feminine   of feminine

Consider, however, the situation when those features are dominated by a feminine norm (as in the examples discussed above):

```
        assumption of feminine norm
              /                    \
    specification            nonspecification
    of feminine              of feminine
```

Here, the left branch of the diagram is redundant, since what is normally the case is specified; similarly, the right branch, representing the simultaneous assumption of a feminine norm and unmarkedness of masculine is contradictory. In general then, reversal might be conceptualized as the situation in which the assumption of a particular norm makes specification of its defining property redundant and nonspecification of the opposite property contradictory. We might assume then that semantic reversals are connected to the dominance of semantic properties in context, which determine the selection of one of two polar features.[37] And we might suggest a tendency to reverse an opposition as context shifts by substituting the polar features, yielding in this case a situation like the one below:

```
        assumption of feminine norm
              /                    \
    nonspecification         specification
    of masculine             of masculine
```

It should be noted that the bifurcation of a polar opposition into two asymmetric ones also provides some options for analyzing gender terms other than *he* and *she*. Examples like *Anyone can succeed if he or she wants to* and *Anyone can succeed if s/he wants to* can be analyzed as a combination of features—for example, as [nonspecification of masculine, nonspecification of feminine]. This option also might work for the analysis of such elements as the *it* of *The baby dribbled its food on its chin*.[38]

NEUTRALIZATION

The definition of markedness in terms of an A versus non-A schema also has consequences for neutralization, which I take to be the suppression of the contrast between A and the narrow sense of the unmarked term in favor of the indefinite or generic sense of the unmarked feature. For example, consider the oppositions *short/long* and *young/old*, where the lesser quantities are marked. The analyses of these relations might be as follows:

short:	[specification of lack of size]
long:	[nonspecification of lack of size] or
	[specification of size]

young: [specification of lack of age]
  old: [nonspecification of lack of age]   or
           [specification of age]

Neutralization, as in "How long is that line?" or "How old is that person?" is the suppression of the specifying options, leaving only the neutral sense. The point to keep in mind is that neutralization is not simply the suppression of a distributional contrast, but rather the suppression of the feature contrast. Similarly, the neutralization of the phonological feature of voicing can be analyzed as

  voiced: [specification of voicing]
voiceless: [nonspecification of voicing]   or
              [specification of nonvoicing]

The contrast between [specification of voicing] and [specification of nonvoicing] is the opposition per se, and [nonspecification of voicing] is the neutral realization when the opposition is suppressed. The pattern shared by both phonology and semantics is that opposition is specification, while neutralization (or suppression) is nonspecification.

MARKEDNESS ASSIMILATION

Unlike reversal and neutralization, assimilation is not a relation between marked and unmarked features but rather a relation between pairs or sets of marked/unmarked categories. There are two versions of this: one the assimilation between expression and meaning, the other the assimilation between units and contexts. In the first case, the marked meaning or function is realized with a marked form; in the second case, the marked element occurs in a marked context.

In both cases, markedness assimilation can be viewed as part of a more general investigation of the diagrammatic nature of language (and of sign systems more generally) outlined in Jakobson's 1966 "Quest for the Essence of Language" (see chapter 2). Though in that article Jakobson provided examples of iconic relations that involve direct qualities of form and meaning, diagrams of value also arise when there is no iconism between direct qualities of signs—that is, when qualities are more subtle than plurality, comparison, temporal sequence, and status. Markedness assimilation can be viewed as one possibility (among several) for expressing the nonarbitrariness of language and other symbolic systems.[39]

The study of such value assimilation is not without pitfalls, however. Care must be taken to avoid tautological assertions. If restricted distribution is taken to be a determining characteristic of marked elements, it is vacuous to "discover" a markedness assimilation relation between a marked category and the restricted context that defines it. Much more convincing are assimilations found between a series of linguistic or cultural categories all of which share a marked or unmarked value and all of which pattern together or demonstrate some diachronic tendency (see Battistella 1990: chapters 5 and 6; Andersen 1972, 1991; Shapiro 1991). Another possible role of markedness assimilation, to which I return below when discussing the apostrophe, is that of creating coherence in a sign pattern by extending a partial pattern.

Since markedness assimilation is a patterning of values, a question that naturally arises is the status of such patterns. What sort of endeavor is the analysis of asymmetries into patterns of assimilation? While the investigation of markedness relations themselves is part of linguistics (when the relations are linguistic), the analysis of patterns is outside the scope of linguistics and falls instead in the domain of other interpretive disciplines.[40] Diagrammaticity in language can be related to Jakobson's Projection Principle, as Andersen (1991: 298) has pointed out. In its original formulation in Jakobson's 1960 article "Linguistics and Poetics," the idea was that the poetic function of language—the function of language that focused on the message in and of itself—involves an extended, patterned use of phonological, morphological, and semantic recurrences (as in Jakobson's example *I like Ike* or its contemporary equivalent *I wanna be like Mike*). The notion that messages or texts cohere in terms of equivalence relations can be extended to the analysis of language itself by showing ways in which patterns of equivalence are projected from the basic paradigmatic relations present in the language onto other paradigmatic or syntagmatic relations.

Viewing markedness assimilation in this way helps to clarify its status. Language can be viewed as an artifact, as a metaphorical message. Such a view allows us to consider grammar, in part, to be a "metalinguistic text" (to use Alan Timberlake's apt phrasing). As a text, grammar is an aesthetic object, an object within which connections can be made about the values of elements in the context of the overall pattern of the language and within which diagrammatic patterns can be discerned or created.

It is worth noting that diagrammatic patterns raise the same question as patterns found in the analysis of literature, culture, or the plastic arts:[41] the question of whether patterns are unconscious preferences for a goodness-of-fit between the parts of an artifact or whether they are deliberate works of design by an author. In the analysis of language, we face the parallel question of whether a particular pattern (of markedness assimilation or diagrammaticity) is an artifact of interpretation or a natural consequence of the nonarbitrariness of language. For any given situation, however, whether goodness-of-fit is a natural consequence or an artifact may be indeterminate (in the short run, at least). Such indeterminacy, however, does not detract from the interest in iconism, and the analysis of sign systems using a uniform, value-based approach both provides an analytic tool not otherwise available and allows for the possibility of a teleology to asymmetry in language and culture.

At this juncture, it may be worthwhile to explore further illustrations of markedness assimilation. The main example I want to develop is one from English punctuation: the use of the *'s* as opposed to the bare apostrophe in English. In terms of distribution, the *'s* is clearly the unmarked sign of the possessive, and the bare apostrophe is the marked sign. The *'s* is, of course, the canonical punctuation associated with possession, and punctuation manuals treat the bare apostrophe in terms of deviation from this pattern. In the singular, the *'s* has the broadest distribution, occurring with stems ending in all consonants except those that end in a pronounced orthographic *s*.[42] The bare apostrophe occurs as the possessive marker in the regular plural (cf. *boys', girls'* vs. *men's, women's*) and in certain classes of singulars ending in *s*. Actual usage varies, as do style manual treatments; depending on the source one consults, the class of *s*-stem nouns that take the bare possessive in the singular includes the following: bi- or polysyllabic words (sources vary), classical or ancient proper names, or proper nouns generally.[43] Other sources cite as conditioning factors the context of the following word (with the bare apostrophe being used if the following word begins in an *s*, as in *Texas' Senators* vs. *Texas's laws*) or the presence of other sibilants within the root *(Dos Passos' poetry* vs. *Dukakis's memoirs)*.[44]

Assuming that the bare apostrophe is the marked case, we can pursue the possibility of markedness assimilation among the conditioning factors for its use. Plural nouns are of course marked as opposed to singular nouns. Similarly, classical names are marked as opposed to contemporary ones, signaling a historical reference (and paralleling the markedness of past tense). Proper nouns are marked in contrast to common nouns, as is suggested by capitalization, which also is marked (see Shapiro 1991: 53). The conditioning factors cohere as a group not in any inherent quality, but in their opposition to more broadly defined unmarked opposites. The possibility of assimilation among these factors, represented as the analogy below, suggests positing further oppositions to complete the pattern.

singular (u)	:	plural (m)
contemporary (u)	:	classical (m)
common (u)	:	proper (m)

We can analyze monosyllabic versus polysyllabic nouns as unmarked versus marked, a conclusion that seems reasonable in terms of the usual assessment of unmarked categories as simpler than marked ones. We can also posit that the repetition of sibilants in a word or across a word boundary is marked as opposed to nonrepetition.[45] Thus, the above pattern can be extended:

nonrepetition (u)	:	repetition (m)
monosyllabic (u)	:	polysyllabic (m)

The utility of markedness assimilation is that it serves as a means of bringing together elements of similar value and determining the identity and value of relevant oppositions. Yet the example also illustrates the limits of markedness assimilation. In my usage (and in the usage of others as well, I suspect), the distinction of proper versus common noun is a rather marginal trigger of the bare apostrophe: I make no distinction between, for example, *the witness's testimony* and *Ms. Furness's testimony*. Even though proper nouns are marked, that does not seem to be enough to make this category a robust component of the possessive rule. Being a marked category is not sufficient to participate in the set of bare apostrophe environments. Markedness is something that we expect of any category that participates in this pattern, though not every marked category is expected to participate. The generalization that we can impute to English to make sense of the bare apostrophe is that *the bare apostrophe is used to signal possession in certain marked cases*. Markedness assimilation thus draws together a variety of conditions that otherwise lack a common principle.

Other, nonlinguistic examples of value assimilation can be taken from commonplace cultural events. Consider, for example, the commencement exercises that signal a student's graduation from some educational institution. As opposed to a student's unmarked interactions with an academic institution, this one involves formal and uniform dress (caps and gowns); it takes place outdoors (ideally), rather than in classrooms; it involves music, speeches, marching, religion (if an invocation is part of the ceremony), explicit symbols of governing authority (trustees, regents, boards of education, etc.), a full complement of faculty and administrative figures (as opposed to a student's usual interaction with individual faculty and staff members), and the presence of family in addition to peers. The language of the ceremony is also marked. Formal language signals the actual conferring of degrees (e.g., "in witness thereof," "by the power vested in me by the trustees"), as do performatives ("I award you the degree of . . . "). And the roll call includes the full (marked) forms of students' names. Such ceremonies can be viewed in terms of the assimilation or coherence of a variety of like-valued elements. The reality of the assimilation is further suggested by the way in which deviations from the ensemble of values weaken the effect of the ceremony (if, for example, it is held indoors or watched on closed-circuit television or if it is disturbed by the wearing of casual dress rather than regalia). To the extent that there is any unpatterned clash of values, the cohesiveness of a ceremony is attenuated.

NAMES

Turning from markedness assimilation back to markedness itself, I consider two further examples of the application of markedness to language. The first example is variation in the structure of names. Names permit a rather wide range of forms, depending on whether full given names or diminutive forms are used and on whether middle names or initials are used. Contraposed to a basic onomastic form are a variety of alternatives, each of which can be considered marked in some way and each of which can be identified, tentatively at least, with a particular conceptual category.

Let us stipulate that the unmarked form of a name in English is the first name plus the surname. This seems reasonable in that this form is the one often used when taking a class roll, writing an invitation or business letter, or when compiling a list of names or a name index. Taking this as a point of departure, we can consider the information carried by various forms of a name. Consider, for example, the following paradigm:

    Gerald Ford
    Gerald R. Ford
    Gerald Rudolph Ford
    Jerry Ford
    G. Ford
    G. R. Ford

As a first approximation, we might speculate that *Gerald R. Ford* differs from the unmarked *Gerald Ford* in being more specific—in distinguishing the referent from *Gerald T. Ford*, for example. The third example, *Gerald Rudolph Ford*, combines specificity with hyperformality, yielding the form used when graduating from an institution or being reprimanded by a parent. The nickname *Jerry Ford* carries the mark of informality. The abbreviation *G. Ford* signals brevity and the form *G. R. Ford* signals both brevity and specificity.[46]

Looking at naming in this way creates a network of marked possibilities that allows us to further investigate ranking among features in other forms and to illustrate contextual reversal. My choice of a president's name was intentional, to suggest a contrast with names like *Jimmy Carter* and *Bill Clinton*, where the marked diminutive is used to achieve a certain effect. Opposed to the alternatives *James Carter* or *William Clinton*, the informal names aim to avoid the distancing neutrality of the unmarked nondiminutives. Conversely, the use of other marked forms—such as *George Herbert Walker Bush*—yield effects of a different sort, distancing the names in question. Note that what is crucial for interpreting the use of names is not merely the fact that certain forms are marked, but which features they are marked for: familiarity is a more highly valued characteristic in campaigning than hyperformality. Once again, markedness tells only part of the story: ranking of values (in context) must also be taken into account to understand a phenomenon.

Naming conventions can also illustrate contextual shifts in markedness: in an informal context—such as between acquaintances or friends—the markedness of the informal name would be redundant (following the reasoning outlined above concerning gender). In such instances, the full form of the name might become marked, with its opposite specifying formality.

PUNCTUATION

My second set of examples concerns the analysis of English punctuation. The set of punctuation signs in English can be analyzed at several levels: at the intersentential level (that is, the level of the independent clause), at the intrasentential level (the level of phrases), and at the word level (involving contractions, compounds, and abbreviations). Putting aside the last set, we can restrict attention to the period, the question mark, the exclamation point, dashes, parentheses, the comma, the semicolon, the colon, and *zero* (the lack of any punctuation).

At the intersentential level, the basic punctuation is the period—a sign that carries no additional information beyond the delimitation of an independent clause (information already signaled by the syntax). The other sentential punctuation marks, the question mark and the exclamation, are more complex, each adding further information. Note too that the question mark and the exclamation can both be replaced by the unmarked period in certain contexts (such as polite imperatives and requests). Tentatively we can analyze these punctuation marks as follows:

Intersentential Punctuation
      period: [specification of separation]
    question: [specification of separation]   and

	[specification of interrogation]	
exclamation:	[specification of separation]	and
	[specification of emphasis]	

The semicolon and the colon function at both the intersentential level and the intrasentential level. But for now let us focus on the content they signal rather than their level. The semicolon supplies the additional information that the separated elements are conjoined, though the nature of the conjunction is left unspecified.[47] The colon typically separates an appositive list or appositive sentence from a preceding complete sentence and can be considered as marked for apposition. Thus both the semicolon and the colon have an additional marked feature in addition to specifying separation:

semicolon:	[specification of separation]	and
	[specification of conjunction]	
colon:	[specification of separation]	and
	[specification of apposition]	

At the intrasentential level the unmarked punctuation is *zero*, the lack of punctuation. The lack of punctuation serves to integrate the material in a sentence or phrase, so typically the propositional core of a clause in English is uninterrupted by punctuation. The comma, by contrast, signals separation between material. This can take the form of a separation of the core of a sentence from peripheral, appositive, or parenthetical material or demarcation of serial or coordinate elements. Dashes serve as a special type of separator to indicate an interruption or break in the flow of the text,[48] while parentheses serve to marginalize text (as when presenting an aside to the reader). These relations can be expressed as follows:

Intrasentential Punctuation

zero:	[nonspecification of separation]	
comma:	[specification of separation]	
dashes:	[specification of separation]	and
	[specification of interruption]	
parens:	[specification of separation]	and
	[specification of marginality]	

Since *zero* is the unmarked nonspecification of separation, it can replace the comma in some instances:

Robin reads Dickens, Achebe(,) and Momaday.
In January(,) we will be moving to new offices.
We all enjoyed the fresh(,) spicy sauce.
Mary went to the play(,) and John went to the symphony.

However, *zero* cannot replace dashes or parentheses because those punctuation marks also carry other information besides mere separation. Notice too that paired commas can substitute for dashes and parentheses, suggesting that the comma is unmarked for interruption and marginality, along with being marked for separation.

> George Washington—the first President of the U.S.—was born in England.
> George Washington, the first President of the U.S., was born in England.

> The party will (I think) be delayed a bit.
> The party will, I think, be delayed a bit.

The punctuation marks that occur at both the intersentential and intrasentential levels are the comma, semicolon, and the colon. Traditionally, the semicolon can be used in lists, as in the following examples:

> There were several project groups: Jan, Tom, and Mary; Bill, Sally, and Fred; and Ann, Robin, and Jim.

> I'd like to invite Mary Smith, my cousin; Fred, her husband; Charles Green, the building supervisor; and Sally Park, the president of the local school board.

In these instances, the semicolon signals conjunction, just as it does when it occurs between sentences. Conversely, the colon may be used between two complete sentences, generally where the second sentence redescribes or summarizes the point of the first (hence its frequency in academic writing).

> Mary was both surprised and pleased with the reaction of her employees: she hadn't expected them to be so willing to work extra hours to meet the deadline.

And of course the comma can also be used to separate sentences, either with or without an accompanying coordinating conjunction:

> Mary went to the play, John went to the symphony.
> Mary went to the play, and John went to the symphony.

The sentence without the "and" of course requires that the conjoined parts be parallel. A bare comma cannot replace the intersentential punctuation between just any pair of clauses (cf. *John went to the concert, they were playing Brahms*). In addition, *zero* can replace the comma before a conjunction if the conjuncts are simple and parallel. Thus the following is also permitted:

Mary went to the play and John went to the symphony.

One way to conceptualize all of this is as follows. Suppose that the opposition that distinguishes the intersentential level from the intrasentential level is [sentential] versus [nonspecification of sentential].[49] The period, exclamation point, and question mark can be analyzed as [sentential] while all other punctuation marks are unspecified for that feature. The expectation is that the period will occur only to delimit sentences, while other marks can occur at either level. An apparent intrasentential period does occur as a stylistic option that signals certain styles of narrative, such as the following:

I waited. For a long time.
He always carried an umbrella. Which was very strange.

One possible analysis of such cases might be that the fragment is an elliptical sentence—that is, it is [sentential]. Another possible analysis is that the period replaces a comma to create a particular effect and that the replacement of the marked period for an unmarked comma could be treated as markedness assimilation, the period signaling foregrounding of a phrase or dependent clause. The comma shows some other interesting asymmetry effects. Its basic meaning is clearly intrasentential, but it can occur between two independent clauses, as in the two examples from above, repeated here:

Mary went to the play, John went to the symphony.
Mary went to the play, and John went to the symphony.

What is not evident in these examples is whether the comma is intersentential (that is, whether the conjuncts are viewed as two separate sentences) or whether it is intrasentential (with the conjuncts viewed as two independent clauses). This indeterminacy is exactly what is expected given the feature definition associated with the comma, nonspecification of sentential status leaving the comma open to interpretation. It may be reasonable, then, to treat the first example above as an instance in which the comma separates two sentences and the second as an example of the comma as an intrasentential punctuation mark. This is consistent with a view that the function of the conjunction is to connect two items into one. It also accounts for the fact that the comma can be replaced by *zero* when the conjunction is present but not when it is absent, and it allows us to preserve the generalization that *zero* is restricted to intrasentential contexts.

We are left then with a picture of punctuation as involving marked features of sentential context, conjunction, and separation, which can be represented as follows (using a minus for the unmarked nonspecification of a feature and a plus for the marked specification of that feature):

	sentential	conjunction	separation
zero	−	−	−
comma	−	−	+
semicolon	−	+	+
colon	−	+	+
period	+	−	+

Here I have listed the period as marked for [separation], but since the expected norm at the sentential level is separation, the period (as well as the question mark and exclamation point) could be unmarked via markedness reversal.

The point of the preceding examples is to show how viewing punctuation in terms of markedness sharpens our understanding of the relations between punctuation signs by forcing us to posit and defend feature specifications. It also enables us to explicate some of the alternations among and constraints on punctuation as consequences of the posited feature relationships that emerge. Together, the examples provided in the last two sections illustrate how the Praguean notion of asymmetry can be used as a tool to explore the relations in both language and culture by encoding nonequivalence as asymmetric features.

CONCLUSION

This chapter has examined various developments and extensions of markedness based on Jakobsonian themes, and an appropriate way to conclude might be to consider the marked/unmarked relation in terms of the underlying structuralist method itself—that is, by analyzing markedness as a concept defined by a feature complex.

Such an analysis begins with the idea of the opposition. Any opposition involves a distinctive or conceptual property and a relation between the two poles of that opposition, which may be characterized as opposites A and B. The effect of markedness is to superimpose onto the opposition A/B an analysis as signalization of A versus nonsignalization of A, where the latter has a double meaning. The polarity A/B is the feature or property defining the opposition, A is the signalization or mark, and markedness is the asymmetric characterization of the relation. Different extensions of markedness may be added onto this basic notion, just as redundant features are imposed on a contrastive opposition. Viewed as a

complex of oppositions, the additional properties of marked and unmarked terms can be schematized as follows:

Signalization of A	*Nonsignalization of A*
specific meaning	general meaning
conceptual complexity	conceptual simplicity
narrowly defined	broadly defined
syncretized	nonsyncretized
subset	superset
figure	ground
abnormal	normal
nonprototypical	prototypical
less frequent	more frequent
implying	implied
low valued	high valued
nonneutralizable	neutralizable
nonoptimal	optimal
overt expression	zero expression

To my knowledge, there is no one view of markedness in which all of
these oppositions are assumed; the above is a summary list of possible
characteristics. Different extensions of markedness select among (and
thus rank) the set of features that characterize markedness, often masking
the original idea of asymmetric opposition and promoting other characteristics. Andrews, Sangster, and van Schooneveld, for example, treat
markedness as characterized by the oppositions A versus non-A and by
specific meaning versus general meaning and subset versus superset; in
addition, they place restrictions on the features, requiring them to be
perceptual or distinctive features. Shapiro and Andersen rank conceptual
complexity and breadth of definition as largely determinative of
markedness, and put aside both general meaning and A versus non-A.
Newfield and Waugh treat markedness in terms of conceptual complexity, breadth of definition, and A versus non-A. Chvany's definition of
inherent markedness ranks A versus non-A high, while her definition of
contextual markedness gives priority to normality, implication, and
value. Though there is considerable variation among approaches,
Greenberg, Croft, Givón, and other typologists and functionalists rank
some combination of frequency, breadth of distribution, syncretization,
overt expression, conceptual complexity, figure/ground, implication, and
prototypicality high as criteria of markedness and develop correspond-
ingly scalar views, eschewing both A versus non-A and general meaning.
    What we have seen in the previous chapter and this one is that Jakob-

son's application of markedness ranges over various, sometimes conflicting criteria and that contemporary Jakobsonian approaches often select
as their guiding theme a particular aspect of Jakobson's work. This results in a set of competing types of markedness, all of which are
grounded in the original notion but all of which diverge. In the next
chapter, we turn to still another version of markedness that arose from
the original notion but which has developed in quite a different way
from the approaches discussed here: markedness in generative grammar.

FOUR

Chomsky on Markedness

Theories of markedness in the Jakobsonian semantic tradition seem quite different from those of Chomskyan syntax. Yet markedness in generative phonology and in Principles and Parameters syntax share the main theme of Jakobson's *Child Language, Aphasia, and Phonological Universals* and *Fundamentals of Language,* that is, language is treated as manifesting an inherent hierarchy that systematically and predictably unfolds in the course of acquisition. To explore this parallel, I begin by recounting the initial introduction of markedness into generative grammar.

THE SOUND PATTERN OF ENGLISH

The term markedness entered generative linguistic theory through phonology. The ninth and final chapter of Chomsky and Halle's *The Sound Pattern of English* (1968; hereafter *SPE*) was an epilogue titled "The Intrinsic Content of Features." That phonological theory was the route by which the notions of marked and unmarked made their way into generative grammar should come as no surprise. The Jakobsonian concept of a category as a complex of distinctive features was a key idea in the phonological theory developed by Chomsky and Halle, serving simultaneously as a means of representing phonemes, formulating generalizations across natural classes, and relating the particular to the universal (see *SPE,* chapters 6 and 7). In early generative phonology, features were also incorporated into what was known as the *evaluation metric.*[1] Recognizing that a language could be described by any number of formal systems, Chomsky set as a goal of linguistic theory to select among descriptions that give an adequate characterization of grammaticality and of essential grammatical relations. The evaluation metric was a theory-internal means of selecting the most highly valued grammar—the grammar best capable of describing the facts of a language.

The earliest published version of such a metric in Chomsky's work was the "condition of generality" described in *Syntactic Structures* (1957: 50), which equated the value of grammars with simplicity.[2] At the same time, Morris Halle was developing a definition of phonological simplicity based on minimization of feature specifications, drawing in part on Jakobson's ideas on information theory and the elimination of redundancy in phonemic representations (see Halle 1959a,b, 1961, 1962, 1964).

Chomsky's 1965 *Aspects of the Theory of Syntax* (hereafter *Aspects*) includes an extended discussion of the evaluation metric. Here Chomsky emphasizes that the evaluation metric is a theory-internal construct—a metatheory—specifying what sorts of generalizations are expected to occur in language and thus what generalizations would be more highly valued by a hypothetical language learner (1965: 37–38). Chomsky notes also that the task

> is that of determining which generalizations about a language are significant ones; an evaluation measure must be selected in such a way as to favor these. . . . The problem is to devise a procedure that will assign a numerical measure of valuation to a grammar in terms of the degree of linguistically significant generalization that this grammar achieves. (1965: 42)

Chomsky emphasizes this point by noting that different notational conventions (which are part of the evaluation metric) provide different definitions of natural processes, remarking that notational conventions such as parentheses and braces imply that certain patterns are typical of language and "are of the type that children learning a language will expect" (1965: 43).[3]

The idea of the evaluation metric was distinct from but related to the notions of substantive and formal universals, terms adopted in *Aspects*. Substantive universals make up the basic material of linguistic description—features and categories of Universal Grammar. Formal universals comprise the architecture of grammatical description—phrase structure rules, transformations, the cycle, rule order, and various abbreviatory conventions and rule-application constraints. Formal universals had a special role in early generative linguistic theory in that they enabled simplification of grammars (compactness of description) to serve as the evaluation measure. In *SPE*, for example, the definition of the evaluation metric was a statement that the value of a grammar was the inverse of the number of features required in that grammar (1968: 304). Abbreviatory devices permitted a more optimal grammatical description to be formulated by eliminating redundancy, in effect permitting certain linguistic generalizations to be represented as shorter grammars.[4]

Substantive universals came to be further connected to the evaluation of grammars through the markedness of phonological features, a step that Stephen Anderson has referred to as "[t]he first line of attack on the SPE program from within the assumptions of generative grammar" (1985: 331).

In chapter 9 of *SPE*, Chomsky and Halle conceded that their account of phonological features, phonological rules, and phonological inventories had the flaw of allowing implausible rules and segment inventories to be as highly valued as natural rules and inventories. The evaluation metric made no distinctions among expected combinations of substantive elements (or processes) and unexpected ones. To deal with this flaw, they introduced markedness into generative phonology as a means of encoding what they, echoing Jakobson and Trubetzkoy, referred to as the "intrinsic content" of features. Chomsky and Halle proposed a set of thirty-nine universal *marking conventions* that would tie naturalness to evaluation. In their system, the unmarked value of a feature was cost-free with respect to the evaluation metric, while the marked values were counted by the metric.[5]

Chomsky and Halle proposed several uses for their theory of marking conventions. Segment inventories were evaluated according to the number of marked features required to characterize them, with more natural inventories evaluated as less costly. In addition, feature sequences and sets of lexical items were evaluated for markedness based on the number of marked features they entailed, producing a cost for the lexical stock of the language. The important concept of *linking* was also posited in *SPE*. Linking is a process by which the number of features required to characterize phonological rules is reduced by allowing marking conventions to apply to the output of phonological rules. Thus, a phonological process that matched the effect of a markedness convention was less costly than one that did not, since linked (that is, unmarked) feature changes could be eliminated from the statement of the rule.[6]

The theories of markedness and linking extended the basic program of *SPE* phonology—that of representing phonological structure and process as a formal system subject to an evaluation metric. Just as formal universals like the abbreviatory conventions fed the metric, so too did the marking conventions, which encoded substantive universals and made natural processes less costly. Chomsky and Halle also saw markedness as a means of opening up the theory of generative phonology to verification through the analysis of historical change and language acquisition. But at the time of *SPE* they provided no clues as to how the idealized language learner constructs a phonological system.

The *SPE* theory of marking conventions differed in several ways from that proposed in Jakobson's *Child Language* and in Jakobson and Halle's *Fundamentals of Language*. One difference was the set of features itself.[7] Another was that Chomsky and Halle presented the markedness conventions as an explicitly formalized hierarchy of features, using the process notation of phonological rules, rather than as a statement of implicational universals, as in Jakobson (1968a [1941]). The *SPE* program also differed with respect to the question of how the markedness hierarchy was determined. While Jakobson provided a rather extensive justification of the markedness values on perceptual grounds, Chomsky and Halle relied instead on typological generalizations, drawing on Trubetzkoy's and Jakobson's work.[8] And while their conventions were in ways similar to those of Jakobson (*pace* the feature definitions and notation), markedness in *SPE* is a way of encoding preference in grammars rather than attempting to explain asymmetries in phonological correlations.

The *SPE* theory of markedness opened up some new avenues for generative phonological theory, and it created some problems as well. The use of the terms marked and unmarked as a way of describing preferred processes was quickly extended to other sorts of "linguistically significant generalizations." Kiparsky, for example, noting that rule reordering favored the maximal utilization of rules (what are known as feeding and counterbleeding orders), posited that such orders were "linguistically simpler" and he adopted the terms *marked order* and *unmarked order* "[a]s a convenient designation for the order types which are shunned and preferred" (1968: 200).[9]

In effect, markedness came to be understood as synonymous with *costly in terms of the evaluation metric* and unmarked with *cheap in terms of the evaluation metric*. But it was not obvious how a marked order or other marked property could be equated to a marked feature in terms of cost. Difficulties also arose with the idea of markedness being part of the evaluation metric. Merely summing the values of marked features in a segment could not directly account for the fact that some features are more likely than others or for the fact that phonological systems have a certain minimal complexity and symmetry.[10]

In her MIT doctoral dissertation, Mary-Louise Kean reformulated the *SPE* marking conventions and clarified the nature of markedness in generative phonology. Kean proposed a set of twenty-five universal marking conventions that "characterize the 'optimal' (most likely) conjunctions of specified features within segments" (1980: i). She also suggested that certain phonological features (the features consonantal, anterior, back, low, labial, and sonorant) are obligatorily marked in any language, where obligatorily marked means that it is obligatory that some segment is marked for that feature. All other features are obligatorily unmarked, meaning that the presence of a segment marked for that feature is not required. The markedness conventions thus state the basic hierarchy of features, and the additional constraints control the distribution of marked and unmarked features to impose a minimal symmetry and complexity on phonological systems, as in the *SPE* system. The result characterizes the optimal phonological system as consisting of the vowels /a/, /i/, and /u/; the consonants /p/, /t/, /k/, and /n/; and a glide.

Kean also discussed the role of markedness in evaluation, adopting the convention that "[t]he 'value' of a segmental system is the reciprocal of the sum of the marked features of its members" (1980: 36). This parallels the evaluation metric of *SPE* but departs from the SPE proposal that "[t]he complexity of a [segmental] system is equal to the sum of the marked features in its members" (*SPE*: 409).

The theories of markedness proposed in *SPE* and in Kean's dissertation were attempts to formulate substantive universals in a way that is compatible with the evaluation metric and the format of generative phonology. In *The Generative Enterprise*, a series of interviews with linguists Riny Huybregts and Henk van Riemsdijk, Chomsky describes the final chapter of *SPE* as "the most interesting" chapter of the book (1982: 109) and adds that the concept of linking is the most significant idea in the *SPE* markedness theory. Interestingly, the concept of linking turns out to be rather similar to the version of markedness that developed in the extended standard theory syntax of the 1970s.

THE EXTENDED STANDARD THEORY

Syntax and phonology have turned out to be organized rather differently, and attempts to carry over the theory of phonological markedness as a framework for analyzing syntax have led to a different sort of research program. In syntax, *SPE*-style markedness using features has received much less attention and has had much less acceptance.

George Lakoff's *Irregularity in Syntax* (1970) applied the idea of markedness conventions to syntactic irregularity, raising the possibility that the markedness notation could be used to encode language-particular syntactic norms. Citing an example of Paul Postal's, Lakoff shows how the noun features *singular* and *countable* can be related in terms of redundancy rules that convert marked and unmarked features into pluses and minuses. Lakoff gives the lexical representations of the count and mass nouns *boy*, *chalk*, *pants*, and *people* as

	boy	chalk	pants	people
singular	u	u	m	m
countable	u	m	m	u

suggesting that the number of *m*'s corresponds to a degree of language-particular naturalness. The features plural and mass are treated as generally marked. *Boy* is thus doubly unmarked, being both singular and countable (e.g., *one boy*); *chalk* is singular but marked as a mass noun *(one piece of chalk* but not *one chalk); people* is marked as plural but is unmarked in that it is countable *(two people,* but *one person); pants* is doubly marked, being both plural and noncountable. In Lakoff's view, singular *boy* is "completely regular," *pants* is "most deviant," and the other items fall in the intermediate range.[11]

Part of Lakoff's idea is that the degree of deviance of a feature combination is encoded by markedness specifications and redundancy rules, with preferred patterns having a relatively higher number of *u*'s while patterns that deviate from the norm have a higher number of *m*'s.[12] With respect to the features singular and countable, Lakoff suggests that it is unmarked for mass nouns to be singular. So *chalk* is unmarked for singularity while *pants*, a plural mass noun, is marked; a rule captures the generalization underlying the preference structure but still allows the less preferred situations to exist. In addition, the rule helps to express the generalization that *chalk, rice, coffee* (etc.) change their senses when they are used in the plural: *chalks, rices, coffees* switch to the unmarked, countable sense when used in the plural.

Similar redundancy rules can be posited for other feature relationships. Also following Lakoff, one might posit that the unmarked situation is for adjectives to realize states and for verbs to realize dynamic actions. In that view, examples like *I am finally leaving* would be unmarked, while ones like *I am finally understanding you* would be marked (since the verb is stative). Similarly, examples like *The tall woman* would be unmarked, while *the standing woman*, with a nonstative adjectival form, would be marked. The use of redundancy rules can be extended naturally to morphology as well. In English plural morphology, the unmarked expression is the morpheme spelled *-s* or *-es*. This can be expressed by using a redundancy rule to specify that the regular plural is unmarked, while the irregular plurals *(geese, feet, oxen*, etc.) are given by marked rules.

This feature approach is also adopted in Robin Lakoff's 1968 *Abstract Syntax and Latin Complementation*.[13] One of her examples concerns English verbs of communication—such as *say, suggest, mention*, and so on—which she treats as unmarked when they select tensed complements. According to Lakoff, instances in which communication verbs select other complements would be marked. Thus all of the following would be marked combinations: *I mentioned Mary's visiting, I declared the meeting to be over, I suggested that everyone be quiet.* Verbs of ordering, on the other hand, are treated as unmarked when they select only infinitives. Marked complementation would be instances where tensed or subjunctive clauses occur: *I ordered that everyone would leave, I command that everyone leave.*

The approach developed in *Irregularity in Syntax* and in *Abstract Syntax and Latin Complementation* presents some intriguing possibilities for encoding the preferred properties of a set of lexical items. However, this approach was overshadowed by the syntactic markedness theory developed by Chomsky in the 1970s.[14]

In work beginning with his "Conditions on Transformations" (1973) and continuing in "Conditions on Rules of Grammar" (1976), "On Wh-Movement" (1977c), and "On Binding" (1980), Chomsky developed a view of generative grammar that attempted to greatly constrain the analytic and theoretical devices available—that is, to decrease the class of possible grammars. The goal was to make progress on the problem of language acquisition by elaborating the structure of formal and substantive universals to permit simplification of particular grammars. Thus, the more work done by substantive constraints and by conditions on levels of representation or conditions on rule application, the less work remained for language-particular grammars. Presumably, with less to do, the set of grammars would have fewer options available. And with fewer options to choose from, the problem of acquisition becomes more tractable.

In "Conditions on Transformations," Chomsky began to shift his research in this direction by developing a relative interpretation of conditions on rules. In this view, conditions like the A-Over-A Condition, the Tensed Sentence Condition, and the Specified Subject Condition do not impose absolute restrictions; instead, rules apply in accordance with conditions unless the rules are specifically complicated to evade them.[15] Chomsky notes that "[t]he logic of this approach is essentially that of the theory of markedness" (1973: 236), implying that the conditions function as part of the evaluation metric by allowing syntactic processes that conform to them to be formally simpler. "Conditions on Transformation" thus treats minimal transformations as unmarked and elaborations of the minimal format as marked complications of the grammar. This approach parallels that of phonological linking: just as linking rules treat linked phonological processes as cost-free and nonlinked processes as incurring some cost, minimal transformations allowed primitive movement processes to be treated as cost-free and complications of them to be assigned a cost.

The rule-based format of transformations permitted this analogue to linking to be formulated straightforwardly. Thus, if a rule like

$$\ldots NP_i \ldots NP_j \ldots \quad \rightarrow \quad \ldots NP_j \ldots [\ ]_j \ldots$$

represents the unmarked format (where the contents of a category NP_j moves to the location of another node NP_i, leaving behind an empty category), then the traditional passive rule

$$\ldots NP_i \text{ Aux V } NP_j \ldots \quad \rightarrow$$
$$\ldots NP_j \text{ Aux be } + \text{ en V } [\ ]_j \ldots$$

would be a marked version of the unmarked format. The linking approach to markedness is echoed and expanded in "On Wh-Movement," where Chomsky suggests that markedness might apply to the definitions involved in conditions on transformations. Discussing some apparent differences in the application of the Specified Subject Condition in different languages, Chomsky raises the possibility that the definition of subject might have marked and unmarked characterizations. Noting Ken Hale's (1976) suggestion for a syntactically "unmarked" subject, Chomsky speculates that "in accordance with [Hale's] approach a language might characterize the notion 'subject' differently, but at a cost in the grammar, in accordance with the logic of markedness" (1977c: 75). This extension is not without potential problems, however. In the "Conditions" framework it is implicitly clear how a marked rule would be evaluated, by way of a parallel with phonology: one can count the number of features or categories required beyond the minimal factorization of the rule. Of course, the idea of counting complications to a minimal factorization is not without problems itself. As Kean (1981) points out, all complications that could be stated in a rule format do not count equally.[16] But once the idea of marked and unmarked definitions of grammatical functions is introduced, the problem of weighting becomes even more complicated. It is unclear, for example, how a marked definition of subject (in, say, the Specified Subject Condition) would fit into an evaluation metric. Such implicit problems would certainly have been another factor impeding the development of a syntactic markedness theory in the generative syntax of the 1970s.

CORE GRAMMAR

In the next phase of syntactic theory, the role of markedness was expanded and new problems arose. The 1977 article "Filters and Control" by Chomsky and Howard Lasnik was in many ways a turning point in post-*Aspects* syntax, falling between "Conditions on Transformations" and *Lectures on Government and Binding* (1981a), both chronologically and theoretically. The focus of research shifted, and markedness began to be treated as part of a theory of *core grammar*.

In "Filters and Control," Chomsky and Lasnik attempt to provide additional architecture for Universal Grammar that is consistent with the goal of reducing the number of options that linguists and hypothetical learners have to draw on; in doing so, they compare a core grammar approach to the earlier *Aspects* theory, which they see as consisting of two parts:

> a universal grammar UG that determines the class of possible grammars and the way they operate, and a system of evaluation that ranks potential grammars in terms of "optimality" or "simplicity." (1977: 427)

Core grammar, by contrast, consists of a set of interacting modules, each posited to be of manageable complexity so as to be more easily learned. The modules proposed by Chomsky and Lasnik are (431):

1. Base
2. Transformations
   (movement, adjunction, substitution)
3a. Deletion   3b. Construal
4a. Filters   4b. Quantifier interpretation
5a. Phonology
6a. Stylistic rules

The base generates underlying representations (Deep Structures), which the transformational component converts to surface representations (Surface Structures). Deletion rules, filters, and phonological and stylistic rules operate on Surface Structures to yield phonological forms; rules of construal and quantifier interpretation operate on Surface Structures to yield logical forms. Grammatical options that fall within this core are free; grammatical options outside of this core incur some cost. Chomsky and Lasnik put it this way:

> We will assume that UG is not an "undifferentiated" system, but rather incorporates something analogous to a "theory of markedness". Specifically, there is a theory of core grammar with highly restricted options, limited expressive power, and a few parameters. Systems that fall within core grammar constitute "the unmarked case"; we may think of them as optimal in terms of the evaluation metric. An actual language is determined by fixing the parameters of core grammar and then adding rules or conditions, using much richer resources, . . . These added properties of grammars we may think of as the syntactic analogue of irregular verbs. (1977: 430)

The "Filters and Control" view departs from the earlier view of markedness as cost in that what is considered unmarked is the entire core grammar of a language—the result of some set of unmarked parameter values being instantiated. Core grammar is contrasted with (and supplemented by) a marked periphery, which Chomsky and Lasnik somewhat vaguely identify with grammatical irregularity.

The two main issues that arise from the treatment of markedness in "Filters and Control" are these: first, how does one determine which constructions are marked (peripheral) and which are unmarked (core); second, what is the relation between the core and the periphery. With respect to the first issue, it should be pointed out that the "Conditions" approach had a guiding principle for determining unmarkedness in terms of minimal factorizations and other notationally based criteria. In the "Filters and Control" model, the focus is shifted so that markedness is determined by the regularity, stability, and centrality of a construction to the core of the language and by cross-linguistic generalizations about construction types. The expansion of markedness away from minimal factorization makes it more difficult to be certain what is and is not marked, since there is no guarantee that formal simplicity will correspond to regularity, stability, and centrality. The analogue of minimal factorization in the "Filters and Control" system would be core grammar, with marked constructions defined as those that fall outside of the core. But this reduces the utility of markedness, since a full theory of core grammar is required in order to know what is marked. Essentially, the role of markedness becomes that of categorizing data as "handled by core grammar" or "not handled by core grammar," with the further expectation that those not handled by core grammar will have some properties that can be characterized as irregular, variable, or otherwise marginal. Markedness goes from being a relatively clear, theory-internal property of rules to being a less clear property shared by grammars and grammatical constructions.

The second issue concerns what the periphery looks like—how it is related to what is in the core. One possibility raised by Chomsky is that the periphery is continuous in some way with the core, differing by degree rather than kind. Another is that the periphery differs in kind from the core, consisting perhaps of any sort of grammatical rule or construction.[17]

Thus, while Chomsky and Lasnik's remarks open some new possibilities, they also leave much unaddressed.

Principles and Parameters

Lectures on Government and Binding (hereafter *LGB*), published in 1981, was a revised and expanded version of Chomsky's 1979 lectures at the Generative Linguists in the Old World (GLOW) conference at the Scuola Normale Superiore in Pisa (the Pisa lectures). In it the notion of the evaluation metric, still evident in "Filters and Control," is minimized further, and core grammar is reformulated as a theory of parameters. The general framework of *LGB* follows from "Filters and Control" in that Universal Grammar is structured as a set of interacting modules (phrase structure theory, Case theory, binding theory, control theory, bounding theory, government theory, etc.) and core language acquisition is viewed as a process of fixing parameters of universal principles rather than of learning rules.[18] But in *LGB* the notion of rule itself is largely eliminated from generative grammar: phrase structure is seen as an inter-action between lexical properties of argument structure and parameters of phrase structure theory (such as head-initial versus head-final, etc.), and traditional transformations are seen as the reflex of a generalized movement option known as "Move alpha." Against this background, Chomsky defines Universal Grammar as "a characterization of the child's pre-linguistic initial state" (1981b: 7) and defines core grammar as the setting of the parameters of Universal Grammar in a particular way.[19]

In *LGB*, markedness is viewed in terms of a description of the initial set of hypotheses available to a language learner. According to Chomsky, the theory of markedness "imposes a preference structure on the parame-ters of UG, and it permits the extension of core grammar to a marked periphery" (1981b: 8). Chomsky's statement identifies two separate as-pects to markedness: markedness within the core and markedness within the periphery. Markedness within the core is what Chomsky refers to as a preference structure, the idea being that certain parameter values are assumed by learners as defaults. These values are unmarked and other core options may be considered marked. This expands the notion of markedness given in "Filters and Control," tying markedness and param-eter setting to the idea of available evidence, since whenever the default is not chosen, the question arises of why it was not selected.

Chomsky remarks in *LGB* that "[i]n the absence of evidence to the contrary," a learner will choose unmarked parameters (1981b: 8), and he speculates about the sort of evidence that would be required to select a marked parameter value. Chomsky suggests that three sorts of experience might enter into the selection of marked parameters: positive evidence (such as the presence of a particular word order), direct negative evi-dence (by explicit correction of the child's speech or perhaps failure to communicate), or indirect negative evidence. With respect to the last, Chomsky writes:

> a not unreasonable acquisition system can be devised with the operative principle that if certain structures or rules fail to be exemplified in rela-tively simple expressions, where they would expect to be found, then

a (possibly marked) option is selected excluding them in the grammar, so that a kind of "negative evidence" can be available even without corrections, adverse reactions, etc. (1981b: 9)

In *LGB*, Chomsky also suggests that unmarked default parameter settings are not automatically equated with order of acquisition, stressing that acquisition is probably more complexly structured. He cautions that although order of acquisition might be related to markedness, "there are many complicating factors: e.g., processes of maturization may be such as to permit certain unmarked structures to be manifested only relatively late in acquisition, frequency effects may intervene, etc." (1981b: 9). In other words, that a particular option is a default does not necessarily mean that it is learned early.

As he develops the idea of markedness of parameter values, Chomsky continues to associate markedness with the periphery itself, positing that "each actual 'language' will incorporate a periphery of borrowings, historical residues, inversions, and so on, which we hardly expect to—and indeed would not want to—incorporate within a principled theory of UG" (1981b: 8). But in *LGB*, Chomsky stresses that the periphery cannot be just an arbitrary dumping ground for irregularities; rather he notes that since marked structures must be learned also, there must be some mechanism for this. In fact, he associates the same categories of evidence with the learning of the periphery as with the core, though the positive experiences are of a different type in the periphery—that is they are made evident by their irregularities as opposed to the presence of a triggering datum.

LGB was followed by Chomsky's only essay devoted specifically to markedness, his "Markedness and Core Grammar" (1981b), a contribution to a volume of articles dealing with *The Theory of Markedness in Core Grammar*, the proceedings of the 1979 GLOW meeting. Here Chomsky reiterates that the markedness of the periphery is manifest in irregularities and other marginal constructions but that these are structured in some way. He suggests that the periphery might be organized such that principles of core grammar are relaxed somehow:

> We might expect that the structure of [the periphery] relates to the theory of core grammar by such devices as relaxing certain conditions of core grammar, processes of analogy in some sense to be made precise, and so on, though there will presumably be independent structure as well: hierarchies of accessibility, etc. (1981b: 127)[20]

Hierarchies of accessibility connect grammar to the type of work pioneered in Jakobson's *Child Language*, to Greenberg's language universals research, and to work like that of Keenan and Comrie on noun phrase accessibility (see Keenan and Comrie 1976). Chomsky's idea that the periphery is related to the core is an intriguing one, bringing the core and periphery closer together. Yet it is also troublesome in one respect, for if there are hierarchies of markedness within the core—an unmarked default and one or more marked options—and if the periphery is defined as a relaxation of conditions of core grammar, can the marked part of the core and the periphery really be distinguished?

In his 1986 book *Knowledge of Language: Its Nature, Origin and Use*, Chomsky again restates and clarifies his views on markedness, suggesting that

> [t]he distinction between core and periphery leaves us with three notions of markedness: core versus periphery, internal to the core, and internal to the periphery. The second has to do with the way parameters are set in the absence of evidence. As for the third, there are, no doubt, significant regularities even in departures from the core principles (for example, in irregular verb morphology in English), and it may be that peripheral constructions are related to the core in systematic ways, say, by relaxing certain conditions of core grammar. (1986: 147)

Chomsky also reiterates his earlier idea that markedness is not a standalone feature of parameters but one that is connected to other factors and that parameters may be interdependent (146). This is a notion similar to the context-sensitivity of markedness developed in *SPE:* just as the markedness value of some phonological feature might depend on its sequential or intrasegmental context, the markedness value of some parameter A may be affected by some other parameter B. So, for example, just as voicing is marked for consonants and unmarked for vowels, we can also analyze certain subject-inversion phenomena as dependent on null subject phenomena (see Hyams 1986 and chapter 5 below).[21]

For many generative grammarians working in the 1980s Principles and Parameters framework, markedness ends up referring to three related things: (1) a distinction between unmarked core and marked periphery; (2) a preference structure imputed to the parameters and parameter values of core grammar; and (3) a preference structure among the rules of the periphery. The preference structures (2) and (3) are not a great divergence from the "traditional" generative theory of markedness and linking developed in *SPE* and in "Conditions on Transformation," where a cost is assigned to possibilities that extend a set of theoretically defined unmarked options. The main difference between later models (such as the core grammar model and the Principles and Parameters model) and earlier ones is that the later models adopt a more complex hierarchy of preferences (ranging from default to a least preferred) while earlier models rely on a simpler (perhaps overly simple) implementation of cost as formal complication. The later models also pay more attention to the problem of evidence for various parametric choices and the triggering of parameter settings, though Chomsky himself does not develop this in any detailed way.

Distinction (1), between core and periphery, does represent a sharp departure from the *SPE* and "Conditions" view of markedness, though it is a distinction present (in different terminology) in Jakobson's *Child Language*, which essentially defines a core grammar for phonology, and it is implied in the *SPE* discussion of optimal phonological systems as well.

EXEMPLIFICATION

To this point we have been looking primarily at Chomsky's discussions *about* the theory of markedness and the evolution of his views. To get a clearer picture of what these discussions mean, it will be helpful to look at some of the constructions and rules he has analyzed as marked and unmarked and at some of the criteria he has used to reach these conclusions.

We have already considered one early exemplification of markedness: in the "Conditions" framework, Chomsky posited minimal transformations as the unmarked case, with additional constants as marked complications. The logic of this approach is that of *SPE*, with minimal transformations embodying an empirical assumption about what constitutes natural syntactic processes.

In later works a number of specific constructions and phenomena are analyzed in terms of markedness—choice of tensed versus infinitive verb, subject control of infinitives, complementizer deletion, and various Case assignment options. In "Filters and Control" for example, Chomsky and Lasnik treat relative infinitival constructions as marked, saying that

> these constructions are rarely found in anything like the variety exhibited in English, and they are a fairly recent phenomenon, in this variety, in English as well. It would not be surprising, then, to discover that special rules are needed for Modern English, departing from what we take to be core grammar. (1977: 470)

In "On Binding," Chomsky also gives several examples of marked and unmarked phenomena. Following Koster (1978), he assumes that unbounded *wh*-movement is "the marked case," with examples like *who do they think Bill will see* permitted by some marked property of English grammar. This means that languages that have strictly local *wh*-movement represent the unmarked case cross-linguistically. In "On

Binding," Chomsky treats this in terms of the bounding principle of Subjacency, positing that in English both S and S' are bounding nodes but that for certain bridge verbs S' "does not count as a bounding node for Subjacency, [which is] a marked property of these verbs" (1980: 15). Chomsky also discusses marked Case assignment and control properties in "On Binding." He treats oblique Case assignment by verbs and Case marking across clauses as marked properties. With respect to constructions like *John believed him to be crazy*, Chomsky says:

> We have so far been considering infinitival complements to verbs with the subject PRO, which we take to be "the unmarked case". But in English, as in some other languages, there are certain constructions with lexical subjects for infinitives. A special marked rule is therefore required to accommodate them. (1980: 28)[22]

In order to encode which verbs allow this marked rule, Chomsky suggests assigning "a certain marked feature" [F] to verbs like *believe* (1980: 28).

Another property identified as marked in "On Binding" is subject control of infinitives, as illustrated in the example *The candidates promised the voters φ to reform the electoral system*. Subject control contrasts with object control examples like *The candidates persuaded the voters φ to reform the electoral system*. Chomsky assumes that the Minimal Distance Principle of Rosenbaum (1967) is the descriptive generalization that covers unmarked control cases. According to this, the closest argument controls the subject of the infinitive—the object if there is one, the subject otherwise. However, verbs like *promise* and a few others require that the main subject control the infinitive even when an object is present. Chomsky treats such verbs as "marked in the lexicon with the feature [+SC] indicating 'assigns subject control' " (1980: 33).

In part, the "On Binding" system is rather traditional, treating marked constructions as requiring specification in the lexicon of marked features like [F] and [SC]. In other respects, however, it departs from earlier practice, assuming the existence of marked rules that are associated with those features and marked parameter options. Moreover, it is not clear whether the "cost" of the marked properties of exceptional Case marking and subject control lies in the lexical specification of the features like [F] and [SC], in the addition to core grammar of marked rules of Case assignment and indexing, or in both.[23]

In *LGB*, Chomsky comments on some other likely marked and unmarked constructions. He notes that the deletion of the complementizer *for* is subject to considerable idiosyncratic variation in English, with some speakers retaining the *for* when it follows the verb and others freely dropping it (cf. *I'd prefer (for) you not to do that; I'd like (for) you to do something*, etc.). The idiosyncracy is taken as evidence that *for*-deletion is a marked rule of English (1981a: 19). However, Chomsky also seems to treat the presence of *for* in infinitival constructions as a marked option restricted to postverbal positions, claiming that null subjects are obligatory in all positions except the postverbal and that "there are no marked exceptions" (1981a: 70). Thus both possibilities with an overt subject are marked, with (presumably) the last as the more marked:

I'd like _____ to do something.   (unmarked)
I'd like for you to do something.   (marked)
I'd like you to do something.   (marked)

In "Markedness and Core Grammar," Chomsky treats the so-called *picture*-NP construction, which he takes as marked. This construction, in which bound anaphors like *each other* occur as the complement of nouns like *picture*, *(letter, book, story*, etc.), generally allows greater possibilities for the binding of *each other* to an antecedent than occur elsewhere. Consider the following examples (from Chomsky 1981b):

They heard the stories about *each other* that had been published last year.

They heard stories about *each other*.

They expected that pictures of *each other* would be on sale.

They expected that several books about *each other* would be on sale.

They think it is a pity that pictures of *each other* are hanging on the wall.

I think it would please *them* that pictures of *each other* are hanging on the wall.

They think it would please me that pictures of *each other* are hanging on the wall.

They think that there are some letters for *each other* at the post office.

Chomsky suggests that the examples above can reasonably be considered marked, noting that they "seem somewhat marginal, judgements tend to vary, and there appear to be differences in judgements depending on lexical choice" (1981b: 143). But he concedes that "[i]n general, this seems to be a rather hazy area, and the construction appears to be a rather unusual one" (143). Chomsky also notes that "nonstructural factors" enter into the acceptability of such examples, with those examples having lexical subjects being more resistant to anaphoric relatedness than those with nonlexical subjects like *it* or *there*.[24]

The binding theory Chomsky was assuming at the time required that anaphors be bound in what was known as their governing category, in this instance in the noun phrase containing the anaphor. To account for the imputed grammaticality of these examples, Chomsky suggests a marked principle of English such that "*each other* may be free in its governing NP if it is not free in the c-commanding domain of a lexical subject," (1981b: 143) where the c-commanding domain of a lexical subject basically means the domain of a lexical subject that precedes the anaphor and is higher in the phrase structure tree. Chomsky emphasizes that relaxations and abstract analogies created by loosening principles of core grammar might in general characterize the periphery.[25] As noted earlier, Chomsky tentatively drops this idea in *The Generative Enterprise*, but proposes it again in *Knowledge of Language*, demonstrating some uncertainty about the relationship of core and periphery.

Chomsky's discussion in connection with the *picture*-NP constructions does clarify one thing by noting that any theory of markedness in a core grammar framework requires two questions to be answered: (1) when is it reasonable to assume that sentences or constructions are marked, and (2) how are marked constructions treated in the grammar? The first question focuses on markedness from the perspective of language, asking what correlative properties one should expect to find in marked constructions. The second question focuses on markedness from the perspective of grammatical theory, asking what options are available for marked rules, principles, and lexical items, and how these options are related to the core.

Overall, Chomsky's practice with markedness shows him tacking about, attempting to characterize it in terms of principles of core grammar but also typologically (as in *SPE* and in his discussions of cross-linguistic syntactic tendencies), language-particularly (via judgments of marginality and regularity), and acquisitionally (by drawing on plausible speculations about acquisition and evidence available to the learner). One thing that should be clear is that the criteria shift and evolve—from the *SPE* focus on phonological universals and typology, to the "Conditions on Transformations" view of unmarked rules as minimal factorizations, to the "Filters and Control" identification of unmarked with core grammar and of marked as the analogue of irregularity, to the *LGB* focus on learnability and defaults. It should also be clear that the problems that arise are essentially the same ones we noted in the Jakobsonian approaches to markedness—distinguishing the marked from the unmarked and integrating markedness into a larger theoretical context.

ECONOMY AND MINIMALISM

In two recent works, "Some Notes on Economy of Derivation and Representation" (1989) and "A Minimalist Program for Linguistic Theory" (1992), Chomsky has proposed a radical departure from the Principles and Parameters framework. He turns once again to the notion of simplicity, though eschewing the evaluation metric. The revived concept of simplicity applies to the relation between levels of grammar.[26] Chomsky suggests that derivations involve "uniqueness" principles that permit, in the best case, only one surface structure for each deep structure. He also adopts principles that encode a preference for logical form operations rather than overt syntactic ones (the "procrastination" principle) and which require that rules do not apply unless their application is necessary (the "last resort" principle). In Chomsky's view, these principles are explicable in terms of economy of representation and economy of derivation. With respect to the procrastination principle, for example, Chomsky remarks that "[t]he intuitive idea is that LF[Logical form]-operations are a kind of 'wired-in' reflex, operating mechanically beyond awareness. They are less costly than overt operations" (1989: 51). Regarding the last-resort principle, Chomsky adds that "[t]he notion of 'last resort' operation is formulable in terms of economy: 'shorter derivations are always chosen over longer ones' " (50).

While economy of representation and derivation sound like the earlier evaluation metric, cost is treated differently than it was in *Aspects* syntax or *SPE* phonology. The *Aspects* and *SPE* notions of evaluation were based on ranking possible grammars (or sets of hypotheses), treating the language learner as a little linguist engaged in theory comparison. The economy proposal, on the other hand, views cost as preference given by Universal Grammar, with economy being similar to the notion of unmarkedness developed in "Conditions on Transformations"—that is, with the principles providing a basic template, and deviations from that template having a cost.

In "A Minimalist Program for Linguistic Theory," Chomsky acknowledges the continuity between his current ideas and earlier approaches, and he associates core grammar directly with economy:

> In early work, economy considerations entered as part of the evaluation
> metric which, it was assumed, selected a particular instantiation of the
> permitted format for rule systems, ... As inquiry has progressed,
> the presumed role of an evaluation metric has declined, and within the
> principles-and-parameters approach, it is generally assumed to be com-
> pletely dispensable: the principles are sufficiently restrictive so that
> PLD [Primary Linguistic Data] suffice in the normal case to set the
> parameter values that determine a language. (1992: 6)

Chomsky adds in an endnote that "[m]arkedness of parameters, if real, could be seen as a last residue of the evaluation metric" (1992: 63), apparently reversing his earlier position concerning hierarchies of accessibility within Universal Grammar.[27]

In connection with recent principles-based and minimalist approaches to syntax, we should note here the current interest in *optimality theory*, pioneered in phonology by Alan Prince and Paul Smolensky and applied to syntax by Jane Grimshaw and others (see Grimshaw 1993 in particular). This approach departs from the more or less traditional view that principles of grammar are independent and posits that principles may conflict. In this view, patterns of grammaticality follow from a ranking of principles that allows conflicts among principles to be resolved. In practice, this involves an evaluation scheme in which the optimal structural representation is that which violates the least important constraints. Thus, to take an example from Grimshaw, consider the contrast between main clause inversion of the auxiliary and its noninversion in English embedded interrogatives, in the (so-called) standard dialects:

When will I see such a sight again?
I wonder when I will see such a sight again.
*I wonder when will I see such a sight again.

Grimshaw proposes that inversion is due to the constraint that heads of phrases must be filled (the Obligatory Head Principle). Since the presence of an operator (like *when*) entails a head position following it, inversion is necessary to fill that head in the first example above. In embedded interrogatives, however, the Obligatory Head Principle is overridden by the higher ranked Projection Principle, which requires that selectional information must be represented at all levels. Inversion, as in the third example, is ruled out on the assumption (developed in Rizzi and Roberts 1989) that this principle rules out movement into the heads of selected constituents. Since the Projection Principle plays no role in main clause examples like *When will I see such a sight again?* inversion is both permitted and required.

Optimality theory shows considerable promise, and should it continue to prove revealing, it might subsume certain aspects of markedness. Since the ranking of constraints implies a preference structure among them, it is possible to treat higher ranked constraints as less marked than lower ranked constraints and to treat the optimal derivations as the least marked result. Moreover, if some nonoptimal derivations are only *less* grammatical than an optimal counterpart (rather than fully ungrammatical), deviations from optimality could be used to characterize the markedness of various violations.

In addition, the notion of markedness may be useful to optimality

theory in some ways. Should it turn out that the ranking of principles
varies from language to language, the framework of markedness may provide a further layer of analysis with which to view the ranking of principles.

OVERVIEW

Almost since its inception, the main theme of generative grammar has
been the problem of explanatory adequacy—the logical problem of language acquisition. The approach to this problem has evolved greatly
since the late 1950s, and markedness, which is important to generative
linguistics insofar as it serves this goal, has evolved along with it. As a
result, Chomsky's work on markedness shows a remarkable flexibility.
Nevertheless, his approach does revolve around and continually return
to two key ideas. One is the (Jakobsonian) idea that certain grammatical
options are more accessible than others and that markedness encodes a
preference structure or default structure for language acquisition. The
other is the idea that these preferences can be formalized in some way—
that markedness reflects the cost of particular analytic options. While
Chomsky's most recent work suggests that the markedness of parameters
is limited, the leading ideas of economy and minimalism are variations
on his earlier views on markedness. And given the rapidity of change
within generative grammar—which has evolved from the *Syntactic Structures* approach to the *Aspects* and *SPE* theories to the retrenchment of
"Conditions on Transformations," "On Wh-Movement," and "Filters
and Control" to the more radical shift in *LGB* and *Knowledge of Language*
to the current focus on economy and minimalism—markedness may
again reemerge as a central aspect of Chomsky's research program.

In light of the above, a working definition of markedness in generative grammar might be the following: given that language acquisition
involves the setting of a series of core parameters based on minimal linguistic input, markedness is the hierarchical arrangement of the parameters and the cost associated with different core choices and with non-core
choices. Yet, while it is easy to define markedness, it is difficult to talk
about there being any elaborately worked out *theory* of markedness in
Chomsky's work, markedness not having been developed in a systematic
and consistent line. Rather, markedness is a theme or leading idea in
generative grammar. And it is a theme that generative grammarians other
than Chomsky have attempted to flesh out and extend. To round out the
picture of markedness in generative grammar, we turn next to some of
these approaches.

FIVE

Departures from the Core

As noted in the previous chapter, Chomsky himself has not developed a detailed, comprehensive theory of markedness in syntax and has moved away from markedness of parameters in his most recent work. Others, however, have attempted to flesh out how a theory of marked and unmarked options in Universal Grammar might work and to examine its consequences. The questions that arise in such discussions revolve around four issues: (1) the nature of core grammar, (2) the existence of marked and unmarked parameters within core grammar, (3) the triggering evidence required to set parameters, and (4) the determination of markedness relations.

With respect to the first issue, we need to delve more deeply into the idea of the core. Some proposals (such as those of Chomsky and Lasnik) suggest that core grammar might be made up of only unmarked options. Alternatively, core grammar can be viewed as including some marked options (just as phonological systems contain marked features). In addition, the distinction between core and periphery and the treatment of the latter as marked raises questions as well: what is the cost of marked peripheral constructions, and how is that cost determined?

The second issue has to do with the idea that parameters within core grammar are themselves marked or unmarked. We need to inquire whether every parameter has an unmarked setting, or whether some parameters are left open. If so, which ones? And if parameters have unmarked and marked values, what is the relation between these and the core/periphery distinction?

The third issue is also related to the question of parameter setting. This is the question of what is required to set a parameter—that is, what sort of evidence do learners use to select among predetermined options? Do unmarked parameters represent the initial state of the language acquisition device? If so, presumably no evidence is required to adopt that parameter setting. However, it remains to be determined what sort of evidence, and how much, is needed to acquire a marked parameter. More generally, we might ask about the role of markedness in grammar development. Do children's grammars begin in an unmarked state and become successively more marked? Or is there the option of setting some parameters with marked values quite early? Parameter setting also has implications for second language acquisition as well, since the question arises of how much access adult speakers have to both the markedness of parameters and the markedness of the periphery.

Finally, for both parametric markedness and core/periphery markedness, the question arises of how markedness hierarchies are determined, that is, what sort of evidence linguists can use to posit that one parameter value is unmarked while others are marked. As we have seen, there are various possibilities for relevant criteria, including cross-linguistic evidence, evidence from acquisition order, properties of grammatical constructions within a language, hypotheses about learning mechanisms, and functional strategies.

We will explore these questions by examining different approaches to markedness that have arisen within the generative framework. As a point of departure, we briefly revisit the notion of the evaluation metric.

THE EVALUATION METRIC

A question that persists in discussions of markedness is the relation of markedness to the evaluation metric. In *Language and Responsibility*, a series of interviews with the French linguist Mitsou Ronat, Chomsky remarks that

> [o]ne must begin by characterizing potential systems of knowledge with the help of principles which express the biological given. These principles determine the type of grammars that are in principle available. They are associated with an evaluation procedure which, given possible grammars, selects the best one. (1977b: 116–7)[1]

In this view, which is basically that of *SPE*, the evaluation metric or procedure draws on the theory of markedness: it incorporates a set of substantive universals that helps select the best grammar. This is also the view of Chomsky and Lasnik (1977), who argue that "systems that fall within core grammar constitute 'the unmarked case'; we may think of them as optimal in terms of the evaluation metric" (1977: 430).[2] Some linguists have noted instances in which the evaluation metric has been extended; Kiparsky, for example, has observed that the evaluation metric shifted to a different theoretical role than was originally intended:

> Rather than just functioning as a procedure for selecting the "right" grammar among a number of grammars that generate the same language, it now is required to define a hierarchy of complexity even among grammars that generate different languages. We can, in fact, think of the evaluation measure as a theory of the order in which alternative hypotheses are entertained in the process of language acquisition. (1974: 263)

Such a definition merges the evaluation metric with markedness.[3] While some linguists have adopted this view, others, such as Kean, explicitly distinguish the evaluation metric from markedness. Kean identifies the former with a simplicity metric and the latter with a ranking of substantive features (1981: 560–1), emphasizing that markedness must do more than simply count deviations from core grammar. Keeping markedness and the evaluation metric distinct seems to me to be the most cogent view and is the one adopted here. In the discussions that follow, the evaluation metric is treated as a means of ranking alternate hypotheses within a language to arrive at the best grammar, while the theory of markedness is taken to be a set of hypotheses about the ranking of grammatical options across languages.

INSTANTIATIONS OF CORE GRAMMAR

One of the earliest attempts to incorporate markedness in the core grammar framework was Henk van Riemsdijk's *A Case Study in Syntactic Markedness* (1982), which analyzed English and Dutch preposition stranding in the core grammar framework (for example, sentences like *Who did you give it to?*).[4] Van Riemsdijk argues that, according to both cross-linguistic criteria and language-internal evidence, preposition stranding must be treated as a marked construction. Stranding is relatively rare in the languages of the world (mainly occurring in Germanic languages), and in Dutch it occurs only with a particular set of pronouns.

Given the assumption that stranding is marked, van Riemsdijk's main concern is how the cost of stranding should be encoded into the grammars of languages that have it. He advances some initial proposals, noting that "[n]o theory is available at the present, however, in which notions such as marked syntactic construction or cost of a syntactic rule are operationalized" (1982: 263). Van Riemsdijk points out that the marked nature of stranding could be associated either with a complication of the phrase structure or with a modification of the binding properties of syntactic categories. In the latter view, the category prepositional phrase would count as a bounding (or cyclic, in van Riemsdijk's terminology) node in the unmarked case. The marked case would be instances where prepositional phrases are not bounding nodes and hence permit movement of a noun phrase that strands the preposition.

Van Riemsdijk eschews this option, arguing that it would require additional complications to account for the instances in Dutch where stranding does not occur. The alternative he adopts is to treat the category prepositional phrase in English and Dutch as containing a complementizer position, which acts as an escape hatch that permits movement (similar to the complementizer in clause initial position). The "cost" of the marked option can thus be evaluated directly as a phrase structure complication.[5] Van Riemsdijk also suggests that the markedness of phrase structure is local, in that it can be established without reference to other components of grammar, and that this allows the evaluation measure to operate in the usual way (1982: 278). The main theme of his approach is to treat the core grammar of a language as the "optimally unmarked syntactic system" (263) and to treat markedness as being determined by a combination of cross-linguistic preference and internal regularity. Markedness is encoded as local phrase structure complexity, and the evaluation metric ranks the preposition stranding option as more complex than nonstranding.

A different approach, though a similar theme, is struck by Jan Koster in his 1978 article "Conditions, Empty Nodes, and Markedness." Koster views marked constructions as ones that show "differentiation across languages, variation in judgement, and susceptibility to lexical and nongrammatical complexity factors" (1978: 571). Cross-linguistic differentiation refers to the Greenbergian idea of occurrence in a wide number of languages. The intralinguistic factors reflect the idea that more costly features of a language will be more easily affected by extragrammatical, lexical, and structural complexities.[6] Koster proposes that marked sentences (those generated by rules outside of core grammar) can be diagnosed "by manipulating the lexical and structural context" of sentences (591). He gives the following as examples of marked sentences (proposing also to designate them with a superscripted m):

  a. ^{m}Who did you see a picture of?
  b. ^{m}What did you say that Bill saw?
  c. ^{m}Mary seems to be likely to win.
  d. ^{m}John is easy to please.

Koster argues that markedness is shown by the fact that changes in the lexical context result in a degrading of grammaticality judgments. So sentences (a) through (d) above contrast with (a') through (d'):

a'. *Who did you destroy a picture of?
b'. *What did you remark that Bill saw?
c'. *Mary seems to be probable to win.
d'. *John is illegal to please.

Koster's view of marked and unmarked sentences suggests that speakers do not have ready intuitions about marked sentences, since all the examples in (a) throught (d) above are straightforwardly grammatical. Interestingly, examples like *To whom did you give the money?* and *From which applicants did you receive reference letters?* seem marginal and variable in precisely the way that Koster suggests for marked structures, suggesting that by his criteria nonstranding is marked in English.

In the framework that Koster assumes, markedness is a property of sentences that is interpreted in terms of the division of labor between core and periphery. Moreover, he suggests that Universal Grammar provides a schema for extending core grammar with a set of auxiliary conditions that generalize core principles (the preferred way of extending core grammar, in his view) and which permit other additions and contextual specifications to core rules (1978: 580).[7]

Hirschbühler and Rivero (1981), in their discussion of relative clauses in Catalan, offer another variant of the core grammar approach. In contrast to the view that the periphery contains marked rules or that it accounts for counterexamples to core predictions, they propose that any rule of grammar "is an aggregate of properties" (1981: 592), some unmarked and others marked, with the marked aspects of rules serving to narrow the set of sentences that could be derived from the core version of the rule.

Hirschbühler and Rivero illustrate their approach with the rule-deleting relative pronouns in the complementizer (COMP) position of a relative clause. They note that the rule is optional in English, while in Catalan it is obligatory. Thus examples like *El tren que va a Barcelona és aquest* ('The train that goes to Barcelona is this one,' their example 15a) cannot occur with a relative pronoun substituting for *que* (that is, there is no parallel of the English 'The train *which* goes to Barcelona is this one'). Hirschbühler and Rivero suggest that optional deletion (and optional rule application more generally) is unmarked and that the requirement that relative pronouns delete in Catalan is the marked aspect of the rule.

Hirschbühler and Rivero's position is interesting in that they imply that the periphery need not have any qualitative difference from the core. Instead of being characterized by irregularity, instability, and mar-

ginality, the periphery represents a subset of the core (they comment
that if Koster's view of marked rules as core counterexamples is also
correct, then such rules as Koster describes might be considered "more
marked" than the part of the periphery that they discuss).[8]

Hirschbühler and Rivero also connect their proposal to learnability,
suggesting that the marked aspect of the deletion rule is learned indi-
rectly. They acknowledge the general learnability problem that negative
conditions create, but suggest that

> access to negative evidence is possible in an indirect way. For example,
> if a WH-NP [such as who] is never found in COMP, but only the que
> complementizer, learners will encounter numerous examples of this sit-
> uation; they can then assume that the presence of the relative pronoun
> is impossible in that situation (622).[9]

Kean (1981) provides yet another perspective on core grammar, arguing that markedness must provide more than an evaluation metric that
simply calculates deviations from core grammar.[10] Rather, she argues, a
theory of markedness must provide a ranking of deviations from core
grammar that captures generalizations. Thus, she points out that any
noun phrase (NP) movement rule that deviates from a core rule by adding a constant term C would be equally costly—regardless of the nature
of the constant. So a rule having the structural analysis . . . C . . . NP
. . . would be equally costly for any value of C (a verb, an adverb, etc.),
unless the theory of markedness provides some evaluation of different
choices of the constant C.[11]

More generally, Kean draws on analogies with her work on phonological systems to describe markedness as "a formal theory of substantive
universals" which would assign probabilities "to the occurrence and variation of substantive elements within and across grammars" (1981: 560).[12]
Her discussion of syntax is cast in terms of grammatical features like
case, tense, and mood and her main syntactic example concerns tense
and mood, inflection: Kean observes that in languages without subjunctive morphology, tense morphology is used in counterfactuals (as in her
English example If I were the queen of Sheba . . .). But in languages
without tense (such as Klamath), there is "apparently invariably" a morphological representation of the indicative versus subjunctive distinction
(564). Kean does not develop a formal proposal, but she does indicate
what a theory of markedness should address. It should capture the generalization that a morphological subjunctive implies a morphological indicative and that the absence of tense inflection implies a mood distinction.
It should also address the cost of having both morphological tense and
mood in a language and the cost of not having morphological tense in

a language. What Kean has in mind, then, is an *SPE*-like project for morphological features.

Kean has also addressed the question of the unmarkedness of core grammar, distinguishing between the possibility that core grammar is "literally" unmarked and that it is "relatively" unmarked (1981: 566). The former means that there would be only a single core grammar for all languages. The latter view, which she adopts, is that core grammar is only *relatively* unmarked. Kean thus argues that core grammar in syntax does not instantiate only unmarked options any more than phonological systems do. Rather, the optimal system is the one that fits the language and uses the fewest marked options, again as in phonology. Kean writes:

> Taking together all the substantive parameters (case, tense, mood, plural/distributive, etc.) along which languages can vary . . . what is suggested is that there will be a finite set of relatively scattered grammars which are core grammars, core grammars being those which involve no relaxing of conditions and constraints, where rules have minimal expressive power, and where the set of substantive elements expressed in the grammar are minimally marked. (1981: 568)

While much of the work on markedness in the late 1970s and early 1980s treats markedness in terms of the relation between the periphery and an adult core grammar,[13] some approaches at this time began to look at markedness in terms of grammar development. Alain Rouveret and Jean-Roger Vergnaud's "Specifying Reference to the Subject," for example, defines the markedness of adult grammars in terms of the child grammars that produce them, saying that "[t]he complexity of a grammar G_L in terms of markedness can be equated with the number of changes which have been made in the [initial grammar] to get the descriptively adequate grammar for L, G_L, i.e., with the length of the sequence G_0, . . . , G_L" (1980: 195). Their position implies that the initial state of learners is a grammar, G_0, and that G_0 instantiates core grammar, though they add in a footnote that their discussion is not intended to serve as a model of acquisition but merely as a neutral characterization of grammatical complexity. Edwin Williams's 1981 article "Language Acquisition, Markedness, and Phrase Structure" goes a step further, positing that "[t]he 'unmarked case' can be understood as the child's initial hypothesis about language (in advance of any data)," with a structured range of other hypotheses defined as marked options that a child successively tries (1981: 8).

These suggestions by Rouveret and Vergnaud and by Williams, while still within the core grammar framework, are precursors to the

shift in the mid-1980s toward markedness as an aspect of learnability, a
shift that was accompanied the Principles and Parameters view of core
grammar.

Parameters

In her 1986 book *Language Acquisition and the Theory of Parameters*, the
first study of language acquisition in the Principles and Parameters
framework, Nina Hyams takes up some of the questions that arise in
incorporating markedness into a model of parameter acquisition. Hyams
eschews the position that markedness is a feature of parameter settings,
maintaining instead that markedness refers only to the separation of unmarked core grammar from a marked periphery and that the theory of
markedness is a mapping function that "provides "the 'least marked' or
'most highly valued' grammar consistent with the data of a particular
language" (1986: 156–7).[14]

Hyams stresses that the shift of generative research away from the
idealization of instantaneous acquisition that characterized early generative research makes markedness unclear, since it can no longer be treated
as an idealized cost but instead must be responsible for evidence concerning acquisition. Pursuing this, she argues that there is no motivation for
treating earlier grammars as less marked than later ones: children may
acquire core structures relatively late in language acquisition because of
the complexity of the constructions themselves or because other developmental or structural prerequisites have not been attained.[15] So, for example, Chomsky and Lasnik (1977) suggest that certain restrictions on infinitival constructions are unmarked; they note, however, but that these
restrictions can arise only after infinitives are acquired, and thus filters
on infinitival constructions will not add to the complexity of the grammar even though they may be acquired late in the course of acquisition.[16]

In adhering to a view of markedness in terms of core versus periphery, Hyams highlights the bifurcation between the markedness of a
grammatical construction and the markedness of the devices that realize
that construction. She notes, for example, that a given construction or
rule may be unmarked in one language and marked in another (where by
"language" she includes stages of acquisition) (1986: 158). She suggests,
for example, that the possibility of postverbal subjects in pro-drop languages (languages that permit subject pronouns to be dropped) is unmarked and that it is determined by an implication relation with the pro-
drop parameter. In non-pro-drop languages, however, the phenomenon
is marked. Thus English constructions like *There walked into the room a
man* are marked, while corresponding constructions in Italian and Span-

ish are unmarked. Another example of a construction that can be in the core in one language and in the periphery in another is the exceptional Case marking construction, exemplified below.

*John believes to be crazy.
John believes Bill to be crazy.

John tried to leave.
*John tried Bill to leave.

John wants to leave.
John wants Bill to leave.

Hyams treats *believe*-type verbs and *want*-type verbs in terms of the marked process of exceptional Case marking in English, noting that the construction is limited to specific subclasses of verbs. She adds, however, that if Case were "systematically assigned to the subject of infinitives, on our view, this would not constitute a marked process in that language" (1986: 160). As Clark (1989) points out, languages like Latin and Irish allow systematic Case assignment to the subject of an infinitive clause, and so are good candidates for such a parameter. Thus, the accusative subjects of infinitives might be unmarked in the following examples, though the English glosses are marked constructions.[17]

credo [eam sapientem esse]
'(I) believe her to be wise'

[eam sapientem esse] creditur
'Her to be wise is believed'

is cuimhneach leo [iad a bheith ar seachran]
'they remembered themselves being lost'

Like van Riemsdijk, Koster, and others, Hyams stresses the need for a definition of markedness that can be tested by the properties of language. She envisions core grammar as a system that accounts in a simple way for the structure and acquisition of natural language while at the same time providing an account of the regularity or marginality of various constructions in a language.[18] But Hyams resists the idea that markedness is a feature of the parameter settings of core grammar themselves (though she ultimately leaves the matter open). She argues further that it is questionable to treat a parameter setting as marked or unmarked "solely on the basis of its position in the developmental sequence and in the absence of any independent evidence" (1986: 158) and that explanations of development based on markedness made under such assumptions

would be viciously circular (161).[19] Instead she assumes that default parameter settings within core grammar have nothing to do with
markedness. She argues, for example, that the pro-drop property is the
initial default parameter for all natural languages: in her view, English
begins as a pro-drop language, but the parameter is reset at a certain
stage. But since both pro-drop and non-pro-drop are permitted within
core grammar, neither value of the parameter should be considered unmarked.[20]

As noted in the previous chapter, Chomsky (1986) approaches the
problem of preference structure within the core differently, distinguishing between markedness within the core and markedness within the periphery. Hyams's view that there is no markedness within the core reflects a minority view among generative grammarians. But the issue that
Hyams raises—that a distinction must be made between core and periphery on the one hand and between preferred and less preferred parameter
settings on the other—is a distinction that must be dealt with if
markedness in generative grammar is to make any sense.

CREOLES

While the common view is that there are a limited number of core grammars defined by Universal Grammar, creolist Derek Bickerton has advanced the idea that there might just be a single, very simple, unmarked
core grammar that is common to all languages. In his *Brain and Behavioral
Sciences* article "The Language Bioprogram Hypothesis" (1984), Bickerton
contrasts the divergent histories of creoles with their common conditions
of origin (arising in a single generation from an impoverished data base)
and with the fundamental structural similarities among creole languages.
This striking uniformity in the face of divergent history leads Bickerton
to suggest that creoles will be one of the best possible testing grounds
for core grammar (and hence for markedness).

Bickerton proposes to explain general creole properties and their acquisition with his Language Bioprogram Hypothesis, and his argument
proceeds on two fronts. First is the idea that what is innovative in creole
grammar arises by invention from children whose linguistic input is a
pidgin and whose output is a creole. Second is the idea that the common
innovations of creole grammar are due to a species-specific language bioprogram (1984: 173). Bickerton proposes in addition that this program
drives language acquisition in non-creole languages as well, suggesting
that

    the role of the bioprogram for children acquiring a "ready-made" lan-
    guage (rather than acquiring a creole) is to furnish elementary forms

and structures from which (guided by input from the target language) they can develop other and more complex forms and structures. (1984: 185)

The Language Bioprogram Hypothesis has a weak form and a strong form. The strong form is that the bioprogram is a single core grammar that underlies the grammars of all natural languages. In this view, of course, there is no need for marked and unmarked parameters, since all parameters are fixed (that is, they are principles rather than parameters). The weaker form of the Language Bioprogram Hypothesis is that the bioprogram is a restricted form of core grammar in which many of the Universal Grammar options are preset and in which modifications and additions to the core are permitted to accommodate peripheral processes (1984: 179).[21] Bickerton suggests that

> various combinations of [parameter] settings would yield all the possible core grammars of human languages. In other words, a human child would have latent in his mind all possible grammars, although differential weighting attached to the various settings would mean that certain types of grammar would have a preferred status. (1984: 178)

The bioprogram grammar would be the set of unmarked settings available to the child, with the unmarked setting being selected in the absence of evidence to the contrary. Bickerton's overall position shares with Chomsky's a commitment to a species-specific language faculty; in addition, the weak version of Bickerton's theory shares the idea that unmarked parameter settings are acquisitionally costless. However, Bickerton's and Chomsky's positions converge in theme but not in details. Bickerton assumes that very little is in the species-specific core. He posits only a minimal phrase-structure schema, representing what he takes to be the common features of the most radical creoles.[22]

Lightfoot (1991) has indicated some problems with Bickerton's proposal regarding the relation of markedness to creole grammar, and focuses especially on Bickerton's suggestion that creole grammar is a pure representation of unmarked parameter settings of Universal Grammar.[23] Lightfoot points out, for example, that Saramaccan, Bickerton's main example of a radical creole, has a marked setting for the parameter that allows wh-movement from subordinate clauses. Like English, Saramaccan allows sentences like *What did they think that you said?*; however, such sentences should be precluded if radical creoles have only unmarked parameter settings. More generally, Lightfoot disputes Bickerton's assumption that radical creoles must have only unmarked parameter settings. He observes that conclusions about marked parameter settings will depend on assumptions about triggering data and that creoles could contain sufficiently robust or salient evidence to set parameters to marked values: parameters of word order, for example, are easily established on the basis of readily available and abundant data (1991: 176).[24] Lightfoot writes that an expectation that radical creoles have only unmarked parameters "presupposes that marked settings require access to more extensive experience, and perhaps to fairly exotic data, and that this is not available to the first speakers of a creole" (176).

Bickerton's view is one instantiation of the position that there are marked and unmarked parameters, and he takes creole properties as a diagnostic of unmarkedness. There are other approaches to the question of determining marked and unmarked parameter values as well, and we turn to some of these in the next section. Following that, we consider the settings of parameters, and finally examine some of the ways that a parameter-setting model might work.

FUNCTIONAL MOTIVATION

How do we know which of two (or more) parameter values of Universal Grammar is unmarked? If, by hypothesis, parameters are part of core grammar, we cannot determine this by appealing to diagnostics of the core/periphery distinction such as irregularity, instability, or marginality. Presumably both (or all) values of a parameter will have core properties, and should be regular, stable, and productive. What then distinguishes a marked from an unmarked parameter setting?

One possibility is to assume, following Chomsky and Lasnik, that unmarked options have a functional motivation. Chomsky and Lasnik propose this for the core/periphery distinction, suggesting that the *[$_{NP}$ NP tense VP] filter (which precludes sentences like *She left was odd*) might be functionally motivated. They argue that the filter is consistent with a plausible sentence-processing strategy—the strategy that structures that can be analyzed as main clauses are analyzed as such. In his article "Learnability, Restrictiveness and the Evaluation Metric" (1981a), Lasnik reemphasizes functional explanations, suggesting that the functional explanation for the filter follows from the Minimal Attachment Strategy of Frazier (1978). He also reiterates the suggestion from Chomsky and Lasnik's "Filters and Control" that the unmarked filters on infinitival structures serve as a means of narrowing the class of possible derivations from a given underlying structure, which is consistent with the possibility that "performance systems 'prefer' a grammar in which the relation between deep and surface structure is as close as possible to biunique" (1981a: 157). In addition, Lasnik suggests that "except in the face of evidence to the contrary, the child will assume that any particular deep structure gives rise to only one surface structure" (157). Moreover, following a suggestion of Kenneth Wexler (1981), he speculates that such a Biuniqueness Principle plays a role in determining markedness generally.

Pursuing this line of thinking within the core, it might be possible as well to connect unmarked parameter settings to functionally motivated grammatical options and to connect marked parameter settings to options that are not so motivated.[25]

POVERTY-OF-STIMULUS ARGUMENTS

Lasnik's work has also developed another possible way to determine what is unmarked, by considering the question of how a learner acquires marked options. If learners require either positive evidence or indirect negative evidence to set marked parameters and to learn the periphery, then it follows that considering the types of evidence that are available to learners will provide information about markedness.

Consider, for example, how a learner acquires a marked option for exceptional Case marking. Lasnik treats exceptional Case marking in terms of a process of S' deletion (which makes an infinitive clause available to Case assignment by a verb in a higher clause). He argues that verbs like *try* must be unmarked, while verbs like *want*, with optional S' deletion, must be marked. This follows from the unavailability of negative data in learning. He writes:

> If the child's initial assumption is that there is never [S'] deletion, he will have guessed right for *try*, and will quickly receive disconfirming evidence for *want* in the form of grammatical sentences such as *[They wanted the men to win]*. On the other hand, if *want* is taken as the unmarked case, the only evidence that *try* is different is the ungrammaticality of such instances as *[They tried Bill to win* and *They tried each other to win]*. But, as has been widely discussed, "negative data" of the required sort does not seem available to the child. (1981b: 165)

This is fairly straightforward. Given two options, one that can be connected to a particular type of positive data and one that requires negative data (or rather esoteric and rare positive data), the logical assumption is that the alternative that can be learned from positive data will be marked while the data-poor alternative will be unmarked. But the unavailability of negative data will not always suffice to determine degrees of markedness, as Lasnik notes. He points out that when exceptional Case marking verbs like *believe* are considered, the question arises of whether *try* or *believe* is the unmarked case (1981b: 165).

It could be, for example, that what is unmarked is lack of S' deletion (i.e., *try*), while obligatory deletion is more marked *(believe)*, and optional deletion is most marked *(want)*. Or it could be that obligatory deletion is unmarked *(believe)*, nondeletion is more marked *(try)*, and optional deletion is most marked. There is no way to tell based on the criterion of positive evidence, and Lasnik suggests that the issue must be resolved (in favor of the former possibility) by examining the context of the phenomenon, which shows that Case marking into a subordinate clause is exceptional in English, and by considering cross-linguistic facts, which reveal that languages such as Vietnamese have verbs that behave like *try* and verbs that behave like *want* but lack verbs like *believe*. So Lasnik uses all three criteria to resolve the markedness decision: the presence versus absence of positive evidence, language-internal evidence, and cross-linguistic implicational facts.[26]

INDIRECT NEGATIVE EVIDENCE AND
STRENGTH MARKEDNESS

The identifying of marked constructions as those that require positive evidence is further attenuated by other factors as well. Lasnik and others have noted instances in which positive evidence alone seems to be insufficient to account for the properties of marked constructions. Lasnik has provided some examples of how indirect negative evidence might work in his article "On Certain Substitutes for Negative Data" (1983). There he discusses the acquisition of the alternation between indirect object sentences like (a) and (b), where the (b) sentences are marked:

   a. John gave the book to Fred.
   b. John gave Fred the book.

As is known, the so-called dative alternation is restricted to a small set of common monosyllabic verbs and also requires the object of the preposition to be a logical indirect object: thus *John donated the library the book* is precluded because *donate* falls outside the designated class of verbs; *John sent New York the book* is also precluded because *New York* is not a possible indirect object in its literal locative sense. The crucial issue, first raised by C. L. Baker (1979), is how this curious alternation is acquired, since negative evidence is not part of the language acquisition environment. Children are not instructed that *donate, New York*, and similar elements are not amenable to the dative alternation. Mazurkewich and White (1984) note that children seem to overgeneralize this process during language acquisition. They argue that acquisition of the dative alternation involves a general rule relating (a) and (b) and that induction from positive evidence allows children to narrow the rule to the appropriate set of objects and verbs.[27] Lasnik points out, however, that positive evidence from grammatical examples should not cause children to abandon an overly general rule. Rather what children must notice is that the alternation does not occur unless the condition is met, that is, they must treat examples with verbs like *donate* and locations like *New York* as indirect negative evidence. If Lasnik is correct and if indirectness can be operationalized further, then indirect negative evidence will be another property associated with marked constructions.[28] And again, this will mean that marked and unmarked cannot be straightforwardly associated with the presence versus the absence of positive evidence.

Steven Pinker's 1989 article on control provides a further perspective on the type of evidence required for the acquisition of marked constructions. Pinker discusses the evidence required for another marked construction, subject-controlled infinitives. Recall that the unmarked control property is for the subject of an infinitive to be controlled by the closest argument of the main verb—the direct object if there is one and the subject otherwise. Thus in (b) below, *Donald* is the object of *tells* and controls the implied subject of *to do*. The marked control property is represented in (a), where the object is irrelevant and the subject of the main clause controls the implied subject of *to do*.

    a.   Bozo promises Donald to do a somersault.
    b.   Bozo tells Donald to do a somersault.

Drawing on Carol Chomsky's (1969) study of the acquisition of these constructions in children between the ages of 5 and 10, Pinker notes that children typically overgeneralize the *tell* pattern, applying it to *promise*. Moreover, Pinker has found that very young children produce *tell*-type sentences spontaneously and with a very small error rate; *promise* sentences like (a) have not been reported in children's early speech, and such sentences show errors even in the usage of older children.

Pinker suggests that *promise* sentences are harder to learn because they represent a marked type, but he asks further how the correct interpretation is learned. To address this, Pinker splits the notion of markedness into two types, which he calls *default markedness* and *strength markedness*. The first is a version of markedness such that a single datum would suffice to trigger a marked construction. The second is a version of markedness such that data must be sufficiently frequent for a marked construction to arise.[29] As he says:

> With default markedness "harder to learn" means "needs an additional kind of information"; with strength markedness, "harder to learn"

means "needs a greater number of exemplars of a single type of information." (1989: 117)

On the default-markedness view, marked constructions like (a) would be relatively easy to learn, requiring only that the learner notice a single example like (a) in a context that reveals who the subject of the infinitive should be. Examples like (b) would arise by default. In the strength markedness view, both marked and unmarked constructions require a threshold of evidence, with the marked construction requiring a higher threshold. Pinker leaves the analysis of *promise* open, observing that the default markedness view cannot be rejected out of hand since examples like (a) are not very common. But while it is possible that many young children might never be exposed to the relevant datum and that a single exposure could trigger the marked construction, Pinker notes that this is much less plausible than the alternative.[30]

He also proposes that both options could play a part in the acquisition of grammar, with strength markedness being more appropriate to global parameters, where setting a parameter incorrectly might yield disastrous results throughout the language, and default markedness being more appropriate to local parameters, where error recovery is less crucial.[31]

One moral of Pinker's example is that the relationship between primary linguistic data and grammar cannot be assumed to be simple. It is likely that both unmarked and marked options will require a threshold of positive evidence in many instances, so it may not be possible to infer that something is marked from the fact that positive evidence of a certain type is needed. Something might be unmarked but simply not yet have reached its appropriate strength threshold.

The question of how to determine markedness from the types of constructions and evidence in a language so far has been answered with a wide range of alternative proposals. Unmarked structures/parameters require less evidence or no evidence. Marked constructions, on the other hand, require some triggering datum or data, require more data than unmarked options, require positive evidence or indirect negative evidence, and (if in the periphery) may require that evidence be structured in a way that facilitates learning. As we see in the next section, within core grammar it may be that marked parameter settings are those that build on the unmarked conditions by relaxing certain restrictions.

MANZINI AND WEXLER ON THE SUBSET PRINCIPLE

The search for functional sources of markedness hierarchies is one possible avenue for explanations; another is the poverty of stimulus and structure of evidence for parameter settings; a further way of determining markedness values lies in properties of the sets of sentences associated with a parameter.

In their 1987 article "Parameters, Binding Theory, and Learnability," Maria Rita Manzini and Kenneth Wexler ask whether the ordering of parameter values can be determined by general principles or whether it is an independent feature of Universal Grammar. Manzini and Wexler develop an approach in which markedness, identified as ordering among the values of a parameter, is defined in terms of the set of sentences that a parameter value produces. Central to their approach is the Subset Principle, which holds that "the learner selects the grammar that generates the smallest possible language that is compatible with the data" (1987: 425).[32]

Following work by Borer (1984), Manzini and Wexler assume that parameters of Universal Grammar are associated with individual lexical items (the Lexical Parameterization Hypothesis); they also assume that only positive data are available to language learners. Manzini and Wexler's main illustration of the Subset Principle involves the theory of binding—that is, the description of the conditions under which anaphors like reflexives and reciprocals can find antecedents and the conditions under which simple pronouns must be disjoint in reference from potential antecedents. They assume a standard description of binding principles, given below:

Principle A: An anaphor must be bound in its governing category.

Principle B: A pronominal must be free in its governing category.

Taking the governing category to be the domain of anaphoric relatedness and disjointness, Manzini and Wexler describe how this domain varies among and within different languages, and they relate this variation to a theory of parameter settings.

To illustrate their approach, we should first consider English anaphors and pronominals. In English sentences like *Mary remembered that Sally had praised herself,* the bound anaphor *herself* has a potential antecedent in the subordinate clause only—it may not refer to *Mary.* The subordinate clause is the governing category in which the anaphor must be bound. Similarly, in *Mary remembered that Sally had praised her,* the pronominal must be referentially free from higher noun phrases (like *Sally*) within the subordinate clause, but it may refer to the noun phrase *Mary,* which is outside of its governing category. For these examples it suffices to treat the governing category as the subordinate clause; other aspects of English require a somewhat more abstract delimitation of governing category. Consider the following examples, where the asterisk indicates that binding of *each other* to *the students* is not possible:

The students believed [*each other* to be smart]
The students borrowed [*each other*'s notes]
**The students* believed [Mary to know *each other*]
**The students* shared [John's notes with *each other*]
**The students* believed [*each other* were smart]
**The students* believed [Mary knew *each other*]
**The students* insisted [that *each other* visit John]
**The students* insisted [that Mary visit *each other*]

Binding is permitted from the subject position of an infinitive clause or the subject position of a noun phrase (the possessive position) but not from the object position of an infinitive or a noun phrase. Moreover, binding is not permitted from either subject or object position of a tensed or subjunctive clause. For English, the governing category can be described (suppressing some details) as the minimal category that contains the anaphor or the pronominal together with its governing element (the head of the phrase containing the anaphor or pronominal) and also contains a subject (distinct from the anaphor or pronominal itself). To account for the ungrammaticality of examples in which anaphors are the subjects of finite clauses (such as **The students believed [each other were smart]* and **The students insisted [that each other visit John]*), it is necessary to treat the inflection element (INFL) of finite clauses as a subject as well (see Chomsky 1981a: 209).[33]

Other languages instantiate different definitions of Governing Category, permitting certain examples paralleling those marked with an asterisk above. Manzini and Wexler point out that in Italian, for example, the relevant governing category is delimited by *inflection* rather than *subjecthood*; in other words, the subject of a noun phrase does not define a governing category, but verbal inflection does. In the first two examples below, reflexive *sè* may refer to either *Alice* or *Mario*, while in the last example, with an inflected subordinate clause, the reflexive may refer only to *Mario:*

Alice guardò i ritratti di *sè* di Mario.
'Alice looked at Mario's portraits of self.'

Alice vide Mario guardare *sè* nello specchio.
'Alice saw Mario look at self in the mirror.'

Alice sapeva che Mario aveva guardato *sè* nello specchio.
'Alice knew that Mario had looked at self in the mirror.'

Manzini and Wexler suggest that in Italian the governing category is the minimal category that contains the anaphor or pronominal together with its governing element and the category Inflection (which is represented as the INFL position in a phrase structure tree).

In Icelandic, however, it turns out to be specifically *Tense* inflection rather than Inflection in general that defines Governing Category for reflexives. In the first example below, the subjunctive clause does not define a governing category, and hence either *Jón* or *Maria* can serve as antecedent for reflexive *sig*. The situation is different for Icelandic pronominals, however. In the second example below the subjunctive does create a governing category for pronominals (hence *hann* may refer to *Jón*). The third example shows that infinitives (which contain untensed inflection) do not define a governing category: *hann* must be disjoint in reference from *Jón* here. Hence, for pronominals in Icelandic, the definition of Governing Category requires inflection to be tensed (indicative or subjunctive), and infinitives with untensed inflection do not create a governing category.

> Jón segir aɗ Maria elskar *sig*.
> 'Jon says that Maria loves (subjunctive) self.'

> Jón segir aɗ Maria elskar *hann*.
> 'Jon says that Maria loves (subjunctive) him.'

> *Jón skipaɗi mér aɗ raka *hann*.
> 'Jon ordered me to shave him.'

Finally, Manzini and Wexler consider examples like the following one from Japanese in which an anaphor can be bound long-distance to the subject of the main clause regardless of the presence of tense in a subordinate clause.[34]

> John-wa Bill-ga *zibun-o* nikunde irujj to omotte iru.
> 'John thinks that Bill hates self.'

Manzini and Wexler suggest that here the notion of "root Tense" is the relevant one for binding; in other words, an anaphor may be bound by a c-commanding antecedent anywhere in the root sentence. Manzini and Wexler synthesize these observations, suggesting that the definition of Governing Category is parameterized as follows:

> γ is a governing category for α iff γ is the minimal category that contains α and a governor for α and
> a. has a subject [English]; or
> b. has an Inflection [Italian]; or

   c. has a Tense [Icelandic reflexives]; or
   d. has a "referential Tense [Icelandic pronominals]; or
   e. has a "root" Tense [Japanese].

Having suggested the plausibility of the above domains for defining governing category, Manzini and Wexler next show that the domains defined by (a) through (e) form subset relations. For anaphors, the most restrictive governing category domain is (a), the minimal category with a subject, since that definition creates the smallest binding domain. The governing category definition (e), the root clause, yields the largest set of sentences for anaphors, because it allows any possible antecedent to be anaphorically related to an anaphor.[35] Choices (b) through (d) define a graduated sequence of sets of sentences between (a) and (e), with each successive parameter choice expanding the class of possible antecedent-anaphor relations. For pronominals, the relation among (a) through (e) is reversed: (e) defines the smallest set of sentences (that in which pronominals are disjoint in reference from all possible antecedents) while (a) defines the largest possible set of sentences (in which disjoint reference is restricted to the domain of phrases with subjects). In Manzini and Wexler's terms, category (a) is the unmarked parameter setting for anaphors, while category (e) is the unmarked setting for pronominals, with the difference between anaphors and pronominals being consistent with the Lexical Parameterization Hypothesis.

As Manzini and Wexler point out, the subset approach makes markedness independent of other types of parameter hierarchization but dependent on the relation of sets of sentences. Their proposal changes the role of markedness considerably, making it derivable from the delimitation of parameters rather than being a primitive notion of linguistic theory. If the class of grammars, or even just a class of parameter values, can be ordered, then markedness can be explained.

In addition to the Subset Principle, which predicts the learnability and markedness of parameters, Manzini and Wexler also propose a Subset Condition, which states that parameter values "generate languages that are in a subset relation" (1987: 414),[36] and an Independence Principle, which says that "the subset relations determined by the values of a parameter hold no matter what the values of other parameters are" (415). Both are claims about the organization of Universal Grammar: the Subset Condition constrains parameters while the Independence Principle assures that the procedure for selecting parameter values can be applied, by treating sets of sentences as projected from different parameters as though there were only one parameter in the language.[37]

Manzini and Wexler consider it an open question whether all parameters of Universal Grammar define sets that fall into the desired relation. The Subset Condition asserts that this is the case, but Manzini and Wexler note that the validity of the condition is a matter to be further investigated. Some parameters, such as the pro-drop parameter, define nonoverlapping sets (if it is assumed that pro-drop is obligatory). Word order parameters will also define nonoverlapping sets (of specifier-head-complement order versus complement-head-specifier order, for example). In cases where no subset relation can be defined for a parameter, the Subset Principle makes no prediction. If markedness relations obtain between parameters not in a subset relation, they must be accounted for in some other way.

Manzini and Wexler also discuss other parameters besides the Governing Category parameter, in particular the parameter of antecedent selection (that is, whether the antecedent of a reflexive must be a subject or whether it can be *any* higher noun phrase). They speculate that lexical items tend to minimize the number of marked parameters that are associated with them. For reflexives, they suggest that the marked choice of antecedent is likely to co-occur with the unmarked governing category while the marked choice of antecedent parameter is likely to co-occur with the unmarked choice of governing category parameter.[38] However they note that this principle is overridden in the case of pronominals, since it could lead to a situation where binding relations could not be expressed when the governing category for pronominals contained that for anaphors (1987: 440).[39]

EXTENSIONS OF THE SUBSET APPROACH

Recent work applying Manzini and Wexler's proposals to language deficits has produced interesting but mixed results. Yosef Grodzinsky's 1990 book *Theoretical Perspectives on Language Deficits* examines the Subset Principle with respect to parallels between acquisition and language deficits, revisiting Jakobson's idea that language decay is the inverse of acquisition. Grodzinsky observes that if language acquisition complies with the Subset Principle in moving from more inclusive sets to less inclusive ones, decay might be expected to follow a principle that restricts affected language to more inclusive sets (a Superset Principle). Grodzinsky's theory shares with Jakobson's the idea of inverse relationship, but while Jakobson treats acquisition in terms of an additive hierarchy of features and phonological distinctiveness, Grodzinsky treats acquisition in terms of parameters. Similarly, in Grodzinsky's scheme, language decay involves parameters being switched to a less marked value rather than features being stripped away.

Grodzinsky looks at available work on the acquisition of binding in light of his Regression Hypothesis, finding support in work by Wexler and Chien (1988; see now Chien and Wexler 1990), who found that children appear to misunderstand sentences like *Is Mama bear touching her?*, allowing coreference between *her* and *Mama bear*. A similar study conducted by Grodzinsky on agrammatic aphasics found aphasics making a parallel misunderstanding. Interestingly, neither children nor aphasics seem to have difficulty with bound quantifiers in the same position: sentences like *Is every bear touching her?*, which have a bound pronoun in the place of a personal pronoun, are understood correctly. Grodzinsky interprets this in terms of Chomsky's speculation that Principle B of the binding theory is initially restricted to bound pronouns but later extended.[40] Overall, Grodzinsky concludes that the Regression Hypothesis for parameters is "vastly underdetermined by the available data" but that it cannot be rejected either (165).[41]

More compelling support for the Subset Principle arises in work on language development among deaf individuals. In a 1990 article in *Language*, Gerald Berent and Victor Samar examine the Subset Principle as it applies to pronoun use among prelingually deaf adults (i.e., those afflicted with deafness before learning language). They tested the hypothesis that, for pronominals, the judgments of prelingually deaf individuals should be characterized by a shift from the normally marked Governing Category parameter for pronominals to an unmarked parameter. Berent and Samar found that in general the grammars of deaf subjects who have low proficiency could be characterized by subset grammars on Manzini and Wexler's Governing Category parameter (1990: 735). Berent and Samar suggest that deaf speakers who have extremely restricted access to the positive language data needed to trigger marked parameter settings instead use unmarked settings provided by Universal Grammar. They remark that

> [t]o the extent that this is true of other markedness hierarchies, a large range of English language errors made by many deaf individuals may be accounted for as atypical settings of a small number of parameters, specifically those parameters whose normal English settings are marked. (1990: 738–9)

Berent and Samar suggest that subject-verb-object (SVO) word order is unmarked and that overgeneralization of this order characterizes the syntactic errors of some prelingually deaf individuals; they also cite the unmarked property of object control of infinitives as overgeneralized, and they note that prelingually deaf individuals experience difficulty with marked relative clause structures (1990: 719).

Another application of Manzini and Wexler's approach has to do with the acquisition of reflexives by nonnative speakers. Finer and Broselow (1986) and Finer (1991) report that speakers of Korean who are learning English select a reflexive parameter midway between the restrictive English parameter and the less restrictive Korean parameter.[42] Finer and Broselow tested subjects' response to picture-identification prompts such as

Mr. Fat thinks that Mr. Thin will paint himself.
Mr. Fat asks Mr. Thin to paint himself.

They found that Korean speakers showed a preference for local antecedents in English sentences in which the reflexive was embedded in a tensed clause. When the reflexive was embedded in an infinitive, however, many selected a nonlocal antecedent. The results, as Finer and Broselow note, suggest neither transfer of the native language parameter nor adoption of the target language parameter.[43] Instead, what is selected is another parameter from the set of parameter values—apparently either parameter choice (c) or (d). Finer and Broselow point out the potential implications of this study for second language acquisition: while the parameter values of Universal Grammar may be available to second language learners, how they are used does not seem predictable.[44]

To summarize, the Manzini and Wexler Subset Principle has some rather nice properties: it is specific and relatively testable and it provides an independent principle with which to approach markedness relations. On the negative side, there is no guarantee that all parameters form subset relations or that the Independence Principle holds in all cases. Moreover, the theory has nothing to say about the triggering experiences that are required to set a marked parameter value.

Triggering Experiences

In his 1991 book *How to Set Parameters*, David Lightfoot explores the issue of triggering experience in detail, an issue toward which he sees a "pathological lack of interest" among generative grammarians (20). Treating markedness as a theory of preference structure for parameter settings, he assumes that the unmarked parameter setting is available in the absence of triggering evidence (that is, it arises innately) and asks what theory of triggering experience could reasonably account for the adoption of marked parameters.

Lightfoot argues that triggering experiences must be both robust and relatively simple. By robust, Lightfoot has in mind data that are both frequent and salient, and he raises the possibility that some parameters might require more triggering experience than others (1991: 19).[45] As Lightfoot emphasizes, robustness will vary among lexical items, with, for example, *give* being more robust than *donate* and thus more likely to allow the double object construction (20). By simplicity of the triggering experience, Lightfoot means to exclude the sort of indirect negative evidence tentatively advanced by Chomsky, Lasnik, and others.

Lightfoot argues that parameters can be set on the basis of evidence provided by local phenomena—what he calls *degree-ϕ learnability*, adopting the terminological schema of Wexler and Culicover (1980). Degree-ϕ learnability entails learners setting marked parameters of Universal Grammar based on evidence gleaned from triggering experiences in an unembedded binding domain, that is, in a single main clause governing category. This domain is essentially the main clause plus the subject position of an infinitival and the head of any subordinate clause (the embedded COMP or INFL). Lightfoot presents several examples of phenomena that seem to require embedded clause triggers but which can be reanalyzed in terms of unembedded binding domains, including long-distance movement in Italian, reflexivization in Chinese, and complementizer phenomena in Dutch and other languages. His discussion of word-order parameters in Germanic is particularly interesting in that he suggests that learners ignore certain types of data in subordinate clauses that conflict with a degree-ϕ parameter setting.

Taking as his point of departure the fact that Old English, Dutch, and German have similar word-order facts—verb-second order in main clauses and subject-object-verb (SOV) order in embedded clauses— Lightfoot raises the issue of how the word-order parameter is set. In standard generative analyses of Germanic verb-second languages, the underlying word order in all clauses is SOV, and the verb in the main clause moves to second position (i.e., to the position following a topicalized element). The movement of the verb thus obscures the underlying OV verb phrase order in main clauses. The learnability problem is whether there is sufficiently robust and salient positive evidence in main clauses to set the word-order parameter as underlyingly OV.

Lightfoot argues that there is. He suggests that various types of abstract positive evidence from main clauses suffice to set the object-verb parameter in Dutch and similar languages. One factor is the Universal Grammar phrase-structure schema itself, which requires that complements be adjacent to their heads underlyingly; Lightfoot argues that this requirement will force learners to hypothesize an underlying verb position adjacent to the verbal complements (1991: 52). So, faced with a sentence like *In Utrecht vonden de mensen het idee gek* ('In Utrecht people found that idea crazy'), a learner would set up verb-final position as basic, due to the final position of the complements *idee* and *gek*. Lightfoot also argues that in sentences like *Jan belt de hoogleraar op* ('Jan calls the professor up'), the location of the particle *op*, which forms a semantic unit with the verb, is further evidence for the underlying verb position. In addition, the location of negative elements, the position of the main verb when a modal is present, and certain colloquial expressions in which verb-final order occurs in main clauses all provide further triggering experiences to set the word-order parameter.

Lightfoot argues that a similar analysis can be adopted for Old English, though he notes that some of the abstract diagnostics (such as evidence from particle and negative position) do not apply. He emphasizes, however, that the main clause evidence for OV order was equivocal in Old English. He argues that it became statistically less robust over time and that this induced a change in the main clause word order to VO order. Lightfoot notes that as OV order in main clauses decreased in frequency, use of separable particles increased in frequency. However, particles never served as a fully reliable diagnostic of underlying verb positions because of their variable position in English. Lightfoot suggests, following Canale (1978), that by the mid-twelfth century the weakening of the main clause evidence caused the parameter setting for word order in English to switch from OV to VO.

The crucial aspect of Lightfoot's argument for degree-ϕ learnability is that while the evidence available for OV order in Old English main clauses was becoming weaker, the embedded clause evidence for OV order remained both robust and obvious (1991: 64). That Old English word order changed despite the counterevidence from subordinate clauses Lightfoot takes as telling support for degree-ϕ learnability.

Like the Subset Principle and other learning-theoretic hypotheses, degree-ϕ learnability provides a means of determining what the marked parameter setting is. The unmarked parameter setting, assumed by Lightfoot to be innate, need not be connected to a particular quality, type, or quantity of evidence. The marked parameter setting is one that requires positive, degree-ϕ evidence. Thus determination of markedness in Lightfoot's view turns out to be a consequence of specifying parameters of Universal Grammar (however determined) and assumptions about the learning theory.

SECOND LANGUAGE ACQUISITION

A number of recent studies have applied the core grammar and Principles and Parameters models to second language acquisition, suggesting how markedness might play a role in the development of grammars constructed by second language learners.[46] The overarching theme of such work—like the theme of the rather different approach of Eckman and his colleagues—is that, via markedness, Universal Grammar provides an inherent learning hierarchy, which is reflected in the process of second language acquisition. As White (1989b: 121–38) notes, markedness has been applied to the sequence in which constructions are acquired, to the difficulty of acquiring certain constructions, and to the transferability of rules across languages. Here I discuss some of the approaches presented in the literature, beginning with the core/periphery distinction.

With respect to the sequence in which structures arise, Mazurkewich (1984a, b) has suggested that structures of core grammar will always arise before those of the periphery. She proposes, for example, that preposition stranding structures will be learned after the core nonstranding structures.[47] To test this, Mazurkewich surveyed Inuktitut Eskimo speakers, whose language lacks prepositions (and hence both stranding and nonstranding). However, the Inuktitut speakers in her study showed a preference for stranding structures in English, disconfirming her initial hypothesis.

In addition, as White emphasizes (1989b: 127), Mazurkewich's thesis also leads one to expect that speakers of one preposition-stranding language who are learning another stranding language would initially avoid stranding. But this does not seem plausible, and as Van Buren and Sharwood Smith (1985) have noted, Dutch speakers learning English as a second language do not avoid stranding.

Mazurkewich's example highlights the difficulties that arise in applying markedness between languages. As we have seen, core grammar can have different instantiations in different languages. Given that a construction might be part of the core in one language and not in another, the question of how core grammar is relevant to learning is problematic. Consider, for example, postverbal subjects in English (such as *There arrived a tired-looking fellow in a uniform*). This is a non-core construction in English, but not in pro-drop languages like Italian. What prediction should be made for English speakers learning Italian? Should we assume that Italian postverbal subjects will be difficult for English speakers to learn because they are part of the periphery in English? Or that they will be easy to learn because they fall within the core in Italian?

A further issue arises when we factor in the distinction between core and periphery on the one hand and unmarked versus marked parameters on the other. With respect to preposition stranding, for example, it might be that the stranding versus nonstranding options are part of the core. It might also be that stranding versus nonstranding reflects a periphery/core distinction. In fact, if we consider the differences between

English, Dutch, French, and Inuktitut, we find four different situations: a language with very free stranding (English), a language with restricted stranding (Dutch), a language with no stranding (French), and a language with no prepositions (Inuktitut). One possibility is that English and French represent parameter values of stranding, while the Dutch restrictions reflect non-core additions to the English parameter. And Inuktitut might be viewed as a situation in which the relevant preconditions for selecting the default are missing and so no parameter value is selected. There are other possibilities as well, but the key point is that it is not easy to determine either how various constructions are to be analyzed or what different acquisition data mean.

Another approach to markedness in second language acquisition has to do with language transfer. Liceras (1985, 1986) has suggested that second language learners begin by transferring the unmarked aspects of their first language grammar to the second language and that overall there is a tendency for unmarked structures rather than marked ones to be transferred into second language grammars.[48]

Liceras presents complementizer deletion as an example. She assumes that there is a default filter in core grammar that precludes an empty complementizer. In this view, English represents the marked value of this filter, in that deletion is permitted (as in *the book I read* from *the book that I read*). Spanish, on the other hand, retains the unmarked value of the filter, in which complementizers are required. The idea that the unmarked structures tend to be transferred predicts that the Spanish property of complementizer retention would be readily transferred to English but that the English property of complementizer deletion would not transfer as readily to Spanish. This was partially borne out, showing up especially in English-to-Spanish translation tasks. Similar results were found in a study by Adjémian and Liceras (1984) that tested English and French speakers who were learning Spanish. However, their studies of French speakers learning English found that subjects had relatively little trouble learning the marked English property. One possible explanation, proposed by White (1989b: 134–5), is that markedness effects in language transfer may be attenuated by such other factors as the particular task subjects are asked to perform and the extent to which they pay attention to marked aspects of the first or second language.

There is another interesting fact about Liceras's analysis of complementizer deletion in Spanish and English. Her assumption about markedness is the opposite of that made in Hirschbühler and Rivero's (1981) analysis of Catalan.[49] Recall that Hirschbühler and Rivero assumed that optional complementizer deletion in relative clauses in English reflects core grammar, with obligatory deletion being marked in relative clauses in Catalan and other Romance languages. In their view, optional deletion rules in general are unmarked and generate a superset of sentences, while obligatory rules reflect marked (peripheral) stipulations to the core to correct overgeneration. Liceras, on the other hand, assumes a core grammar model in which English represents the marked parameter value, and the default filter precluding complementizer deletion would arise automatically. Thus, the marked situation (the deletion of a complementizer) would require positive evidence. Assuming that the data about the transfer of complementizer deletion are correct, we find that the conclusions one reaches about the role of markedness in language transfer will vary depending on whether the phenomenon in question is treated as marked or unmarked.

Finally, let us mention some research that connects the ease of learning to parameter settings. Phinney (1987) has suggested that unmarked parameter settings will be easier to learn than marked ones and that it should be easier to switch from a marked L1 (first language) parameter value to an unmarked L2 (second language) value than from an unmarked L1 value to a marked L2 one. Phinney exemplifies with the pro-drop phenomenon, which she takes to be unmarked. She reports that Spanish speakers who are learning English have, more difficulty learning to retain subject pronouns than English speakers learning Spanish have in learning to drop them. However, the same indeterminate conclusion is possible here as we found with respect to stranding and complementizer deletion. The conclusion depends on whether pro-drop is treated as marked or unmarked. White (1986), for example, assumes that pro-drop is the marked parameter value rather than the unmarked one. The same observations—that it seems more difficult for Spanish speakers to learn to retain English subject pronouns than it is for English speakers to learn to omit them—is interpreted by White as suggesting that marked parameters should be easier to learn.

There is a rationale to this: if marked parameters can be easily set by learners' recognizing positive data (the omission of a subject pronoun), then marked constructions in a second language should be amenable to the same ease of learning. Similarly, if the data required to motivate unmarked parameter values are more diffuse and degenerate, it should be harder to find the appropriate evidence in a second language to overtly select an unmarked parameter. On the other hand, Phinney's view is also plausible: unmarked values could have acquisitional priority if they are somehow given by Universal Grammar, and if second language learners retain access to unmarked values, these values could affect second language development as well. What seems to be needed to resolve the issue is a better understanding of the extent to which speakers of a language have access to judgments about markedness—in other words, firmer conclusions about the status of constructions like pro-drop.

I have not attempted here to provide an exhaustive survey of the application of generative markedness to second language acquisition, but merely to give a sense of the direction of such work and some of the problems that arise. What emerges from even such a brief survey as this is that although markedness provides a way of associating generative linguistic theory with second language acquisition research, the fruitfulness of this association depends on the development of more comprehensive theories that relate markedness to triggering data, agreement on what is and is not marked, and further study of the accessibility of core grammar by adult second language learners. In particular, the distinction between markedness of parameters (a feature of Universal Grammar) and the markedness of the periphery (which is language-particular) needs to be pursued to determine how each is relevant to second language acquisition and to ascertain where a particular construction in a particular language falls. Other questions that need to be raised are whether adult learners retain access to parameter settings not adopted in their native language (see Kean 1986) and what the balance is between the saliency of marked constructions and the inherent preference for unmarked constructions.

Conclusion

In this chapter, we have looked at some of the main questions that arise in working out a theory of markedness. These revolve around three key issues: the relationship of markedness to core grammar, the existence of marked and unmarked parameters within core grammar, and the triggering evidence required to set parameters. Cutting across all of these is the problem of determining markedness relations, which involves such criteria as cross-linguistic implicational laws, internal regularity, possible triggering evidence, and so on. My purpose here has been not to devise a theory of markedness, but rather to inquire into what a theory of markedness in generative grammar must attempt to do within the conceptual framework of Chomsky's program. At this point, we are in a good position to sketch an answer to this question.

Suppose that grammatical theory consists of a set of core principles and parameters and, further, a set of schemata for rules of the periphery (additions to and relaxations of the core). We can then view Universal Grammar as a set of biologically provided options $\{F, P, R\}$, where F is the set of fixed principles of the core (essentially closed parameters), P is the set of true parameters, and R is the class of possible relaxations or peripheral modifications of the core.[50] The theory of markedness will specify the nature of *P* and *R* and the relative costliness of different options in *P* and *R*. Since the set *F* will be fixed by Universal Grammar directly, it will be independent of the theory of markedness.

As part of the specification of *P*, markedness theory must indicate what the parameters of Universal Grammar are and whether they have a designated unmarked setting. The theory of markedness will also need to indicate the hierarchization of parameters and any contextual dependencies that exist among them, just as hierarchy and contextual dependency were specified in the *SPE* theory.

Markedness theory must also address the relation of parameter settings to the initial state of Universal Grammar—that is, what it means to say that unmarked options are "given." And it will need to further concretize the triggering issue to determine the quality and quantity of triggering evidence required for parameters and to determine whether parameters differ in this regard. Ultimately, for each parameter *p*, some trigger condition *t* will need to be specified.[51]

In addition, the study of markedness in generative grammar must show how parameters and their marked and unmarked values are determined.[52] It remains uncertain to what extent cross-linguistic tendencies determine markedness (see Lightfoot 1991: 176–7). And as we have seen, recent work in the Principles and Parameters framework has moved away from the position that markedness is correlated with such properties of "language" as regularity, stability, and productivity; instead, markedness has been associated with learnability of grammars and with comparative work that shows how proposed parameters account for co-occurring properties of diverse languages and diverse constructions. It remains an open question whether properties of language can be tied to parameter values or whether core grammar markedness will have only an indirect connection to properties of constructions.

There is also a parallel set of questions for the rules of the periphery. The theory of markedness will need to address the issues of hierarchy and dependency among the set of options *R* of the periphery, and specify what constraints are on *R* (or whether the rules of *R* are unconstrained and can be anything at all). This will entail investigating the relation of *R* to *P* and *F*, that is, clarifying whether the periphery is an extension of the core or whether the periphery (or some portion of it) is an entirely separate type of system.

The way in which the rules of *R* are learned will also need to be described—in terms of both how the rules of *R* arise and what data trigger them. This will involve providing some metric for the "costliness" of the elements of *R*. Perhaps this metric will be compatible with the notion of complexity that arises in the selection of marked parameter values as well, and the compatibility issue will help us to decide whether we are dealing with one theory of markedness ranging over both the core and the periphery or with two distinct theories. Moreover, as with core markedness, the relation between properties of language (regularity, stability, productivity) and the periphery remains to be clarified.

There is still, then, plenty of interesting work to do.

SIX

Jakobson and Chomsky: Bridging Invariance and Variation

In this concluding chapter, I want to summarize briefly some of the key aspects of the evolution of markedness that have emerged in this book and contrast Jakobson's and Chomsky's approaches to linguistics and to markedness one final time. It should be apparent by now that both Jakobson and Chomsky expanded and refined their views on markedness over the course of many years of work. Jakobson's early work, concerned with the structuring of oppositions, applied the distinction between marked and unmarked primarily to grammatical oppositions. In later work, markedness emerged as a property of phonological universals as well, and ultimately as a global structural principle. But while Jakobson's work continually hinted at an integrated theory of asymmetry, he never delineated a full-fledged account of semantic and phonological markedness.

Chomsky and Halle introduced markedness as a factor in evaluating grammars, that is, as part of what a linguist (or a hypothetical language learner) draws on in choosing among descriptively adequate models of linguistic competence. Initially, markedness existed within a general theory of natural language grammar and a methodology of grammar selection. As Chomsky's views developed, it was extended as a syntactic cost metric and as a set of defaults and preferences in language acquisition. However, the further markedness has been extended from a concrete set of conventions like those of *SPE*, the less it can be said to be a systematic "theory," and the more it has become a fragmented set of proposals about the structure of Universal Grammar.

Neither Jakobson nor Chomsky developed markedness in an in-depth dedicated study, each relying on it instead as a principle in the service of a larger research program. For Jakobson, this larger research agenda was to determine a general system of oppositions and antinomies across language and other domains; for Chomsky, the overall goal is to construct a linguistic theory that can account for language acquisition.

If we examine what Chomsky and Jakobson have said about markedness, we find some important pieces of a larger picture, but only pieces. In *Knowledge of Language*, Chomsky's comments suggest what markedness theory can do, but not what it would be like. His article "Markedness and Core Grammar" was as much about binding theory as about markedness, and his speculative proposal that the periphery consisted of relaxations of the core was never developed further. Similarly, Jakobson's discussions of markedness usually arose in the context of some other topic, such as analysis of the Russian nominal or verbal categories, or the totality of the sound shape of language. His work that dealt specifically with markedness tended to take the form of short retrospective pieces, such as the chapter titled "The Concept of the Mark" in his *Dialogues with Krystyna Pomorska* and the chapter "Markedness" in *The Sound Shape of Language*, coauthored with Linda Waugh. In both essays, Jakobson reiterates and emphasizes the bifurcation between phonological and semantic markedness while also describing markedness in a broadly unified way. In *Dialogues*, he says that "[t]he conception of a binary opposition at any level of the linguistic system as a relation between a mark and its absence carries to its logical conclusion the idea that a hierarchical order underlies the entire linguistic system and all its ramifications" (1980: 97); in *Sound Shape*, Jakobson and Waugh describe markedness simply as "the preeminence of one of the two opposites" (1979: 94). To move from such a general perspective to an understanding of what generative and structuralist markedness share, it will be helpful to briefly consider some of the other key themes in the work of Jakobson and Chomsky.

Beyond Formalism

Both Jakobson and Chomsky began their careers as formalists—that is, with a concern for purely formal aspects of language. Jakobson, as a cofounder of the Moscow Linguistic Circle, was a member of the Russian Formalist school of criticism. This school's approach departed from the previous century's orientation toward the writer and focused instead on the linguistic devices used in the craft of writing, pioneering such ideas as Shklovsky's concept of defamiliarization. The formalists adopted ideas from such avant garde movements in art as futurism and cubism (influences found in Jakobson's later analysis of the Russian case system).[1] Jakobson's formalist contributions included his studies of "marked time" in his 1921 book *Recent Russian Poetry* and his 1935 lecture on "the dominant" in literature. The latter defined a dominant as that which dominates not only the work of a particular artist but potentially the work of an entire period: "the focusing component of a work of art [which] . . . rules, determines, and transforms the remaining parts . . . [and] which guarantees the integrity of the structure" (1935: 41). With the development of the dominant, Jakobson treats literariness not merely as a *set* of formal devices but as a *hierarchy* of devices, a hierarchy that both permits and defines possible changes in literary genres, much in the way that markedness in language permits and defines possible language change (see Scholes 1974: 90).

As Moscow formalism gave way to Prague structuralism and his work was increasingly influenced by collaboration with Trubetzkoy, Jakobson's main theoretical interests shifted from literariness to language function and the relational nature of oppositions as they concerned issues of typology, universals, and the integration of synchrony and diachrony. In Prague, Jakobson's focus was on phonological and morphological systems and on relations and distinctive features; markedness was conceived primarily as a property of linguistic and cultural relations in the consciousness of the speakers of a language. In the late 1930s, Jakobson looked increasingly to the role of a universal, binary phonological hierarchy in language acquisition, work that found its main expression in *Child Language, Aphasia and Phonological Universals*. In the last phase of his linguistic studies, Jakobson focused on the iconism between sounds and meanings and on the function of sound in language, expanding his system of distinctive and conceptual features ultimately to encompass what he called the total sound shape of a language. It is thus no surprise that the last phase of Jakobson's career dealt once again with questions of verbal art and the grammar of poetry.

Throughout his life, Jakobson was strongly influenced by art and by the connection of art and science (see Waugh and Monville-Burston 1990). In his early years this was manifest in an interest in relativity in physics and in topology in mathematics, fields where he saw the ideas of invariance and variation. He also continuously stressed the importance of both universal definitions and general principles, but he remained concerned with language use and with historical and social variation in language as well, concerns that led away from formalism. In addition, Jakobson's view was an expansive one, tacking about among art, science, and linguistics, but with language always a focus, since he saw language as being at the heart of social communication (see his "Linguistics in Relation to Other Sciences", 1970).[2]

Chomsky too began his career as a formalist, though a formalist of a different sort. His early work, influenced by the Bloomfieldian tradition in linguistics (especially as practiced by his teacher Zellig Harris) and by the tradition of logical positivism in philosophy, adopted the mathematical tools of recursive function theory to arrive at a radically different research agenda than that typical among American linguists of the 1950s.[3] During the 1950s, as a junior fellow at Harvard, Chomsky studied formal properties of mathematical models for abstract languages and applied those principles both to linguistic description and to the methodological underpinnings of linguistic theory. The eventual result was a series of arguments that formal grammars could serve as models for natural language syntax and that models of a particular type (transformational generative models) were required to adequately describe the sentences of natural languages and their properties.[4] In addition, Chomsky suggested that using formal grammars as models raised the possibility of stating a system of general principles and procedures for selecting grammars (see his *The Logical Structure of Linguistic Theory*, 1975: 32).[5]

At Harvard during the 1950s, Chomsky had been exposed to Jakobson's work and there he also began his collaborations with Morris Halle. Jakobson's and Halle's influence provided Chomsky with new perspectives on the importance of universals and on the psychological reality of linguistic constructs. These new perspectives were quite different from those prevailing in American linguistics and philosophy at the time and helped to determine the direction of generative grammar in the 1960s. With the publication in 1959 of Chomsky's review of B. F. Skinner's *Verbal Behavior* and later with the publication of *Aspects of the Theory of Syntax* and *The Sound Pattern of English (SPE)*, interest shifted from methodological questions to the psychological interpretation of generative grammar. Universal Grammar began to move from being defined as a general linguistic theory to being a description of the initial state of a hypothetical language learner. And with the development of a substantive evaluation measure in *SPE*, Chomsky and Halle took a first step away from formalism.[6]

As generative grammar took hold in the United States in the 1960s, its research agenda expanded and transformational analyses were applied to an ever increasing set of phenomena in syntax, phonology, and (with the rise of generative semantics) semantics as well. The period of the 1970s, by contrast, saw the beginnings of a theoretical retrenchment. The focus of Chomsky's work moved from showing that the transformational-generative model was descriptively necessary to the goal of constraining the class of grammars made possible by linguistic theory. Along with this shift came less interest in formal language theory and in notations for formalizing particular grammars and an increasing interest in properties of Universal Grammar.[7] The evaluation metric, with its notion of cost, remained a consideration in the syntax of the 1970s, though in a modified form, and it eventually gave way to his view of grammar construction as a selection of parameters from a menu of options provided by Universal Grammar. Later Chomskyan approaches often involved showing that particular choices of parameters can account for contrasts between or among languages or that the choice of parameters is consistent with plausible assumptions about available triggering data. In more recent work, Chomsky has moved to constrain grammatical parameters or to replace their effects with principles, restricting parameterization to the lexicon or to a designated set of categories (see Chomsky 1992, 1994).

Along with parallel formalist origins, Jakobson's and Chomsky's work shows other parallel themes as well. Both embrace the reality of abstract mental constructs, rejecting a prevailing methodological conservatism in favor of the view that linguistic descriptions are psychologically real in some sense, rather than simply procedural redescriptions of data. Moreover, both Jakobson and Chomsky also see the goal of linguistic research as the search for universals, though (apart from phonological features) they view universals quite differently. But each is committed to cutting through the apparent diversity of the world's languages to find a small set of general linguistic quanta—oppositions for Jakobson, parameters for Chomsky.

In addition, Chomsky's Principles and Parameters approach and Jakobson's child language studies share the idea that a universal hierarchy determines the initial hypotheses of children learning language. And the notion of parameter itself reflects the theme of variability within a set of invariant boundaries. While syntactic parameters are much different in detail from Jakobsonian distinctive features and general meanings, they reflect a common interest in analyzing linguistic diversity in terms of a small set of substantive elements. John Lyons, in his introduction to Chomsky's work, emphasizes this parallel, noting:

> Like Jakobson, Chomsky believes that there are certain phonological, syntactic and semantic units that are *universal*, not in the sense that they are necessarily present in all languages but in the somewhat different, and perhaps less usual, sense of the term "universal," that they can be defined independently of their occurrence in any particular language and can be identified when they do occur in particular languages, on the basis of their definition within the general theory. (1977a: 126)

Jakobson recognized the similarity between his and Chomsky's goals, viewing Chomsky's goal of explanatory adequacy as similar to his own goal of "elicitation and interpretation of the entire network" of language (see "Retrospect" in his *Selected Writings II*, 1971a: 713). And, as Waugh and Monville-Burston (1990: 37) note, Chomsky makes an implicit comparison between his and Jakobson's goals when he writes that for Jakobson linguistics was "a science that sought to discover something fundamental, something real and invariant, in the real world—something analogous . . . to the laws of physics," and that Jakobsonian linguistics has as its goal "the task of discovering explanatory principles."[8]

Another common theme is that of the autonomy of linguistics and language. Jakobson and his Prague colleagues rejected the Neogrammarian view that sound laws were statements about individual sounds, replacing it with the view that sound laws were statements about interconnected systems of oppositions. Jakobson's earliest analyses of language and literature embraced the idea of autonomy—the analysis of formal "literariness" being autonomous from content, biography, and history, and the text and its properties being the sole object of study. However, this autonomy thesis was an aspect of his thought that was attenuated rather early, and his linguistic work increasingly embraced the integration of language with extralinguistic properties and an isomorphism of levels of language. As Holenstein (1976: 104) emphasizes, Jakobson viewed both autonomy and integration as guiding principles. As he wrote in "The Role of Phonic Elements":

> Each level of language from its ultimate discrete components of the totality of discourse and each level of speech production must be treated with respect both to intrinsic, autonomous laws and to the constant interaction of diverse levels as well as to the integral structure of the verbal code and messages (alias LANGUAGE and SPEECH) in their permanent interplay. (1968b: 716)[9]

For Chomsky, as an intellectual inheritor of the American structuralist proscription against mixing levels, the analysis of syntax has always been separated from semantics. Moreover, the analysis of language itself, in his view, can only be carried out autonomously from the vagaries of its use. This means that grammatical competence is the object of linguistic study rather than actual corpora or aspects of performance (see Chomsky 1965). In recent work, the idealization of autonomy has been extended to the view that languages themselves may be epiphenomena (Chomsky 1986) and that the proper object of study is a set of possible mental grammars. Autonomy is also connected to the modularity of Chomsky's view—both generally, in that grammatical competence is a module of human mental faculties, and more specifically, in that grammars themselves are modular, consisting of a set of interacting subtheories for grammatical case, thematic roles, binding, and so on.

As Waugh and Monville-Burston emphasize, Jakobson saw aspects of the strong autonomy thesis of generative grammar as misguided. In the separation of competence and performance, for example, he saw a "disregard for the functional, pragmatic, social and communicative basis of language" (Waugh and Monville-Burston 1990: 28), which he viewed as a misstep. Jakobson also saw the modularity of the standard theory as problematic, preferring a holistic approach that would emphasize the mutual dependence of sound and meaning as well as the connections among language, literature, and other fields. In addition, he argued that generative descriptions of language should encompass the poetic function of language as well as idealized competence (see Holenstein 1976: 108–9).

There are other important differences in the linguistic philosophies of Jakobson and Chomsky as well, especially with regard to language acquisition. Jakobson took a weaker position than Chomsky with respect to the role of innate principles in language acquisition (see Jakobson 1970).[10] Jakobson's skepticism about the modularity of mental faculties and his commitment to broad communicative principles led him away from the position that acquisition is driven largely by domain-specific mechanisms. Jakobson preferred to think of the principles of linguistics (opposition, binarism, invariance within variation, projection, markedness, dynamic synchrony, similarity vs. contiguity) as global—as integrated in all sign systems but exemplified most sharply in language. In addition, the minimalism of his own theoretical architecture—consisting of a phonological level and a semantic level organized according to oppositions—made him resistant to intratheoretic modularity and to abstract linguistic levels.

Chomsky and Jakobson also differ on the place of linguistics among other disciplines. Both view linguistics as part of the sciences and as requiring an abstract deductive model rather than an inductive one. Chomsky views linguistics as a branch of psychology (in turn a branch of biology) and as a field that is interesting primarily in that it presents the possibilities of significant results for the study of the mind. For Jakobson, on the other hand, linguistics is at the center of the social sciences—surrounded by semiotics, anthropology, and communication—and the principles of language structure and function are generalizable to much broader domains. Jakobson's and Chomsky's views on the place of linguistics are consonant with their views on autonomy and learning, Jakobson taking the broad, integrative view and Chomsky taking the more narrowly focused, modular position.

Despite such differences, Jakobson "probably exerted a greater influence on transformational generative grammar than any other linguist," as Frederick Newmeyer remarks in his *Linguistic Theory in America* (1986:

32). Certainly, Jakobson's rejection of the naive empiricism of American structuralism was one of the influences on Chomsky's methodology. And in addition to the philosophical and methodological contact between Jakobson and Chomsky, technical aspects of Jakobson's approach were adapted into generative grammar: the notation of Jakobson's "Russian Conjugation" (1948) and the implicit evaluation procedure made possible by Jakobson's use of binary features and archiphonemes, and emphasized in his work on information theory, were influential in the phonological evaluation metric developed in *SPE*.[11]

TWO MODELS OF MARKEDNESS

As we have seen, both Jakobsonian and Chomskyan linguistics connect markedness to hierarchy, universals, and language development. Each linguistic tradition, however, reflects the intellectual orientation of its founder—Jakobson's in phenomenology, semiotics, and poetry, and Chomsky's in mathematics, psychology, and philosophy. In continually expanding and reshaping markedness, Jakobson and Chomsky have produced a cluster of overlapping ideas that range from the formal description and representation of language to its acquisition to its value and use.

Having contrasted the overall frameworks of Jakobson and Chomsky and reemphasized the evolving nature of markedness in each, I want to end with a final résumé of how the two men's approaches to markedness differ, beginning with Jakobson's. In its narrowest version, in which language is viewed as made up of a small set of universal, binary (semantic or phonological) features, Jakobson's system can be viewed as a highly restricted but very abstract theory of relations between feature values, with markedness as a property of features.[12] In its broader conception, where asymmetry ranges over all oppositions (semantic, phonological, grammatical, contextual, cultural, aesthetic, and so on), markedness becomes much less constrained, since features can be based on loose semantic or cultural relations (such as working days vs. holidays, etc.), and features are justified primarily insofar as they succeed in organizing properties of the elements they describe.[13] In its totality, Jakobson's model extends phonological and morphological binarism and asymmetry to relations between actual or potential features that characterize any aspects of sign structure—that is, anything from basic phonological distinctions to morphological categories to opposites in literature, art, and culture. His view implies that learning about the world involves the construction of oppositions and rankings, and it assumes an integration and interdependency between the levels of language and between language and other sign systems. This interdependency in turn is the basis for the

isomorphism of levels and the extension of the notion of value from inherent linguistic features to created cultural ones. For the linguist, critic,
or philosopher whose interests include the organization of sign systems
and the possibility of general structural principles that are relevant across
systems, Jakobson's approach to markedness has much appeal.

Chomsky's approach, like Jakobson's, treats markedness as a principle
of hierarchy (within Universal Grammar), but it involves a more intricate
theoretical architecture and a determination of markedness by studying
details of comparative syntax and language acquisition. The two main
strands of Chomsky's approach—conceiving of markedness as cost and
as part of a learner's initial state—yield a number of differences from
the Jakobsonian approach. First, markedness has been applied to many
different sorts of theoretical constructs besides features—to parameters
of Universal Grammar, rules, features, constraints on rules and representations, and ways of organizing and applying rules. Second, markedness
relations are not necessarily binary but may be multivalued. Third,
markedness is embedded in a modular framework of grammar and a
modular approach to the mind—subsystems are organized according to
different principles; the expectation is that markedness in one area of the
grammar need not have commonalities with markedness in other modules. Connected to this is the idea that markedness is an aspect of a
theory of Universal Grammar—a theory aimed at explaining the acquisition of language. Given this specific connection of markedness to a particular type of mental faculty, attention has been given to the triggering
mechanisms for marked parameters and to the role of markedness as part
of the mapping from linguistic data onto grammars.

While it is possible to identify particular constructions as marked, the
main role of markedness in current generative models involves explaining
language acquisition. The broader perspective of viewing marked and
unmarked as *values* of linguistic elements that are separate from acquisition is not included in Chomsky's view of markedness. In addition, there
have been few attempts at extending markedness to other analytic goals,
though such extensions are possible, both in the cost version and in the
default version. An attempt at using markedness to characterize departure from the norm in scientific and cultural belief systems is made by
McCawley (1985), who posits marked and unmarked features for different options in beliefs or theory systems and sets up an evaluation metric
to measure the cost of adopting noncanonical beliefs. If belief systems
can be analyzed on the model of grammars, then such an approach holds
some promise as a descriptive technique. McCawley's approach is in the
tradition of the *SPE* version of markedness and the feature-oriented proposals of George Lakoff and Catherine Chvany for syntax, all of which

evaluate the cost of systems of rules with respect to sets of background conventions. Another possible extension of markedness would be to explore the idea of parameters in domains other than language; while this has not yet (to my knowledge) been attempted, it is worth investigating whether we can construct core grammars for such domains as music, delineating marked and unmarked parameters of music appreciation or performance.

Until such extensions are worked out further, Chomsky's model of markedness will have a much different sort of appeal than Jakobson's, requiring a commitment to an intricate parametric model and limiting its claims to the logical problem of language acquisition.

Conclusion

In chapter 1, we set out two tasks: to ascertain whether there is a theory of markedness and to determine to what extent the concept is the same in two different linguistic traditions. We also noted several issues in need of exploration—issues of definition, correlation, and consistency. In examining not only the work of Chomsky and Jakobson but also developments of markedness by others working in the Chomskyan and Jakobsonian traditions, we ultimately must conclude that there is no theory of markedness per se. Rather, the picture of markedness we arrive at is one merging a number of different domains of markedness, different technical proposals, and different analytic goals.

We have seen, for example, that the domain of markedness—what it refers to—includes both the intrinsic content and the normative value of elements. The idea of intrinsic content cuts across Jakobsonian and Chomskyan approaches, referring both to the default values of parameters, features, or categories in a theory of Universal Grammar and to the intrinsic feature hierarchy connected to biological and experiential properties of perception or conceptualization. The latter may include our inherent ways of categorizing the world—in terms of opposition, maximal contrast, and specification versus nonspecification.

The normative (nonintrinsic) focus of markedness refers to the idea that one pattern, element, or feature takes priority over another. We speak of what is normal, typical, or basic as being unmarked, even though this might not be intrinsically or universally the case. Normative markedness arises from our expectations and conceptual rapport with patterns of language: some forms, features, or patterns are viewed as more foregrounded, atypical, or more informative than others. The markedness of norms is especially evident in the analysis of lexical contrasts—for example, the treatment of a more informative lexical item such as *love* as a marked version of a more neutral items such as *like*. The most important aspect of the markedness of norms is its relation to our conceptual rapport. We have more of an affinity with neutral terms than with ones that require a greater information commitment. Conversely, items that carry more information have a foregrounding and highlighting effect: the short and long forms of names, topicalized or inverted word orders, academic punctuation, and other marked choices are all used with specific effects.

The markedness of norms is also reflected in the idea of redundancy and economy in a system. A prototypical pattern, such as the pattern of nouns having distinct singular and plural forms, is something against which other patterns are measured, and less general grammatical patterns (such as mass nouns or irregular plurals) will be marked to the extent that they depart from the conceptually neutral main pattern.

Both the inherent and normative nonequivalence of categories may be linked to distribution, variability, and regularity. We might talk about *blue* as being a less marked, more general version of *neptune blue* or *sky blue*. Or we might consider strong verbs or non-*s* plurals as being more marked because they exhibit less internal regularity. Syntactic properties like exceptional Case marking or subject control of infinitives are considered more variable among speakers than related unmarked constructions. Even the idea that marked and unmarked are connected to subset relations among sets of sentences entails positing a correlation between grammar and language. In both generative and structuralist linguistics, correlations reflect the tendency for hierarchy to be implemented in the distributional properties of the languages themselves.

Various technical proposals have been advanced for the inherent and normative aspects of markedness. These include how the markedness of features is implemented—whether as an A versus non-A approach, as a looser ranking of equipollent binary choices, or as a scale encoding implicational relations. If markedness is viewed as cost, as in some generative approaches, technical questions include whether it is calculated in terms of parameter values, symbol counting, or weighting, or whether it is tied to particular unmarked rules or unmarked organizations of grammar. In addition, whether reversal, assimilation, and neutralization exist are technical questions that arise for structuralist approaches to markedness. The determination of markedness values is a final technical issue, with the range of approaches including determination by invariance, by distribution and meaning, by mutual dependence with other pattern values, by the structure of Universal Grammar, or by specific properties of constructions or sets of sentences.

The goals of markedness are a final locus of variability. For some, the goal of markedness research is to determine or uncover the relations between values at different levels of grammar, relations that make grammar into a better or worse object aesthetically or semiotically. For others, the goal of markedness is to encode relations in the structure of language and other sign systems by delineating the asymmetries among general meanings and the connection of these asymmetries to language use and function. In some instances, markedness has retained a strong descriptive focus, its job being to facilitate the statement of norms and redundancies in a language in the context of modeling systems of knowledge. In others, the goal is to document hierarchies and correlative properties and to tie those hierarchies to descriptive typological universals. And for many structural and generative linguists, the goal of markedness is to encode abstract parameters that might play a part in a solution to the logical problem of language acquisition.

We have seen that there is no single comprehensive theory of markedness. As we end, it is time to return to the other question raised in chapter 1: is there a common core to Jakobson's and Chomsky's views of markedness? In the broadest context of twentieth-century linguistics, I am tempted to answer the question positively. Certainly Jakobsonian and Chomskyan linguistics share a perspective of markedness as both an evaluation of linguistic structure and as a factor in its acquisition. At the level of detail, however, I think there is not a common core, but only a shared history. While robust parallels are apparent in Chomsky's and Jakobson's thought, from their formalist origins to their broader biological interests, we must recognize markedness as a concept that is unified only at an abstract, thematic level. At the level of concrete applications, diversity rules, and it is necessary to distinguish many views and themes. But such diversity, while daunting, need not be a cause for pessimism. In diversity there is discovery. And in the development of markedness we discover much that is useful and revealing about the structure of language and culture.

Notes

CHAPTER I

1. The term *deep structure* is often confused with a similar term coined by Wittgenstein and is sometimes paraphrased within generative grammar as "underlying structure." It has been misconstrued as a representation of "underlying meaning" or as being universal or otherwise invariant. On misunderstandings of the notion of deep structure, see Chomsky (1975, 1977b). *Logical form* has also been variously construed, depending on what properties of meaning are associated with that level of representation (cf. Katz 1980). The term *phoneme* has different definitions depending on theoretical assumptions (see Anderson 1985), and the terms *grammar* and *rule* mean different things to prescriptive and descriptive grammarians.

2. The nominalization *markedness* seems to have been first used by Chomsky and Halle in *The Sound Pattern of English* (1968), where they placed the term in quotation marks (a practice continued by Chomsky and Lasnik 1977). Jakobson and Waugh also adopt the nominalization in *The Sound Shape of Language* (1979); in prior works Jakobson's practice seems to have been to use only the terms *marked* and *unmarked*.

3. See, for example, Moravcsik and Wirth (1986), Tomić (1989), Andersen (1989), Mufwene (1991), and Gvozdanović (1989), among others. Pessimism has also been expressed by Bickerton (1984), who sees no "clear objective criteria" for syntactic markedness values and by Lightfoot (1991: 186) who notes that "[t]he notion of 'markedness' has led to much confused discussion." See also Waugh (1982) and Lyons (1977b: 305).

4. The quote is from Jakobson's translation of Trubetzkoy's letter (Jakobson and Pomorska 1983: 95; the Russian original can be found in Trubetzkoy 1975: 162–4.; see also Andersen 1989).

5. George Lakoff, in his *Irregularity in Syntax* (1970), equates unmarkedness with both "naturalness" or "normalcy" and identifies "marked" features with exceptions to syntactic norms. See also Robin Lakoff (1968) and Green (1974). The idea of unmarked as norm also arises in Roland Barthes's *Elements of Semiology;*

Barthes remarks that "[s]ome linguists have identified the mark with the exceptional and have invoked a feeling for the normal in order to decide which terms are *unmarked*; according to them, the *unmarked* is what is frequent or banal, or else derived from the *marked* by a subsequent subtraction" (1967: 76).

6. Abstract syntactic markedness is described by Zwicky as marking by syntactic or morphosyntactic features, however these features are established. His point seems to be that such marks need not be connected to semantic features. Gazdar, Klein, Pullum, and Sag (1985) have also applied markedness to syntactic features, identifying markedness conventions with Feature Specification Defaults among features.

7. Greenberg's criteria for determining marked and unmarked categories include neutralization of a contrast (either phonological or semantic), semantic dominance (as in the use of the Arabic dual form of *fathers* for *father and mother*), defectivation or syncretism (the unmarked category showing more subdistinctions than the marked), facultative expression/*par excellence* representation (the ability of a category to be used for both oppositions, as in Greenberg's example of the use of the singular pronoun in Chinese to refer to both singular and plural), agreement *a potiori* (the use of the unmarked form as a common modifier for two conjoined forms), text frequency, frequency across languages, greater variability and irregularity within a language (the unmarked category showing more variation in phonological or morphological patterning), presence versus lack of a secondary articulation, zero expression, implied versus implying in universal relations, or realization as the basic allophone of a phoneme or as the base form of a paradigm. See Andersen (1989) for discussion and Croft (1990) for a new synthesis of Greenberg's diagnostics.

8. In some instances neutralization is connected to the notion of substitutability of the unmarked for the marked. This is one of the main criteria used in treatments of antonyms (see Lehrer 1985, among others). Henry Kučera (1980, 1984) in particular has analyzed the role of neutralization and substitution beyond the domain of antonymy.

9. Cairns (1969), e.g., following Trubetzkoy, describes marked sounds as those deviating from a neutral position.

10. See Battistella (1990: chapter 2).

11. Taraldsen (1981) argues that marked extractions in Norwegian are determined by deviation from an optimal pattern of rule interaction (in which extraposition precedes *wh*-movement). Muysken (1981) argues that rules that translate syntactic representations to Logical Forms are unmarked while rules that translate morphological forms to Logical Forms are marked; Quechua causatives, on his view, are marked because causative interpretation operates at Logical Form.

12. Thus, the unmarked term is the one used to represent the generic property in questions like *How tall is that building?* But an interesting question is posed by expressions like *How is it?* where a zero adjective occurs but the presupposition can be good or bad depending on context.

13. Finegan and Besnier suggest a set of tests for unmarked color terms, proposing that unmarked words are often monomorphemic while more marked

color terms are the result of the metaphorical usage of other terms (they give the example of *saffron*). Of course this would require us to conclude that *orange* is also marked, patterning with *indigo, saffron, royal blue, aquamarine,* and *bisque* rather than with *blue, red, yellow, green, black,* and *purple.*

14. See Battistella (1990: chapter 6) for other examples. See also Liszka (1989), who analyzes both spatial orientation of figures and facial expressions (of surprise, anger, and so on) in terms of marked and unmarked features, and Brown and Witkowski (1980) who suggest, among other things, that circles are the unmarked geometric figures, while squares are marked. Lambrecht (1994: 17) argues that certain types of focus structures are pragmatically marked, equating that notion to the breadth-of-discourse function that a sentence type serves.

CHAPTER 2

1. The idea appears to have been nascent at the time. As Viel (1984) notes, Jakobson had already used a concept similar to markedness in his study of marked time in his 1921 work *Recent Russian Poetry*, adapting ideas from Paul Verrier's 1909 work on metrics. See also Holenstein (1976: 129). For some discussion of the intellectual climate of eastern European linguistics in the first half of this century, see Toman (1995).

2. Trubetzkoy went on to characterize the marked members of the correlation as "positive" and "active" and the unmarked members of the correlation as "negative" and "passive."

3. See Andersen (1989: 22) and Cairns (1969).

4. See in particular Trubetzkoy (1931; and 1969 [1939]: 146–7).

5. See Trubetzkoy's 1936 "Die Aufhebung der phonologischen Gegensätze."

6. Jakobson credits Peškovskij with the idea of "zero categories." As Henning Andersen has pointed out in his article "Markedness: The First 150 Years," something much like the concept of marked and unmarked predated the actual coining of the terms in the 1930s, going back to work by G. M. Roth in the early 1800s and by Theodor Kalepky in the late 1800s.

7. Jakobson notes that the use of the marked in place of the unmarked is also possible, but states that such replacements should in general be interpreted figuratively. He returns to this in "Zero Sign," giving it the term "hypostasis."

8. Jakobson remarks here that "[r]esearch on aphasia shows that marked categories are lost before unmarked ones" and that "[t]he same phenomenon is known from child language" (1968a [1941]: 11).

9. Hjelmslev's early work used the terminology *intensive* versus *extensive* (rather than *marked/unmarked*), though in later work he seems to have used these terms differently (see Hjelmslev 1969 [1953]). See Andersen (1989) for a lucid summary of Hjelmslev's phonological views.

10. Crucially, the notion of inclusion is logical and relational, rather than semantic. Interestingly, inclusion is sometimes attributed to Hjelmslev (see Andersen 1989) and sometimes to van Schooneveld (see Waugh 1976a: 94; Andrews 1990), and it plays a large role in approaches such as those of Lyons (1977b),

Kučera (1984) and Andrews (1990). As Andrews (1985) notes, an inclusion-like analogue of semantic markedness can be found in Edward Sapir's article "Grading: A Study in Semantics" (1944).

11. See Jakobson (1984: 62–6).

12. The apparent difference between zero degree and zero phonemes is whether zero serves as part of a morphological alternation or not.

13. Another theme concerns restrictions on marked categories. Jakobson suggests that marked number and marked tense undergo restrictions not imposed on their unmarked counterparts (1957a: 53).

14. Moreover, the genitive singular and the nominative plural, each of which bears a single mark for quantity, tend to be expressed by a difference in word stress. Jakobson speculates that the markedness of the categories genitive and plural is reflected in the patterned expressions of these categories.

15. This is implicit in his treatment of markedness shifts in Russian gender forms (just discussed) and also in the bifurcation of the features compact and diffuse. Jakobson also points out that Polish has an opposition between objective and nonobjective in the singular, but between personal and nonpersonal in the plural. This theme of bifurcated features arises again in chapter 3.

16. See in particular "The Identification of Phonemic Entities" (1949b) and "Notes on the French Phonemic Pattern" (with John Lotz, 1949). Jakobson also used a double specification in some instances (see Jakobson, Cherry, and Halle 1953).

17. In prompting this reformulation, Stanley (1967) was an early and crucial work, arguing that zeroes in phonological representations led to difficulties; work in underspecification theory in phonology, however, has revived the idea.

18. See the essays in *Studies on Child Language and Aphasia* (1971b), which include Jakobson's articles on "The Sound Laws of Child Language and Their Place in General Phonology" (1949a), "Aphasia as a Linguistic Topic" (1955), "Two Aspects of Language and Two Types of Aphasic Disturbances" (1956), and "Toward a Linguistic Classification of Aphasic Impairments" (1964). See also his "On Aphasic Disorders from a Linguistic Angle" (1975).

19. Jakobson is explicit about this in later works, such as Jakobson and Waugh 1979.

20. There are exceptions; see Kean (1980).

21. It is worth emphasizing that there is not a fixed order of sounds but a fixed order of oppositions, and that oppositions can be implemented and combined in different ways.

22. See also Menn (1986), Blache (1978), Kiparsky and Menn (1977), and Halle (1977: 135).

23. A literary example that does not quite follow Jakobson's hierarchy is Technical Sergeant Garp in John Irving's novel *The World According to Garp*. Sergeant Garp retains possession of only his name and then loses that in the sequence GARP, ARP, AR, A. Perhaps Irving's intuition here reflects a different kind of phonological hierarchy, involving loss of syllable onset, then coda, followed by reduction of the syllabic nucleus.

24. Blumstein reports that this tendency is less robust for patients suffering from conduction aphasia.

25. He also suggests that the marked nature of the passive voice accounts for the behavior of children and aphasics:

> [A]phasics and little children erroneously understand the inverted sentence, "*Mamu* (acc.) *ljubit papa* (nom.)", as "Mom loves dad", because the former word order is neutral, unmarked, whereas the latter is marked as expressive, and only the unmarked order is grasped by these listeners. Dr. Goodglass' example, "the lion was killed by the tiger", tends to be interpreted by aphasics as "the lion killed the tiger", because in the usual, most normal, word order the subject functions as an agent, whereas here it becomes the victim, and moreover, because the passive is a superstructure upon the active. (1980: 105–6)

For another view, see Kean (1977).

26. Jakobson did of course recognize language-particular phonological relations and universal grammatical ones.

27. Jakobson and Waugh, who intended their book as a counterpoint to Chomsky and Halle's *The Sound Pattern of English*, have as a main goal the defense of the traditional autonomous phoneme as opposed to the purely distinctive systematic phoneme adopted by Chomsky and Halle.

28. See Timberlake (1987) for further discussion of Jakobson's consistency.

CHAPTER 3

1. See also Haiman (1980, 1983, 1985).

2. See Andersen's dissertation (1966) and his *Language* article on Indo-European **s* (1968). Shapiro (1972) notes that the concept was present also in Schachter (1969) and Stewart (1967). It may also be possible to trace the idea of value assimilation in positions of neutralization to Trubetzkoy's comments on dissimilative neutralization (1969 [1939] 229–31).

3. Andersen's other example involves assimilation of the English verb *do*. For another view of the correctness of the example involving the subjunctive, see Andrews (1990: 149). For more discussion of *do* from the perspective of markedness, see Battistella (1985).

4. Shapiro adopts the markedness values of nouns and verbs from Jakobson (1980: 105). For another option, see Andrews (1990).

5. Reversal is a type of assimilation in that a ranking that obtains in the unmarked context is reversed in the marked context; the markedness of the context is assimilated to the value of the unmarked feature (unmarked becomes marked) and reverses the marked feature (marked becomes unmarked). This leads to an apparent paradox: if assimilation characterizes the situation in which the marked features occur in the marked context (and unmarked features in the unmarked context) and if a marked context reverses the normal markedness values of an opposition, then how do we know which feature is expected in a marked context—the *normally* marked feature (expected by assimilation) or the *normally*

unmarked feature (treated as marked by reversal)? The spirit of the idea of reversal seems to be that markedness assimilation is the basic pattern but a *further* marked context can reverse assimilation.

6. Shapiro (1983, 1991) also equates markedness to C. S. Peirce's notion of interpretant, viewing it as a type of logical interpretant. I set aside discussion of Peirce's system of signs and the idea of a Peircean linguistics, focusing instead on exemplification of the principles of markedness assimilation and reversal. See also Andrews (1990).

7. What, for example, would be the analysis of the diminutive *Mickey?* Would this be treated as an augmented form of a truncated diminutive *(Michael > Mike > Mickey)* or as a different type of marking *(Michael > Mickey)*. More analysis of diminutives is needed, it would seem.

8. Contrast the situation in English with the allomorphs *a* and *an*. If the closed syllable version of the article is considered marked and if the vowel-initial form of the following words is also considered marked, we arrive at a pattern of m + m *(an* + vowel) and u + u *(a* + consonant). (To some extent the same pattern holds for the definite article if we consider the long *e* as marked and the schwa as unmarked.) The question is what this means: do English and Japanese differ in terms of complementarity versus replication of values, or should the analysis be revised to look for an underlying complementarity?

9. In Shapiro's view, markedness complementarity may interact with markedness reversal to explain morphophonemic alternation. Consider the analysis of Russian vowel/zero alternations given in Shapiro 1983. Shapiro treats the zero ending of the nominative singular as a marked ending that combines with an unmarked stem, and he treats alternations in stem shape as markings or unmarkings in accordance with the principle of complementarity. So, for example, nominative singular *voš* + ϕ 'louse' is analyzed as an unmarked stem plus a marked zero. The genitive singular *vši* is analyzed as an unmarked ending *i* plus a marked stem form *vš*. This is fairly straightforward, if one assumes the correctness of nominative singular as marked (see Shapiro 1972). However, other examples are treated in terms of double reversals: the nominative singular of the word 'gaff,' *bagór* + ϕ, is treated as a marked stem combined with a marked ending because of "the discrepancy in the stem shape between the maximally unmarked form and the other forms in the paradigm," leading Shapiro to conclude that "the markedness values are reversed *in the pre-zero shape only*" (1983: 149). This reversal of stem markedness is restricted to the masculine, however, because its form is unmarked as opposed to the feminine. On the other hand, examples like *lob* 'forehead' are re-reversed to unmarked status because "the fact that nonsyllabic stems are marked for syllabicity, . . . effects yet another reversal in markedness values" (1983: 149). Ultimately, words like *bagór* + *šč* + *ik* 'gaffer' and *lob* + *ov* + *oj* 'forehead' (adj.) are successfully analyzed as complementary forms, and the principles of complementarity and reversal make it possible, in Shapiro's view, to "comprehend the peculiarities of the Russian declensional system" (1983: 148). But the success of the endeavor depends on the soundness of the initial markedness assignments and the various reversals posited, which are not always transparent.

10. A related application of markedness assimilation and reversal developed by Andersen and Shapiro concerns the organization of feature hierarchies. Andersen has restated Brøndal's Law as a principle of *markedness compensation* of hierarchies, which says that

> the marked sign in the paradigm will not be combined with subordinate signs unless its unmarked opposite is. . . . [I]f a subordinate opposition is combined with a marked term of a superordinate opposition, then it will be combined with the unmarked terms of that opposition, but not conversely. (1979: 379)

Shapiro (1972) extends markedness assimilation and reversal to the phonological features in a hierarchy, positing a replication of higher level markedness values in unmarked branches of a phonological feature hierarchy and a reversal of higher level values in marked branches. Thus, in his view, if there are superordinate features +A and −A, where +A is unmarked, organization of the features subordinate to +A will replicate the association of the unmarked term with the positive feature; the marked branch of the hierarchy (the −A branch) will reverse this pattern so that the unmarked is associated with the opposite value. These principles are consistent with an overall Jakobsonian view of language organized by similarity and difference. However, Shapiro's main examples of reversal and complementarity in hierarchy involve the phonological distinctive features set adumbrated by Jakobson and Halle (1956). Other nonphonological feature hierarchies given in Shapiro (1983) and Battistella (1990) seem not to conform to this schema, so it may be that it is noncompulsory as well. For other treatments of complementarity, see Kean (1980) and Woisetschlaeger (1985).

11. In developing the idea of the invariant, Jakobson was also influenced by turn-of-the-century physics, notably the theory of relativity; by artistic movements like cubism, which stressed abstract relationships; and by topology, which deals with transformations of mathematical shapes (see Waugh and Monville-Burston 1990: 5).

12. For more detailed exemplifications of van Schooneveld's theory, see Andrews (1990), van Schooneveld (1991) and Tobin (1991).

13. Tobin also suggests that marked verbs may be related iconically to morphological irregularity. Tobin (1994) develops a comparative study of semantic invariants in English and Hebrew, arguing that the two languages use different invariants for such structures as mass and count nouns, quantifiers, possessives, prepositions, and deixis. While Tobin's approach is in the Jakobsonian tradition, drawing on the concepts of markedness and invariance, it also owes much to the approaches of Dwight Bolinger, Gustave Guillaume, and the linguists of the Columbia (Diverian) School as well (see Tobin 1994: 41–5).

14. Sangster adds that markedness relations "must be established in abstracto from the individual classes of phenomena with respect to which they occur" (1991: 146). Andrews (1990) also argues that the determination of semantic markedness relations should eschew distributional criteria. She concedes, however, that examination of distribution is permitted in order to make an initial assignment of markedness values, noting that distributional facts "may be used

initially to help determine which form is marked or unmarked, but they have no place at the most fundamental axiomatic base" (1990: 125–6).

15. Cf. *Robin died young* vs. *Robin died old*. This contrast suggests that there are contexts in which the opposition is suppressed in a different way, with the usually unmarked form marginalized.

16. A different sort of example is the contrast between *That it was raining surprised me* and **φ it was raining surprised me*. Here we have a syntactic rather than a semantic neutralization, the contrast between the complementizer *that* and its absence being suppressed when the complementizer introduces a noun clause in subject position. One way to approach such examples is to inquire what information is supplied by *that* or by φ and what is suppressed when the contrast is neutralized.

17. In his 1982 book, Sangster, elaborating on Elmar Holenstein's observation that the markedness relation between *close* and *far* differs depending on whether the words refer to emotions or to distances (Holenstein 1976: 131), writes:

> the effect of context upon the markings themselves, and the resulting relationships can be explained in terms of semantic COMPATIBILI-TIES: that member of a semantic opposition will be unmarked which conforms more closely to the inherent nature of the concept being expressed. (1982: 75)

With respect to Holenstein's example, Sangster suggests that spatial relationships use distance as the unmarked term while interpersonal relations use closeness. He thus identifies unmarked properties with those that are the "neutral or more natural quality, defined with respect to a particular context" (1982: 75).

18. Andrews argues that "generally, conceptual features in grammar and morphology cannot reverse synchronically," though she mentions of the possibility of diachronic reversals (1990: 148).

19. See also Weinreich (1966: 469) and Wierzbicka (1980: xv–xvi).

20. Newfield and Waugh's position is shared by a number of other researchers working in the Jakobsonian tradition, which reflects a majority view that conceptual complexity is not a fixed relationship and that distribution and meaning are integrated. Waugh's earlier article on "Marked and Unmarked" (1982) strongly emphasizes the reversibility of markedness and the connection of markedness to context. As noted, Shapiro and Andersen are adherents of reversibility, in a Jakobsonian-Peircean framework. In addition, the various typologically oriented approaches of, for example, Greenberg, Haiman, Croft, Givón, and others, treat markedness as context-sensitive, as do the German naturalists. Tiersma (1982) and Witkowski and Brown (1983) also make use of the notion of reversal to explain the brevity of marked forms and lexical changes. With respect to reversal in phonology, see Jakobson and Waugh's treatment of contextual markedness, Greenberg (1966: 24), Chomsky and Halle (1968), Kean (1980), and Gamkrelidze (1989, 1991).

21. Kučera (1984) also allows reversal but notes that it requires a feature

bifurcation. Kučera's treatment of markedness emphasizes the substitutability of the unmarked term for the marked as a defining criterion, following work by Dokulil (1958). Kučera remarks that Jakobson's definition entails that "the meaning of the marked member is included in the (general) meaning of the unmarked member but not vice versa. The logical consequence of this is that the implication relation between the marked and unmarked member of the Jakobsonian opposition is a unilateral one" (1984: 63). See also Kučera (1980) and Lyons (1977b: 291–5).

22. Chvany (1992: 53) also treats Government and Binding parameters as contextually "U" and "M", suggesting that the initial state of a language learner is "U" and reset parameters are "M".

23. Chvany's notation suggests that one or the other ranking of values will always be contextually basic or "U".

24. Shapiro (personal communication) has suggested that words like *student* can in some cases apply to females as well as males. See also Rothstein (1973).

25. Another example would be the relation between zero pronouns and overt ones. In languages such as English, Russian, and French, overt pronouns are probably more frequent than null pronouns; in other languages (such as Czech, Italian, Chinese), the opposite is the case. But presumably one or the other option is more common cross-linguistically.

26. In a recent article, Greenberg reiterates the idea that when "an implicational relation exists, the unmarked category is the implied one. But marking involves a whole cluster of other characteristics, such as nonzero expression of the marked category in morphology, its lesser text frequency in both morphology and phonology, etc." (1991: 422).

27. Croft notes (1990: 92) that the structural criterion does not apply to all distinctions. He also rejects neutralization as a criterion (contra, e.g., Greenberg).

28. As Gundel, Houlihan, and Sanders (1986) note, typological markedness often (but not always) correlates with wider distribution in a particular language. They provide several examples of phonological and syntactic constructions in which distribution is skewed.

29. On diachronic implications, see Greenberg (1966, 1978, 1991) and Croft (1990: 213–8).

30. Croft notes that psychological and philosophical theories might be self-fulfilling to the extent that they are based on assumptions about language structure, and he speculates that the real utility of iconism might be to help to propose psychological hypotheses.

31. The universals approach overlaps somewhat with the semiotic approach of Shapiro and Andersen in viewing rules in terms of the sign relations they implement and in searching for a sense to patterns. However, as Dressler (1985: 286) notes, his approach differs from other semiotic approaches because it views naturalness as based on universal functional principles. See Andersen (1980: 202) for other discussion.

32. If the generalization that semantically marked categories are quantita-

tively greater than unmarked ones is correct, then this would be a direct relation rather than an inverse one.

33. The purely practical role of markedness is sometimes overlooked. Consider something as commonplace as driving. In the U.S., the unmarked side of the road is the right; in Britain and many other places, it is the left. When crossing the street, the unmarked behavior in the U.S. is to look to the left first; in Britain it is to look to the right. Such practical behavior as crossing the street safely is influenced by the unmarked norm. This view of unmarked as a norm can be applied in various ways: to aspects of driving (what is the unmarked behavior at a yellow light or a four-way stop sign?) and styles (of writing, speaking, proxemics, dress, etc.).

34. This approach shares some similarity with Greimas's idea of semiotic squares. See Greimas (1983 [1966]), Liszka (1982), Schleifer (1987), and Utaker (1974).

35. A separate issue is whether the generic and the specific meanings can be separated. It seems unlikely that one could use a generic *he*, for example, without also triggering the specific meaning.

36. As Treichler and Frank note, use of the generic feminine pronoun may signal other information as well in certain contexts: a challenge of the use of generic *he*, a reinforcement of sex role stereotypes (as with the use of *she* in traditionally female occupations), or part of a larger discourse pattern (as with the use of *she* for Speakers and *he* for Hearers in some linguistic usage).

37. A question that remains is whether true equipollent (truly equally valued) oppositions are possible. For that to occur, context would need to be equalized—there would need to be either no background norms or equivalent background norms. In principle there is no reason it could not be the case, though I know of no examples.

38. Unisex *guys* might be analyzed similarly, as [nonspecification of feminine] in the plural. Singular *guy*, on the other hand, would more appropriately be analyzed as [specification of masculine]. The term *he-she* might be analyzed as the combination [specification of masculine, specification of feminine].

39. My view contrasts with that of Shapiro (1983), who takes markedness assimilation to be a separate diagrammatic principle, independent of a larger diagrammaticity.

40. Most naturally, this approach to markedness fits into semiotics or aesthetics. See Shapiro (1983: 9; 1991), Battistella (1990: 114–5) and Andersen (1991) for discussion.

41. On markedness in meter, see Shapiro (1988), and for a treatment of music, see Hatten (1994). For discussion of marked and unmarked features of facial expression, see Liszka (1989).

42. Thus, a silent *s* does not trigger the bare apostrophe: the correct form is *Camus's work*, rather than *Camus' work*.

43. See Battistella (1993) for more on the bare apostrophe. The most entertaining bare apostrophe rule, pointed out to me by James Rachels, is the prescription to use the bare apostrophe "when a word rhymes with *sneezes*."

44. Some distinctions appear to be fairly robust: cf. the Biblical *Jesus' life* vs.

contemporary Hispanic *Jesus's friend*, classical *Aristophanes' comedies* vs. modern *Onassis's fleet*, and mythical *Mars' wrath* vs. astronomical *Mars's orbit*.

45. Repetition in general may be marked.

46. The form *Jer* seems to be both informal and personal, usually occurring only by itself (not in combination with a last name).

47. The nature of the conjunction may of course be supplied by a conjunctive adverb like *however* or a transitional phrase like *in addition*.

48. Hyphens share the feature of interruption with dashes.

49. An alternative is to set up marked features [intersentential] and [intrasentential], but it is preferable, I think, to explore the consequences of the more economical hypothesis first.

CHAPTER 4

1. The evaluation metric was also sometimes referred to as the *evaluation procedure* or *evaluation measure* or as the *simplicity criterion*.

2. It also figured in then unpublished work that later appeared in Chomsky's *The Logical Structure of Linguistic Theory* (1975 [1955]) and *Morphophonemics of Modern Hebrew* (1979 [1951]).

3. Chomsky remarks, by way of example, that the question of whether rule ordering is highly valued or not depends on "the factual question of expressibility of linguistically significant generalizations in terms of one or the other theory, not on any presumed absolute sense of 'simplicity' " (1965: 40).

4. The evaluation metric of *SPE* seems to combine Halle's views on economy of lexical representation and segment inventory, which were developed in conjunction with Jakobsonian work on information theory and redundancy, with Chomsky's view of notational conventions as ways to express linguistically significant generalizations.

5. See *SPE*, chapter 8, where Chomsky and Halle define the evaluation procedure as a set of notational conventions plus a definition of *value:* "The 'value' of a sequence of rules is the reciprocal of the number of symbols in its minimal representation" (334).

6. While the marking conventions themselves were substantive universals, the operation of linking was a formal universal—an inherent convention that allowed natural phonological processes to be represented more minimally.

7. See *SPE*, chapter 7, for discussion of Chomsky and Halle's set of features.

8. Chomsky later also cites Greenberg's typological work approvingly: see, for example, *The Generative Enterprise* (1982: 111) and *Lectures on Government and Binding* (1981a: 95).

9. Chomsky and Halle cite a 1966 article by Kiparsky ("Über den deutschen Akzent") as an example of "an interesting discussion" of the idea of optimal rule orderings (*SPE*, 1968: 402).

10. See Vennemann (1972) for more discussion.

11. Lakoff gives *scissors, binoculars,* and *spectacles* as examples, to which we can add: *shears, clippers, tweezers, glasses,* etc.

12. Lakoff's proposal is not fully clear to me. Presumably, plurals in general

will be more marked than singulars. It seems then that the example should be extended to make the plural *people* as more marked than, for example, the plural *boys*. Nevertheless, the overall direction of Lakoff's approach is evident.

13. She applies this approach, combined with the notion of rule-government, to Latin complementation (1968: 80–82).

14. The approach was perhaps also a casualty of the conflict between the generative semantics approach advocated at that time by the Lakoffs and others and the interpretive semantics approach of Chomsky. Its failure may also have been due in part to the fact that a theory of feature-based markedness in the *SPE* mold would have required a received view of what the set of syntactic features was.

In current syntactic frameworks, the idea of the unmarked feature specification as a default is most prominent in Generalized Phrase Structure Grammar. As Gazdar, Klein, Pullum, and Sag note, the restrictions expressed by marking conventions in *SPE* are treated in their approach by Feature Co-occurrence Restrictions and Feature Specification Defaults, some of which express universal restrictions and some of which express "parochial" (i.e., language-particular) restrictions (1985: 27–30).

15. The A-Over-A Condition prevents a rule from affecting a category (A) contained within a like category (A) that could also be affected by the rule. The Tensed Sentence Condition states that the presence of tense makes a clause opaque to rule application and the Specified Subject Condition states that the presence of a subject in a category blocks the application of rules to other constituents in that category. See Chomsky (1973), Chvany (1978), and Newmeyer (1986) for more discussion.

16. This is the analogue of the problem of phonological weighting raised by Vennemann and others.

17. It has also been suggested that the periphery might be highly structured, perhaps more structured than the core (see Baker 1991).

18. Briefly, phrase structure theory deals with the ordering of specifiers, heads, and complements; Case theory with the privileges of occurrence of overt noun phrases as opposed to null ones; binding theory with coreference and disjoint reference; control theory with the interpretation of zero pronouns, bounding theory with the structural conditions on movement applications; and government theory with the definition of basic structural relations.

19. In *Knowledge of Language* (1986), Chomsky adopts a circuit board metaphor (which he attributes to James Higginbotham) to describe the core, speculating that each parameter may have as few as two values.

20. He also makes this point in *LGB* (see page 9); in *The Generative Enterprise* (1982: 108), Chomsky tentatively drops the idea.

21. Chomsky and Lasnik also speculate that the filters that characterize the English relative infinitival construction may "constitute the 'unmarked case' when the language permits the full range of base generated infinitival constructions," suggesting that the relevant filters would be learned automatically (1977: 470).

Chomsky and Lasnik's idea illustrates the context-sensitive nature of markedness in which a superordinate marked option (having the full range of infinitival constructions) is associated with an unmarked strategy (particular filters). This, in essence, permits the language to make the best analysis of marked constructions.

Discussing the idea that rules that refer to the content of categories are "highly marked," Chomsky and Lasnik also reassert the context-sensitivity of markedness, suggesting that "some extensions of the grammar that are 'highly marked' when regarded in isolation may still be the 'unmarked case' for broader reasons" (1977: 477, note 92).

22. Chomsky supports this evaluation by noting that the overt subject of the infinitive is an "idiosyncratic property" of English because the cognates of *believe* in French and German lack this property (1980: 29).

23. The same idea applies to the Subjacency violations associated with English sentences like *Who did they think Jane saw?* These might represent duplicate complications to the grammar of English, if long-distance *wh*-movement requires both the existence of a special rule (say, converting *S'* to *S*) and a lexical feature designating the class of verbs that trigger the rule.

24. He adds that judgements shift when the reciprocal is replaced by a reflexive, suggesting further marked instability (1981b: 143).

25. In "Markedness and Core Grammar" Chomsky also suggests that in the Government and Binding system sentences like *John read his books* and *They'd prefer each other's writing the book* are unmarked, while sentences like *They read each other's books* are marked. He notes that in the "On Binding" system the reverse would be the case (1981b: 141). Chomsky tentatively assumes the *Government and Binding* conclusion, that is, that *They read each other's books* is marked.

It is worth noting also that in "Conditions of Transformations" he treats the interpretation of reciprocals in such constructions as *The candidates believed that pictures of each other were on sale* as unmarked, specifically designing the conditions to allow the rule of "*each* movement" (as reciprocal interpretation was then conceived) to operate into the subject of an embedded clause.

26. These ideas are hinted at in "Filters and Control," where Chomsky and Lasnik suggest that "it seems reasonable to assume that a one-to-one mapping of deep and surface structures will be optimal for language processing" and may provide a functional explanation of certain conditions (1977: 470).

27. Chomsky's remark here refers to markedness of parameters, that is, to hierarchy within core grammar. Presumably, the marked/unmarked distinction between the periphery and the core remains as before.

Chapter 5

1. Chomsky notes further that sufficiently restrictive principles would constitute a discovery procedure, presumably making evaluation unnecessary.

2. Chomsky and Lasnik here seem to be using the expression "the unmarked case" figuratively to mean the least marked possible grammar, since the opposition marked to unmarked cannot apply literally to grammars.

3. White (1982: 93) identifies markedness with the evaluation of grammars also; see White (1989b) for a more recent view. For additional discussion of the relation between markedness and the evaluation metric, see the articles in Lasnik 1990, especially Lasnik and Freidin's "Core Grammar, Case Theory, and Markedness" (1981) and Lasnik's "Learnability, Restrictiveness and the Evaluation Metric" (1981a).

4. Van Riemsdijk's book was originally published in 1978 and reissued in 1982; citations are to the 1982 publication.

Another early application of markedness to the extended standard theory model was Chvany's 1978 article on the A-Over-A Principle, which developed the idea that violations of the principle meet criteria of markedness such as economy and preference.

5. There are other possibilities as well: Hornstein and Weinberg (1981) treat stranding as a consequence of a marked (non-core) rule reanalyzing prepositional phrases as complex verbs. Kayne (1981) argues that reanalysis follows from the government and Case assignment properties of languages, and, following Kayne, Stowell (1981) suggests that both stranding in English and nonstranding in French should be analyzed as unmarked.

6. Koster does not, however, explain *why* marked structures should be affected by extragrammatical, lexical, and structural complexities.

7. Lightfoot (1979) also defines markedness as distance from core grammar, treating language change as a process of increasing markedness followed by a restructuring that decreases the markedness of the grammar by reanalyzing marked structures as core ones. He describes his approach to change as one in which "less highly valued grammars" are reanalyzed in a way that increases their value. Lightfoot remarks that in this view of change "the real work is done by the theory of grammar and by the set of perceptual mechanisms, which together define 'less highly valued' grammars in accordance with the logic of markedness" (1979: 150). For Lightfoot's current views on change, see Lightfoot (1991), discussed later in this chapter.

8. Thus their position on subset relations contrasts with that of Manzini and Wexler, discussed later.

9. Hirschbühler and Rivero treat core grammar as a set of invariant properties. In their words:

Core grammar specifies the principles that account for unmarked aspects of a language; these are invariant across languages, and are not learned by the language learner or are extremely easy to learn. Peripheral grammar includes language-particular rules and marked processes. (1981: 591)

10. Note, of course, that Kean's argument parallels Chomsky and Halle's argument for phonological markedness in *SPE*.

11. The structural analysis of the core rule would be $X\ NP\ Z$, with no constant specified.

12. Kean adds that the theory of markedness should include "non-

parameterized constraints which provide the substantive definition of possible grammar" and that it should "set parameterized constraints which set the limits on the substantive variation among languages" (1981: 560). However, it is not clear why these constraints are part of markedness theory and not Universal Grammar.

13. See also Cinque (1982) and the articles in Belletti, Brandi, and Rizzi (1981).

14. Hyams's description suggests that she identifies markedness with the evaluation metric.

15. Hyams also stresses that the markedness of a grammar (or a stage of development) should be considered relative to the set of sentences generated at that stage, paralleling Kean's thinking about relative markedness. If a grammar that generates only part of a language needs to be made more complex to account for a larger fragment of the language, it makes no sense to consider this a less highly valued grammar than a grammar that does not handle all the data.

16. The same point should hold for markedness of parameters—that a marked parameter setting may have associated with it some unmarked consequences.

17. Another example might be constructions in Chinese like *Ta yao ta qu* 'He wants him to go'. Li (1990: 131–4) suggests analyzing these as following from a special property of Chinese.

18. Hyams does not, however, elaborate on the diagnostics that would distinguish the core from the periphery.

19. She argues instead that pro-drop represents the default setting of the parameter in terms of an isomorphism of deep and surface structure levels, but that this is not to be equated with markedness.

20. Lightfoot (1991: 49) and Phinney (1987), for example, characterize Hyams as treating pro-drop as unmarked.

21. Bickerton explicitly excludes from the periphery substitution and deletion of core options.

22. Bickerton's version of core grammar consists of the following rules plus the transformation Move α, restricted in the core to moving N^3 or V (see 1984: 179):

$S^1 \rightarrow$ COMP, S
$S \rightarrow N^3$, INFL, V^3
$N^3 \rightarrow S^1$
$N^3 \rightarrow$ (Determiner), N^2
$N^2 \rightarrow$ (Numeral), N^1
$N^1 \rightarrow$ (Adjective), N
$V^3 \rightarrow V^2$, (S^1)
$V^2 \rightarrow V^1$, (N^3)
$V^1 \rightarrow$ V, (N^2)

23. For further discussion, see the peer commentary published with Bickerton (1984); see also Mufwene (1991).

24. Given Lightfoot's view of triggering data for marked parameter settings,

it could easily be the case that creoles contain sufficiently robust positive, main clause (degree-ϕ) evidence to set parameters.

25. Hyams also proposes a version of biuniqueness that she calls the Isomorphism Principle to support the hypothesis that pro-drop is the Universal Grammar default. She writes:

> All else being equal, the least complex grammatical system is the one which allows for the greatest degree of isomorphism between the levels of representation, D-structure, S-structure, PF and LF. (1986: 162)

Since Hyams assumes that pronouns are represented as phonologically null sets of features at D-structure, the parameter setting in which pronouns remain null at S-structure would be preferable in terms of isomorphism. In a framework in which pro-drop and non-pro-drop are, respectively, unmarked and marked settings, isomorphism might be advanced as a functional explanation for markedness. Similarly, functional explanations might be pursued for other unmarked core parameter settings.

William O'Grady, in his *Principles of Grammar and Learning*, also treats markedness in the Principles and Parameters approach as arising from extragrammatical, functional factors. O'Grady suggests that processing factors related to the continuity and discontinuity of information may determine some markedness hierarchies, remarking that "[a] continuity preference of this sort supports predictions about markedness based on the types of phrases and clauses that can be discontinuous" (1987a: 201). He illustrates his suggestion using "markedness hierarchies" that treat the following examples as ranked from least to most marked:

> Who did John see?   (least marked)
> Who did John sit near?
> Who did John read a book about?   (most marked)

O'Grady also identifies less marked structures with frequency and naturalness, pointing out that "[s]ome structures, which are usually referred to as 'marked,' occur relatively infrequently and seem to involve grammatical devices that are unusual or special in some way" (1987a: 200). Here we begin to see overlaps with the functionalist approaches described in chapter 3.

26. Another option is to treat *want* in terms of S' deletion and *believe* in terms of the insertion of a null complementizer that can assign Case. In this instance the difference in markedness might be attributed to a difference in the marked processes themselves.

27. Actually, Mazurkewich and White's rules relate to the subcategorization frames of the verbs, but this does not affect the point under discussion.

28. In addition, see Lasnik (1981a), where he suggests that positive data from examples like *Do not be careless* might suffice to trigger a contextual restriction on the rule of auxiliary verb raising. For additional discussion of the English auxiliary system, see Lasnik (1981c).

29. The latter is a version of markedness in which control rules are given a

strength value that is incremented each time an example of the relevant type is encountered (see Pinker 1989: 116–7).

30. See also Pinker (1984) and Gropen, Pinker, Hollander, Goldberg, and Wilson (1989).

31. This criterion would suggest that *promise* falls under default markedness since the parameter involved is not one (like choice of bounding node) that will affect the grammar globally but rather is local to a lexical item.

32. See Angluin (1980), Dell (1981), and Berwick (1985) for background discussion of the Subset Principle.

33. Chomsky's rationale is that the features of INFL are nominal and INFL is the most prominent element in a tensed clause, hence the subject (his SUBJECT).

34. Korean and Chinese behave similarly. See O'Grady (1987b), Battistella and Xu (1990), and Cole, Hermon, and Sung (1990).

35. By "set of sentences" I mean a set of structural descriptions. Thus a single sentence with different binding possibilities or other structural differences would count as different structural descriptions or, in this usage, different sentences. Thus the ambiguous *The women introduced the men to each other* would represent two sentences, one in which *each other* refers to *the women* and one in which *each other* refers to *the men*.

36. Manzini and Wexler leave it as an open question whether all parameters adhere to the Subset Condition (1987: 429).

37. Note that the Subset Principle and the Subset Condition are distinct.

38. There is of course an interesting parallel with the "principle of compensation" discussed in chapters 2 and 3.

39. Other applications include Weinberg's analysis of the doubly filled COMP filter (1990).

40. Grodzinsky (1990: 126) attributes this suggestion to Chomsky. Yet as Grodzinsky himself notes—and as Crain (1992) emphasizes—this proposal demands special assumptions about the development of Principle B, including the speculative assumption that children first limit the application of Principle B to bound pronouns like *everyone* and only later expand it to personal pronouns.

41. Cf. Ingram's conclusion concerning Jakobson's regression hypothesis (see chapter 2).

42. Finer and Broselow also studied Japanese and Hindi speakers, with similar results. See Finer (1991) for details.

43. See Thomas (1991) for discussion of Finer and Broselow 1986 and Finer 1991. Other studies that apply the Subset Principle to second language acquisition have investigated configurationality (Zobl 1988) and Case assignment (White 1989a). See White (1989b) and Gair (1988) for some discussion.

44. See the section in this chapter on Second Language Acquisition for more discussion.

45. Lightfoot does not define salience, however Bardovi-Harlig (1986) equates it with the availability of crucial data. Her discussion arises in the con-

text of the conflict between markedness as an aspect of core grammar and intra-linguistic markedness. Discussing the fact that preposition stranding is the norm in the adult grammar of English and is apparently learned more rapidly than nonstranding, she suggests that ease of acquisition is associated with salience as well as with universal markedness conventions. She concludes that the effects of salience refute the strong expectation that the unmarked construction is acquired first and the weaker view that both a nonsalient unmarked construction and a salient marked one would be acquired simultaneously.

46. Among these are Liceras (1986), Flynn (1987), White (1989b), Sharwood Smith (1994), and the articles in Flynn and O'Neil (1988), Eubank (1991), Gass and Schachter (1989), Rutherford (1984), Kellerman and Sharwood Smith (1986), Pankhurst, Sharwood Smith, and Van Buren (1988), Eckman, Bell, and Nelson (1988). See also Bley-Vroman, Felix, and Ioup (1988), Eubank (1989), Hilde-brand (1987), Kellerman (1985), Klein (1993), Phinney (1987), Liceras (1988), White (1985, 1986, 1987, 1989a), and Zobl (1983). My survey in this section adopts the distinctions made by White (1989b).

47. Mazurkewich also tested French speakers who were learning English. But, as White notes (1989b: 126), the preference of French speakers for stranding could just as well be explained by the transference of the native French structure as by a preference for core grammar.

48. As White (1989b) notes, this entails the assumption that second language learners have access to judgments about marked and unmarked constructions in their first language.

49. See also Liceras (1988).

50. By biologically provided I don't mean that principles and parameters are necessarily innate in the form in which they are discussed by linguists, merely that these principles arise as a consequence of biologically provided mechanisms and strategies.

51. The triggering issue may turn out to be especially crucial in instances where a phenomenon might be either part of the marked core or part of the periphery (such as, for example, preposition stranding). If there are clear trig-gering differences between the marked core and the periphery, then presumably the learning context will distinguish the two situations.

52. The way in which markedness values are determined is not part of "markedness theory," any more than the way in which a grammar is determined is part of linguistic theory. There is no discovery procedure for markedness values.

CHAPTER 6

1. See Chvany (1984, 1986), among others, for discussion of Jakobson's case system.

2. In "Linguistics in Relation to Other Sciences," Jakobson speculates that the organization of language is parallel to the organization of biological informa-tion systems. See Waugh and Monville-Burston (1990) and Halle (1992) for some discussion.

3. Chomsky himself was a contributor to recursive function theory, as the reader of almost any beginning programming text will find.

4. See Chomsky (1975 [1955]), Lyons (1977b), Newmeyer (1986), and Haley and Lunsford (1994).

5. In developing this line of investigation further, Chomsky proposed various idealizations—the idealization of the homogeneous speech community, the bifurcation of sentences into grammatical and ungrammatical, and later the distinction between competence and performance.

6. Not surprisingly, *The Sound Pattern of English* is dedicated to Jakobson, though it is richly allusive to Trubetzkoy and others as well.

7. There are of course many notable exceptions, such as Lasnik and Kupin's work (1977), Generalized Phrase Structure Grammar, Lexical Functional Grammar, Montague Grammar, and other frameworks that have ties to information technology.

8. The comment is from Chomsky's remarks in *A Tribute to Roman Jakobson* (1983: 82).

9. Jakobson did maintain that linguistics should be autonomous from a priori psychological or biological explanations, as Holenstein emphasizes. Holenstein notes that the central issue for Jakobson was not how elements of language can be explained psychologically, but what the mind must be like "to be capable of producing and receiving a system that is constituted upon specific, intrinsic laws" (Holenstein 1976: 115), a position similar to Chomsky's.

10. See Waugh and Monville-Burston (1990: 28). Jakobson's position is consistent with the holism of his approach.

11. Newmeyer (1986: 31) also notes that "the attraction of most of the leading Prague School members to phenomenology made them suspicious of formalism and dubious that the goals and methods of linguistic theory could be identified with those of the natural sciences."

12. It could in fact be argued that a Jakobsonian system is a more constrained framework than that found in generative grammar since linguistic structure is reduced to a handful of universal features. But what is missing are the connecting links to the idea that grammars generate sentences.

13. This criterion is too subjective for some, since it involves an idealization and abstraction of meaning, which is ultimately interpretive. Note, however, that the basic idealizations of the generative approach (such as judgments of well-formedness) are in practice open to interpretation as well.

References

Adjémian, Christian, and Juana Liceras (1984) "Accounting for Adult Acquisition of Relative Clauses." In *Universals of Second Language Acquisition*, F. Eckman, L. Bell, and D. Nelson (eds.), 101–18. Rowley, Mass.: Newbury House.

Angluin, D. (1980) "Inductive Inference of Formal Languages from Positive Data," *Information and Control* 48, 117–35.

Andersen, Henning (1966) *Tenues and Mediae in the Slavic Languages: A Historical Investigation*. Ph.D. diss., Harvard University.

Andersen, Henning (1968) "IE *s after *i, u, r, k* in Baltic and Slavic," *Acta Linguistica Hafniensia* 11, 171–90.

Andersen, Henning (1972) "Diphthongization," *Language* 48, 11–50.

Andersen, Henning (1979) "Phonology as Semiotic." In *A Semiotic Landscape*, Seymour Chatman, Umberto Eco, and Jean-Marie Klinkenberg (eds.), 377–81. The Hague: Mouton.

Andersen, Henning (1980) "Summarizing Discussion." In *Typology and Genetics of Language*, Torben Thrane, Vibeke Winge, Lachlan Mackenzie, Una Langer and Niels Ege (eds.), 197–210. Copenhagen: Linguistic Circle of Copenhagen.

Andersen, Henning (1989) "Markedness—The First 150 Years." In *Markedness in Synchrony and Diachrony*, O. M. Tomić (ed.), 11–46. Berlin & New York: Mouton de Gruyter.

Andersen, Henning (1991) "On the Projection of Equivalence Relations into Syntagms." In *New Vistas in Grammar: Invariance and Variation*, Linda Waugh and Stephen Rudy (eds.), 287–311. Philadelphia: John Benjamins.

Anderson, Stephen R. (1985) *Phonology in the Twentieth Century*. Chicago: University of Chicago Press.

Andrews, Edna (1985) "Markedness Reversals in Linguistic Sign Systems." In *To Honor Roman Jakobson: Papers from the 1984 Mid-America Linguistics Conference*, Gilbert Youmans and Donald Lance (eds.), 169–80. Columbia: University of Missouri.

Andrews, Edna (1990) *Markedness Theory: The Union of Asymmetry and Semiosis in Language*. Durham, N.C.: Duke University Press.

Baker, C. L. (1979) "Syntactic Theory and the Projection Problem," *Linguistic Inquiry* 10.4, 533–81.

Baker, C. L. (1991) "The Syntax of English *not*," *Linguistic Inquiry* 22.3, 387–429.

Baltaxe, Christiane A. M. (1978) *Foundations of Distinctive Feature Theory*. Baltimore: University Park Press.

Bardovi-Harlig, Kathleen (1987) "Markedness and Salience in Second-Language Acquisition," *Language Learning* 37.3, 385–407.

Barthes, Roland (1967) *Elements of Semiology*, Annette Lavers and Colin Smith (trans.). New York: Hill and Wang.

Battistella, Edwin L. (1985) "Markedness Isomorphism as a Goal of Language Change," *Lingua* 65.4, 327–42.

Battistella, Edwin L. (1990) *Markedness: The Evaluative Superstructure of Language*. Albany, N.Y.: SUNY Press.

Battistella, Edwin L. (1993) "*s's*," *SECOL Review* 17.2, 127–41.

Battistella, Edwin L. (1995) "Jakobson and Chomsky on Markedness." In *Travaux du Cercle Linguistique de Prague* n.s. 1, 55–72. Amsterdam & Philadelphia: John Benjamins.

Battistella, Edwin L., and Yonghui Xu (1990) "Remarks on the Reflexive in Chinese," *Linguistics* 29, 205–40.

Belletti, Adriana, Luciana Brandi, and Luigi Rizzi, eds. (1981) *Theory of Markedness in Core Grammar* (Proceedings of the 1979 GLOW Conference). Pisa: Scuola Normale Superiore di Pisa.

Benveniste, Emile (1966) *Problèmes de linguistique générale*. Paris: Gallimard.

Berent, Gerald, and Victor Samar (1990) "The Psychological Reality of the Subset Principle," *Language* 66.4, 714–41.

Berretta, Monica (1995) "Morphological Markedness in L2 Acquisition." In *Iconicity in Language*, R. Simone (ed.), 197–233. Amsterdam & Philadelphia: John Benjamins.

Berwick, Robert (1985) *The Acquisition of Syntactic Knowledge*. Cambridge: MIT Press.

Bickerton, Derek (1984) "The Language Bioprogram Hypothesis," *Brain and Behavioral Sciences* 7.2, 173–203.

Birnbaum, Henrik (1984) Review of Rodney Sangster's *Roman Jakobson and Beyond*. *Language* 60.2, 412–16.

Blache, Stephen (1978) *The Acquisition of Distinctive Features*. Baltimore: University Park Press.

Bley-Vroman, R., S. Felix, and G. Ioup (1988) "The Accessibility of Universal Grammar in Adult Language Learning," *Second Language Research* 4, 1–32.

Blumstein, Sheila (1973) *A Phonological Investigation of Aphasic Speech*. The Hague: Mouton.

Brøndal, Viggo (1943) *Essais de Linguistique Générale*. Copenhagen: Munksgaard.

Borer, Hagit (1984) *Parametric Syntax*. Dordrecht: Foris.

Brown, Cecil H., and Stanley R. Witkowski (1980) "Language Universals." In

Toward Explaining Human Culture, David Levinson and Martin J. Malone et al., 359–84. New Haven, Conn. HRAF Press.

Cairns, Charles E. (1969) "Markedness, Neutralization, and Universal Redundancy Rules," *Language* 45.4, 863–85.

Canale, Michael (1978) *Word Order Change in Old English: Base Reanalysis in Generative Grammar.* Ph.D. diss., McGill University.

Caramazza, Alphonse, and Edgar Zurif (1978) *Language Acquisition and Language Breakdown.* Baltimore: Johns Hopkins University Press.

Chien, Y.-C., and Kenneth Wexler (1990) "Children's Knowledge of Locality Conditions in Binding as Evidence for the Modularity of Syntax and Pragmatics," *Language Acquisition* 1, 225–95.

Chomsky, Carol (1969) *Acquisition of Syntax in Children 5 to 10.* Cambridge: MIT Press.

Chomsky, Noam (1957) *Syntactic Structures.* The Hague: Mouton.

Chomsky, Noam (1959) Review of B. F. Skinner's *Verbal Behavior. Language* 35, 26–58.

Chomsky, Noam (1965) *Aspects of the Theory of Syntax.* Cambridge: MIT Press.

Chomsky, Noam (1973) "Conditions on Transformations." In *A Festschrift for Morris Halle*, S. R. Anderson and P. Kiparsky (eds.), 232–86. New York: Holt.

Chomsky, Noam (1975 [1955]) *The Logical Structure of Linguistic Theory.* New York: Plenum.

Chomsky, Noam (1976) "Conditions on Rules of Grammar." In *Essays on Form and Interpretation*, 163–211. Amsterdam: Elsevier-North Holland, 1977.

Chomsky, Noam (1977a) *Essays on Form and Interpretation.* Amsterdam: Elsevier-North Holland.

Chomsky, Noam (1977b) *Language and Responsibility.* New York: Pantheon.

Chomsky, Noam (1977c) "On Wh-Movement." In *Formal Syntax*, Peter Culicover, Thomas Wasow, and Adrian Akmajian (eds.), 71–132. New York: Academic Press.

Chomsky, Noam (1979 [1951]) *Morphophonemics of Modern Hebrew.* London & New York: Garland.

Chomsky, Noam (1980) "On Binding," *Linguistic Inquiry* 11.1, 1–46.

Chomsky, Noam (1981a) *Lectures on Government and Binding.* Dordrecht: Foris.

Chomsky, Noam (1981b) "Markedness and Core Grammar." In *Theory of Markedness in Core Grammar*, A. Belletti, L. Brandi, and L. Rizzi (eds.), 123–46. Pisa: Scuola Normale Superiore di Pisa.

Chomsky, Noam (1982) *The Generative Enterprise: A Discussion with Riny Huybregts and Henk van Riemsdijk.* Dordrecht: Foris.

Chomsky, Noam (1983) [Reminiscence]. In *A Tribute to Roman Jakobson, 1896–1982*, 81–3. Berlin: Mouton.

Chomsky, Noam (1986) *Knowledge of Language: Its Nature, Origin and Use.* New York: Praeger.

Chomsky, Noam (1989) "Some Notes on Economy of Derivation and Representation," *MIT Working Papers in Linguistics* 10, 43–74.

Chomsky, Noam (1992) "A Minimalist Program for Linguistic Theory," *MIT Working Papers in Linguistics*, Occasional Papers in Linguistics, 1. Cambridge: MIT.

Chomsky, Noam (1994) "Bare Phrase Structure," *MIT Working Papers in Linguistics*, Occasional Papers in Linguistics, 5. Cambridge: MIT.

Chomsky, Noam, and Morris Halle (1968) *The Sound Pattern of English*. New York: Harper and Row.

Chomsky, Noam, and Howard Lasnik (1977) "Filters and Control," *Linguistic Inquiry* 8.3, 425–504.

Chvany, Catherine V. (1978) "Adjusting and Justifying the A-Over-A Principle (with Evidence from Second Language Acquisition)." In *Studies in Honor of Horace G. Lunt*, Part 1, Ernest Scatton, Richard Steele, and Charles Gribble (eds.), 71–80. Columbus, Ohio: Slavica. (Also published in *Folia Slavic 2*, 1–2.)

Chvany, Catherine V. (1984) "From Jakobson's Cube as *objet d'art* to a New Model of the Grammatical Sign," *International Journal of Slavic Linguistics and Poetics* 29, 43–70.

Chvany, Catherine V. (1985) "Backgrounded Perfective and Plot Line Imperfectives: Toward a Theory of Grounding in Text." In *The Scope of Slavic Aspect*, Michael Flier and Alan Timberlake (eds.), 247–73. Columbus, Ohio: Slavica.

Chvany, Catherine V. (1986) "Jakobson's Fourth and Fifth Dimensions: On Reconciling the Cube Model of Case Meaning with the Two-dimensional Matrices for Case Form." In *Case in Slavic*, R. D. Brecht and J. Levine (eds.), 107–29. Columbus, Ohio: Slavica.

Chvany, Catherine V. (1992) "Multi-level Markedness in Russian, English and Bulgarian." In *Papers in General and Computational Linguistics in Honor of Henry Kučera*, Andrew Mackie, Tatyana McAuley, and Cynthia Simmons (eds.), 1–22. Ann Arbor: Michigan Slavic Publications.

Chvany, Catherine V. (1993) "The Evolution of the Concept of Markedness—From the Prague Circle to Generative Grammar." In *Tradition and Change in Central and Eastern Europe*, Henrietta Mondry and Paul Schveiger (eds.), 41–57. Johannesburg: University of Witwatersrand.

Cinque, Guglielmo (1982) "On the Theory of Relative Clauses and Markedness," *Linguistic Review* 1, 247–94.

Clark, Herbert (1970) "The Primitive Nature of Children's Relational Concepts." In *Cognition and the Development of Language*, J. R. Hayes (ed.), 269–78. New York: John Wiley and Sons.

Clark, Robin (1989) "Causality and Parameter Setting," *Brain and Behavioral Sciences* 12.2, 337–8.

Cole, Peter, Gabriella Hermon, and L.-M. Sung (1990) "Principles and Parameters of Long-Distance Reflexives," *Linguistic Inquiry* 21.1, 1–22.

Comrie, Bernard (1986) "Markedness, Grammar, People, and the World." In *Markedness*, Fred R. Eckman, Edith A. Moravcsik, and Jessica R. Wirth, (eds.), 85–106. New York: Plenum.

Crain, S. (1992) Review of Yosef Grodzinsky's *Theoretical Perspectives on Language Deficits*. *Language* 68.3, 624–33.

Croft, William (1990) *Typology and Universals*. Cambridge: Cambridge University Press.

Dell, F. (1981) "On the Learnability of Optional Phonological Rules," *Linguistic Inquiry* 12.1, 31–7.

Dokulil, M. (1958) "K Otazce Morfologickych Protikladu," *Slovo a Slovesnost* 19, 81–103.

Donaldson, Margaret, and Roger Wales (1970) "On the Acquisition of Some Relational Terms." In *Cognition and the Development of Language*, J. R. Hayes (ed.), 235–68. New York.: John Wiley and Sons.

Dressler, Wolfgang (1985) *Morphonology: The Dynamics of Derivation*. Ann Arbor, Mich.: Karoma.

Dressler, Wolfgang (1989) "Markedness and Naturalness." In *Markedness in Synchrony and Diachrony*, O. M. Tomić (ed.), 111–20. Berlin & New York: Mouton.

Dressler, Wolfgang (1995) "Interactions Between Iconicity and Other Semiotic Parameters in Language." In *Iconicity in Language*, R. Simone (ed.), 21–37. Amsterdam & Philadelphia: John Benjamins.

Dressler, Wolfgang, Willi Mayerthaler, Oswald Panagl, and Wolfgang Wurzel (1987) *Leitmotifs in Natural Morphology*. Amsterdam & Philadelphia: John Benjamins.

Eckman, Fred R. (1977) "Markedness and the Contrastive Analysis Hypothesis," *Language Learning* 27.2, 315–30.

Eckman, F., L. Bell, and D. Nelson, eds. (1988) *Universals of Second Language Acquisition*. Rowley, Mass.: Newbury House.

Eubank, Lynn (1989) "Parameters and L2 Learning: Flynn Revisited," *Second Language Research* 5, 43–73.

Eubank, Lynn, ed. (1991) *Universal Grammar in Second Language Acquisition*. Amsterdam & Philadelphia: John Benjamins.

Ferguson, Charles, and Carol B. Farwell (1975) "Words and Sounds in Early Language Acquisition," *Language* 51.2, 419–39.

Finegan, Edward, and Niko Besnier (1989) *Language: Its Structure and Use*. New York: Harcourt Brace Jovanovich.

Finer, Daniel (1991) "Binding Parameters in Second Language Acquisition." In *Universal Grammar in Second Language Acquisition*, Lynn Eubank (ed.), 351–74. Amsterdam & Philadelphia: John Benjamins.

Finer, Daniel, and Ellen Broselow (1986) "Second Language Acquisition of Reflexive Binding." In *Proceedings of the Sixteenth Meeting of the North East Linguistic Society*, S. Berman, J.-W. Choe, and J. McDonough (eds.), 154–68. Amherst, Mass.: Graduate Linguistics Student Association.

Flynn, Suzanne (1987) *A Parameter Setting Model of L2 Acquisition*. Dordrecht: Reidel.

Flynn, Suzanne, and Wayne O'Neil, eds. (1988) *Linguistic Theory and Second Language Acquisition*. Dordrecht: Kluwer.

Frazier, Lynn (1978) *On Comprehending Sentences*. Ph.D. diss., University of Connecticut.

Freud, Sigmund (1953 [1891]) *On Aphasia*. New York: International Universities Press.

Gair, James W. (1988) "Kinds of Markedness." In *Linguistic Theory and Second Language Acquisition*, S. Flynn and W. O'Neil (eds.), 225–50. Dordrecht: Kluwer.

Gamkrelidze, Thomas V. (1989) "Markedness, Sound Change and Linguistic Reconstruction." In *Markedness in Synchrony and Diachrony*, O. M. Tomić (ed.), 87–101. Berlin & New York: Mouton de Gruyter.

Gamkrelidze, Thomas V. (1991) "Language Typology and Diachronic Linguistics." In *New Vistas in Grammar: Invariance and Variation*, Linda Waugh and Stephen Rudy (eds.), 465–72. Amsterdam & Philadelphia: John Benjamins.

Gass, Susan, and Jacqueline Schachter, eds. (1989) *Linguistic Perspective on Second Language Acquisition*. Cambridge: Cambridge University Press.

Gazdar, Gerald, Ewan Klein, Geoffrey Pullum, and Ivan Sag (1985) *Generalized Phrase Structure Grammar*. Cambridge: Harvard University Press.

Givón, Talmy (1990) *Syntax: A Functional-Typological Introduction* (Vol. 2). Amsterdam & Philadelphia: John Benjamins.

Goodglass, Harold (1968) "Studies on the Grammar of Aphasics." In *Developments in Applied Psycholinguistic Research*, S. Rosenberg and J. H. Koplin (eds.), 177–208. New York: Macmillan.

Green, Georgia (1974) *Semantics and Syntactic Regularity*. Bloomington: Indiana University Press.

Greenberg, Joseph (1963) "Some Universals of Grammar with Particular Reference to the Order of Meaningful Elements." In *Universals of Language*, J. Greenberg (ed.), 73–113. Cambridge: MIT Press.

Greenberg, Joseph (1966) *Language Universals*. The Hague: Mouton.

Greenberg, Joseph (1978) "Diachrony, Synchrony and Language Universals." In *Universals of Language*, J. Greenberg (ed.), Vol. 1, 61–91. Stanford: Stanford University Press.

Greenberg, Joseph (1991) "Two Approaches to Language Universals." In *New Vistas in Grammar: Invariance and Variation*, Linda Waugh and Stephen Rudy, (eds.), 417–35. Amsterdam & Philadelphia: John Benjamins.

Greimas, A. J. (1983 [1966]) *Structural Semantics: An Attempt at Method*, Daniele McDowell, Ronald Schleifer, and Alan Velie (trans.). Lincoln: University of Nebraska Press.

Grimshaw, Jane (forthcoming) "Minimal Projection, Heads, and Optimality," *Linguistic Inquiry*.

Grodzinsky, Yosef (1990) *Theoretical Perspectives on Language Deficits*. Cambridge: MIT Press.

Gropen, Jess, Steven Pinker, Michelle Hollander, Richard Goldberg, and Ronald Wilson (1989) "The Learnability and Acquisition of the Dative Alternation," *Language* 65.2, 203–57.

Gundel, Jeanette K., Kathleen Houlihan, and Gerald K. Sanders (1986)

"Markedness and Distribution in Phonology and Syntax." In *Markedness*, F. Eckman, Edith A. Moravcsik, and Jessica R. Wirth (eds.), 107–38. New York: Plenum.

Gvozdanović, Jadranka (1989) "Defining Markedness." In *Markedness in Synchrony and Diachrony*, O. M. Tomić (ed.), 47–66. New York: Mouton de Gruyter.

Haiman, John (1980) "The Iconicity of Grammar," *Language* 56.3, 515–40.

Haiman, John (1983) "Iconic and Economic Motivation," *Language* 59.4, 781–819.

Haiman, John (1985) *Natural Syntax*. Cambridge: Cambridge University Press.

Hale, Kenneth (1976) "Linguistic Autonomy and the Linguistics of Carl Voegelin," *Anthropological Linguistics*, 18, 120–8.

Haley, Michael, and Ronald Lunsford (1994) *Noam Chomsky*. New York: Twayne.

Halle, Morris (1959a) "Questions of Linguistics," *Nuovo Cimento* 13, 494–517.

Halle, Morris (1959b) *The Sound Pattern of Russian*. The Hague: Mouton.

Halle, Morris (1961) "On the Role of Simplicity in Grammatical Description." In *The Structure of Language and its Mathematical Aspects*, Roman Jakobson (ed.), 89–94. Providence, R.I.: American Mathematical Society.

Halle, Morris (1962) "Phonology in Generative Grammar." In *The Structure of Language*, Jerry Fodor and Jerrold J. Katz (eds.), 334–52. Englewood Cliffs, N.J.: Prentice Hall, 1964.

Halle, Morris (1964) "On the Bases of Phonology." In *The Structure of Language*, Jerry Fodor and Jerrold J. Katz (eds.), 324–33. Englewood Cliffs, N.J.: Prentice Hall, 1964.

Halle, Morris (1977) "Roman Jakobson's Contribution to the Modern Study of Speech Sounds." In *Roman Jakobson: Echoes of His Scholarship*, Daniel Armstrong and C. H. van Schooneveld (eds.), 123–43. Lisse, Netherlands: Peter de Ridder.

Halle, Morris (1992) Review of Roman Jakobson's *On Language*. *Language* 68.1, 182–6.

Hatten, Robert (1994) *Musical Meaning in Beethoven: Markedness, Correlation, and Interpretation*. Bloomington: Indiana University Press.

Hildebrand, J. (1987) "The Acquisition of Preposition Stranding," *Canadian Journal of Linguistics* 32.1, 65–85.

Hirschbühler, Paul, and Maria-Luisa Rivero (1981) "Catalan Restrictive Relatives," *Language* 57.3, 591–625.

Hjelmslev, Louis (1935) *La catégories des cas*. Aarhus, Denmark: Universitetsforlaget.

Hjelmslev, Louis (1969 [1953]) *Prolegomena to a Theory of Language*, Francis J. Whitfield (trans.). Madison: University of Wisconsin Press.

Holenstein, Elmar (1976) *Roman Jakobson's Approach to Language: Phenomenological Structuralism*, Catherine and Tarcisius Schelbert (trans.). Bloomington: Indiana University Press.

Hornstein, Norbert, and Amy Weinberg (1981) "Case Theory and Preposition Stranding," *Linguistic Inquiry* 12.1, 55–91.

Hyams, Nina (1986) *Language Acquisition and the Theory of Parameters.* Dordrecht: D. Reidel.

Ingram, David (1988) "Jakobson Revisited: Some Evidence from the Acquisition of Polish," *Lingua* 75, 55–82.

Jakobson, Roman (1921) "Recent Russian Poetry" [in Russian]. In *Selected Writings V: On Verse, Its Masters and Explorers,* 299–354. Berlin, New York, & Amsterdam: Mouton, 1979.

Jakobson, Roman (1928) "Proposition au Premier Congrés International de Linguistes." In *Selected Writings I: Phonological Studies,* 3–6. The Hague: Mouton, 1962 (exp. ed. 1971).

Jakobson, Roman (1932) "The Structure of the Russian Verb." In *Russian and Slavic Grammar Studies, 1931–1981,* Linda R. Waugh and Morris Halle (eds.), 1–14. Berlin, New York, & Amsterdam: Mouton, 1984.

Jakobson, Roman (1935) "The Dominant." In *Language in Literature,* Krystyna Pomorska and Stephen Rudy (eds.), 41–6. Cambridge: Harvard University Press, 1987.

Jakobson, Roman (1936) "Contributions to the General Theory of Case: General Meanings of the Russian Cases." In *Russian and Slavic Grammar Studies,* 59–103, 1984.

Jakobson, Roman (1939) "Zero Sign." In *Russian and Slavic Grammar Studies,* 151–60, 1984.

Jakobson, Roman (1948) "Russian Conjugation." In *Russian and Slavic Grammar Studies,* 15–26, 1984.

Jakobson, Roman (1949a) "The Sound Laws of Child Language and Their Place in General Phonology." In *Studies on Child Language and Aphasia,* 7–20. The Hague: Mouton, 1971.

Jakobson, Roman (1949b) "The Identification of Phonemic Entities." In *Selected Writings I,* 418–25, 1962.

Jakobson, Roman (1955) "Aphasia as a Linguistic Topic." In *Selected Writings II: Word and Language,* 229–38. The Hague: Mouton, 1971.

Jakobson, Roman (1956) "Two Aspects of Language and Two Types of Aphasic Disturbances." In *Selected Writings II,* 239–59, 1971.

Jakobson, Roman (1957a) "Shifters, Verbal Categories, and the Russian Verb." In *Russian and Slavic Grammar Studies,* 41–58, 1984.

Jakobson, Roman (1957b) "The Relationship Between Genitive and Plural in the Declension of Russian Nouns." In *Russian and Slavic Grammar Studies,* 135–40, 1984.

Jakobson, Roman (1958) "Morphological Observations on Slavic Declension (The Structure of Russian Case Forms)." In *Russian and Slavic Grammar Studies,* 105–33, 1984.

Jakobson, Roman (1959) "On the Rumanian Neuter." In *Selected Writings II,* 187–9, 1971.

Jakobson, Roman (1960a) "The Gender Pattern of Russian." In *Russian and Slavic Grammar Studies,* 141–3, 1984.

Jakobson, Roman (1960b) "Linguistics and Poetics." In *Selected Writings III:*

Poetry of Grammar and Grammar of Poetry, 18–51. The Hague: Mouton, 1981.

Jakobson, Roman (1963) "Implications of Language Universals for Linguistics." In *Universals of Language*, Joseph Greenberg (ed.), 263–78. Cambridge: MIT Press, 1963.

Jakobson, Roman (1964) "Toward a Linguistic Classification of Aphasic Impairments." In *Selected Writings II*, 289–306, 1971.

Jakobson, Roman (1966a) "Linguistic Types of Aphasia." In *Selected Writings II*, 307–33, 1971.

Jakobson, Roman (1966b) "Quest for the Essence of Language." in *Selected Writings II*, 345–59, 1971.

Jakobson, Roman (1968a [1941]) *Child Language, Aphasia and Phonological Universals*, Allan R. Keiler (trans.). The Hague: Mouton.

Jakobson, Roman (1968b) "The Role of Phonic Elements." In *Selected Writings I* (exp. ed.), 705–19, 1971.

Jakobson, Roman (1970) "Linguistics in Relation to Other Sciences." In *Selected Writings II*, 655–96, 1971.

Jakobson, Roman (1971a) "Retrospect." In *Selected Writings II*, 711–22, 1971.

Jakobson, Roman (1971b) *Studies on Child Language and Aphasia*. The Hague: Mouton.

Jakobson, Roman (1972) "Human Communication." In *Selected Writings VII: Contributions to Comparative Mythology: Studies in Linguistics and Philology, 1972–1982*, 81–92. The Hague: Mouton, 1985.

Jakobson, Roman (1974) "Mark and Feature." In *Selected Writings VII*, 122–4, 1985.

Jakobson, Roman (1975) "On Aphasic Disorders from a Linguistic Angle." In *The Framework of Language*, 93–111. Ann Arbor: Michigan Studies in the Humanities, 1980.

Jakobson, Roman (1980) *The Framework of Language*. Ann Arbor: Michigan Studies in the Humanities.

Jakobson, Roman (1981) "Notes on the Declension of Pronouns." *Russian and Slavic Grammar Studies*, 145–9, 1984.

Jakobson, Roman (1984) *Russian and Slavic Grammar Studies, 1931–1981*, Linda R. Waugh and Morris Halle (eds.). Berlin: Mouton de Gruyter.

Jakobson, Roman (1987) *Language in Literature*. Krystyna Pomorska and Stephen Rudy (eds.). Cambridge: Harvard University Press.

Jakobson, Roman (1990) *On Language*. Linda R. Waugh and Monique Monville-Burston (eds.). Cambridge: Harvard University Press.

Jakobson, Roman, E. Colin Cherry, and Morris Halle (1953) "Toward a Logical Description of Languages in Their Phonemic Aspect." In *Selected Writings I*, 449–64, 1962.

Jakobson, Roman, and Morris Halle (1956) *Fundamentals of Language* (2nd rev. ed.). The Hague: Mouton, 1971).

Jakobson, Roman, and John Lotz (1949) "Notes on the French Phonemic Pattern." In *Selected Writings I*, 426–34, 1962.

Jakobson, Roman, and Krystyna Pomorska (1983 [1980]) *Dialogues with Krystyna Pomorska*. Cambridge: MIT Press.

Jakobson, Roman, and Linda Waugh (1979) *The Sound Shape of Language*. Berlin, New York, & Amsterdam: Mouton.

Katz, Jerrold J. (1980) "Chomsky on Meaning," *Language* 56.1, 1–41.

Kayne, Richard (1981) "On Certain Differences Between French and English," *Linguistic Inquiry* 12.3, 349–71.

Kean, Mary-Louise (1977) "The Linguistic Interpretation of Aphasic Syndromes," *Cognition* 5, 9–46.

Kean, Mary-Louise (1980) *The Theory of Markedness in Generative Grammar* [Ph.D. diss., Massachusetts Institute of Technology, 1975]. Bloomington: Indiana University Linguistics Club.

Kean, Mary-Louise (1981) "On a Theory of Markedness: Some General Considerations and a Case in Point." In *Theory of Markedness in Core Grammar*, A. Belletti, L. Brandi, and L. Rizzi (eds.), 559–604. Pisa: Scuola Normale Superiore di Pisa.

Kean, Mary-Louise (1986) "Core Issues in Transfer." In *Cross Linguistic Influence in Second Language Acquisition*, E. Kellerman and M. Sharwood Smith (eds.), 80–90. Oxford: Pergamon.

Keenan, Edward, and Bernard Comrie (1976) "Noun Phrase Accessibility and Universal Grammar," *Linguistic Inquiry* 8.1, 63–99.

Kellerman, E. (1985) "Dative Alternation and the Analysis of Data: A Reply to Mazurkewich," *Language Learning* 35, 91–106.

Kellerman, E., and M. Sharwood Smith, eds. (1986) *Cross Linguistic Influence in Second Language Acquisition*. Oxford: Pergamon.

Kiparsky, Paul (1966) "Über den deutschen Akzent," *Studia Grammatika* 7, 69–98.

Kiparsky, Paul (1968) "Linguistic Universals and Language Change." In *Universals in Linguistic Theory*, E. Bach and R. Harms (eds.), 170–202. New York: Holt.

Kiparsky, Paul (1974) "Remarks on Analogical Change." In *Historical Linguistics* (Vol. 2), J. M. Anderson and Charles Jones (eds.), 257–75. Amsterdam: North Holland.

Kiparsky, Paul, and Lise Menn (1977) "On the Acquisition of Phonology." In *Language Learning and Thought*, J. MacNamara (ed.), 47–78. New York: Academic Press.

Klein, Elaine C. (1993) *Toward Second Language Acquisition: A Study of Null-Prep.* Dordrecht: Kluwer.

Koster, Jan (1978) "Conditions, Empty Nodes, and Markedness," *Linguistic Inquiry* 9.4, 551–93.

Kučera, Henry (1980) "Markedness in Motion." In *Morphosyntax in Slavic*, Catherine V. Chvany and Richard Brecht (eds.), 15–42. Columbus, Ohio: Slavica.

Kučera, Henry (1984) "The Logical Basis of the Markedness Hypothesis." In *Language and Literary Theory*, B. Stolz, J. Titunik, and L. Doležal (eds.), 61–75. Ann Arbor: Michigan Slavic Publications.

Kuipers, Aert H. (1975) "On Symbol, Distinction and Markedness," *Lingua* 36, 31–46.

Lakoff, George (1970) *Irregularity in Syntax*. New York: Holt.

Lakoff, George (1987) *Women, Fire and Dangerous Things*. Chicago: University of Chicago Press.

Lakoff, Robin Tolmach (1968) *Abstract Syntax and Latin Complementation*. Cambridge: MIT Press.

Lambrecht, Knud (1994) *Information Structure and Sentence Form*. Cambridge: Cambridge University Press.

Lapointe, Steven G. (1986) "Markedness, the Organization of Linguistic Information in Speech Production, and Language Acquisition." In *Markedness*, F. Eckman, E. Moravcsik, and J. Wirth (eds.), 219–39. New York: Plenum.

Lasnik, Howard (1981a) "Learnability, Restrictiveness and the Evaluation Metric." In *Essays on Restrictiveness and Learnability*, H. Lasnik (ed.), 146–62. Dordrecht: Kluwer, 1990.

Lasnik, Howard (1981b) "On a Lexical Parameter in the Government-Binding Theory." In *Essays on Restrictiveness and Learnability*, 163–71, 1990.

Lasnik, Howard (1981c) "Restricting the Theory of Transformations: A Case Study." In *Essays on Restrictiveness and Learnability*, 125–45, 1990.

Lasnik, Howard (1983) "On Certain Substitutes for Negative Data." In *Essays on Restrictiveness and Learnability*, 184–97, 1990.

Lasnik, Howard, ed. (1990) *Essays on Restrictiveness and Learnability*. Dordrecht: Kluwer.

Lasnik, Howard, and Robert Freidin (1981) "Core Grammar, Case Theory, and Markedness." In *Essays on Restrictiveness and Learnability*, 172–83, 1990.

Lasnik, Howard, and Joseph Kupin (1977) "A Restrictive Theory of Transformational Grammar." In *Essays on Restrictiveness and Learnability*, 17–41, 1990.

Lehmann, Christian (1989) "Markedness and Grammaticalization." In *Markedness in Synchrony and Diachrony*, O. M. Tomić (ed.), 175–90. New York & Berlin: Mouton.

Lehrer, Adrienne (1985) "Markedness and Antonymy," *Journal of Linguistics* 21, 397–429.

Li, Yen-hui Audrey (1990) *Order and Constituency in Mandarin Chinese*. Dordrecht: Kluwer.

Liceras, Juana (1985) "The Role of Intake in the Determination of Learners' Competence." In *Input in Second Language Acquisition*, S. Gass and C. Madden (eds.), 354–73. Rowley, Mass.: Newbury House.

Liceras, Juana (1986) *Linguistic Theory and Second Language Acquisition*. Tübingen: Narr.

Liceras, Juana (1988) "L2 Learnability: Delimiting the Domain of Core Grammar as Distinct from the Marked Periphery." In *Linguistic Theory and Second Language Acquisition*, S. Flynn and W. O'Neil (eds.), 199–224. Dordrecht: Kluwer.

Lightfoot, David (1979) *Principles of Diachronic Syntax*. Cambridge: Cambridge University Press.

Lightfoot, David (1991) *How to Set Parameters*. Cambridge: MIT Press.

Liszka, James Jakób (1982) "A Critique of Levi-Strauss' Theory of Myth and the Elements of a Semiotic Alternative." In *Semiotics 1981*, Michael Herzfeld and Margo Lenhart (eds.), 297–306. New York: Plenum.

Liszka, James Jakób (1989) *The Semiotic of Myth*. Bloomington: Indiana University Press.

Lyons, John (1977a) *Noam Chomsky*. New York: Penguin.

Lyons, John (1977b) *Semantics* (2 vols.). Cambridge: Cambridge University Press.

Manzini, M. Rita, and Kenneth Wexler (1987) "Parameters, Binding Theory, and Learnability," *Linguistic Inquiry* 18.3, 413–44.

Mayerthaler, Willi (1988 [1981]) *Morphological Naturalness*, Janice Seidler (trans.). Ann Arbor, Mich.: Karoma.

Mazurkewich, Irene (1984a) "The Acquisition of Dative Questions by Second Language Learners and Linguistic Theory," *Language Learning* 34, 91–109.

Mazurkewich, Irene (1984b) "Dative Questions and Markedness." In *Universals of Second Language Acquisition*, F. Eckman, L. Bell, and D. Nelson, (eds.), 119–31. Rowley, Mass.: Newbury House.

Mazurkewich, Irene, and Lydia White (1984) "The Acquisition of the Dative Alternation," *Cognition* 16.3, 261–83.

McCawley, James D. (1985) "Kuhnian Paradigms as Systems of Markedness Conventions." In *Linguistics and Philosophy: Studies in Honor of Rulon S. Wells*, Adam Makkai and Alan Melby (eds.), 23–43. Amsterdam & Philadelphia: John Benjamins.

Menn, Lise (1986) "Language Acquisition, Aphasia, and Phonotactic Universals." In *Markedness*, F. Eckman, E. Moravcsik, and J. Wirth (eds.), 241–69. New York: Plenum.

Moravcsik, Edith, and Jessica Wirth (1986) "Markedness—An Overview." In *Markedness*, F. Eckman, E. Moravcsik, and J. Wirth (eds.), 1–11. New York: Plenum.

Mufwene, Salikoko (1991) "Pidgins, Creole, Typology and Markedness." In *Development and Structures of Creole Languages*, Frank Byrne and Thom Huebner, (eds.), 123–43. Amsterdam & Philadelphia: John Benjamins.

Muysken, Peter (1981) "Quechua Causatives and Logical Form: A Case Study in Markedness." In *Theory of Markedness in Core Grammar*, A. Belletti, L. Brandi, and L. Rizzi (eds.), 445–73. Pisa: Scuola Normale Superiore di Pisa.

Newfield, Madeleine, and Linda Waugh (1991) "Invariance and Markedness in Grammatical Categories." In *New Vistas in Grammar: Invariance and Variation*, Linda Waugh and Stephen Rudy (eds.), 221–38. Amsterdam & Philadelphia: John Benjamins.

Newmeyer, Frederick J. (1986) *Linguistic Theory in America* (2nd ed.). New York: Academic.

O'Grady, William (1987a) *Principles of Grammar and Learning*. Chicago: University of Chicago Press.

O'Grady, William (1987b) "The Interpretation of Korean Anaphora," *Language* 63.2, 251–77.

Pankhurst, James, Michael Sharwood Smith, and Paul Van Buren, eds. (1988) *Learnability and Second Languages: A Book of Readings*. Dordrecht: Foris.

Phinney, Marianne (1987) "The Pro-drop Parameter in Second Language Acquisition." In *Parameter Setting*, T. Roeper and E. Williams (eds.), 221–38. Dordrecht: Reidel.

Pinker, Steven (1984) *Language Learnability and Language Development*. Cambridge: Harvard University Press.

Pinker, Steven (1989) "Learnability and Linguistic Theory." In *Learnability and Linguistic Theory*, Robert Matthews and William Demopoulos (eds.), 107–27. Dordrecht: Kluwer.

Postal, Paul (1968) *Aspects of Phonological Theory*. New York: Harper and Row.

Prince, Alan, and Paul Smolensky (1993) *Optimality Theory: Constraint Interaction in Generative Grammar*. Piscataway, N.J.: Technical Report of the Rutgers Center for Cognitive Science.

Rizzi, Luigi, and Ian Roberts (1989) "Complex Inversion in French," *Probus* 1.1, 1–30.

Rosenbaum, Peter (1967) *The Grammar of English Predicate Constructions*. Cambridge: MIT Press.

Ross, John R. (1987) "Islands and Syntactic Prototypes." In *Papers from the 23rd Annual Regional Meeting of the Chicago Linguistic Society* (Part 1: The General Session), B. Need, Eric Schiller, and Anna Bosch (eds.), 309–20. Chicago: Chicago Linguistic Society.

Rothstein, Robert (1973) "Sex, Gender and the October Revolution." In *A Festschrift for Morris Halle*, S. R. Anderson and P. Kiparsky (eds.), 460–6. New York: Holt.

Rouveret, A., and J.-R. Vergnaud (1980) "Specifying Reference to the Subject," *Linguistic Inquiry* 11, 97–202.

Rutherford, William, ed. (1984) *Language Universals and Second Language Acquisition*. Amsterdam & Philadelphia: John Benjamins.

Sangster, Rodney (1982) *Roman Jakobson and Beyond: Language as a System of Signs*. Berlin: Mouton.

Sangster, Rodney (1991) "Two Types of Markedness and Their Implications for the Conceptualization of Grammatical Invariance." In *New Vistas in Grammar: Invariance and Variation*, Linda Waugh and Stephen Rudy (eds.), 133–51. Amsterdam & Philadelphia: John Benjamins.

Sapir, Edward (1944) "Grading: A Study in Semantics." In *Selected Writings of Edward Sapir in Language, Culture, Personality*, David G. Mandelbaum (ed.), 122–49. Berkeley: University of California Press, 1963.

Schachter, Paul (1969) "Natural Assimilation Rules in Akan," *International Journal of American Linguistics* 35, 342–55.

Schleifer, Ronald (1987) *A. J. Greimas and the Nature of Meaning*. Lincoln: University of Nebraska Press.

Scholes, Robert (1974) *Structuralism in Literature*. New Haven: Yale University Press.

Shannon, Thomas (1986) Book notice of Michael Shapiro's *The Sense of Grammar.* *Language* 62.1, 233–4.

Shapiro, Michael (1972) "Explorations into Markedness," *Language* 48.2, 343–64.

Shapiro, Michael (1983) *The Sense of Grammar.* Bloomington: Indiana University Press.

Shapiro, Michael (1988) "The Meaning of Meter." In *Russian Verse Theory*, B. Scherr and D. S. Worth (eds.), 331–49. Columbus, Ohio: Slavica.

Shapiro, Michael (1991) *The Sense of Change.* Bloomington: Indiana University Press.

Sharwood Smith, Michael (1994) *Second Language Learning: Theoretical Foundations.* London & New York: Longman.

Silverstein, Michael (1976) "Hierarchy of Features and Ergativity." In *Grammatical Categories of Australian Languages*, Robert M. W. Dixon (ed.), 112–71. Canberra: Australian Institute of Aboriginal Studies.

Stanley, Richard (1967) "Redundancy Rules in Phonology," *Language* 43, 393–437.

Stewart, J. M. (1967) "Tongue Root Position in Akan Vowel Harmony," *Phonetica* 16, 185–204.

Stowell, Timothy (1981) *Origins of Phrase Structure.* Ph.D. diss., Massachusetts Institute of Technology.

Taraldsen, Tarald (1981) "The Theoretical Interpretation of a Class of Marked Extractions." In *Theory of Markedness in Core Grammar*, A. Belletti, L. Brandi, and L. Rizzi (eds.), 475–516. Pisa: Scuola Normale Superiore di Pisa.

Thomas, Margaret (1991) "Do Second Language Learners Have 'Rogue' Grammars of Anaphora?" In *Universal Grammar in Second Language Acquisition*, Lynn Eubank (ed.), 375–88. Amsterdam & Philadelphia: John Benjamins.

Tiersma, Peter (1982) "Local and General Markedness," *Language* 58.4, 832–49.

Timberlake, Alan (1987) "Grammar as Metalinguistic Text," *International Journal of Slavic Linguistics and Poetics* 25/26, 267–84.

Tobin, Yishai (1991) "Invariant Meaning: Alternative Variations on an Invariant Theme." In *New Vistas in Grammar: Invariance and Variation*, Linda Waugh and Stephen Rudy (eds.), 61–82. Amsterdam & Philadelphia: John Benjamins.

Tobin, Yishai (1993) *Aspect in the English Verb: Process and Result in Language.* London & New York: Longman.

Tobin, Yishai (1994) *Invariance, Markedness and Distinctive Feature Analysis.* Amsterdam & Philadelphia: John Benjamins.

Toman, Jindřich (1995) *The Magic of a Common Language: Jakobson, Mathesius, Trubetzkoy, and the Prague Linguistic Circle.* Cambridge: MIT Press.

Tomić, Olga M. (1989) *Markedness in Synchrony and Diachrony.* Berlin & New York: Mouton.

Treichler, Paula A., and Francine Wattman Frank (1989) "Introduction: Scholarship, Feminism, and Language Change." In *Language, Gender and Professional Writing*, Francine Frank and Paula Treichler (eds.), 1–32. New York: Modern Language Association.

Trubetzkoy, Nikolai (1931) "Die phonologischen Systeme," *Travaux du Cercle Linguistique de Prague* 4, 96–116.

Trubetzkoy, Nikolai (1936) "Die Aufhebung der phonologischen Gegensätze," *Travaux du Cercle Linguistique de Prague* 6, 29–45.

Trubetzkoy, Nikolai (1969 [1939]) *Principles of Phonology*, Christiane A. M. Baltaxe (trans.). Berkeley & Los Angeles: University of California Press.

Trubetzkoy, Nikolai (1975) *Letters and Notes*, Roman Jakobson (ed.). The Hague: Mouton.

Utaker, Arild (1974) "On the Binary Opposition," *Linguistics* 134, 73–93.

Van Buren, P., and M. Sharwood Smith (1985) "The Acquisition of Preposition Stranding by Second Language Learners and Parameter Setting," *Second Language Research* 1, 18–26.

van Langendonck, W. (1986) "Markedness, Prototypes and Language Acquisition," *Cahiers de l'institut de linguistique de Louvain* 12.3/4, 39–76.

van Riemsdijk, Henk (1982) *A Case Study in Syntactic Markedness*. Dordrecht: Foris.

van Schooneveld, Cornelius H. (1978) *Semantic Transmutations*. Bloomington, Ind.: Physsardt.

van Schooneveld, Cornelius H. (1991) "Praguean Structure and Autopoiesis: Deixis as Individuation." In *New Vistas in Grammar: Invariance and Variation*, Linda Waugh and Stephen Rudy (eds.), 341–62. Amsterdam & Philadelphia: John Benjamins.

Vennemann, Theo (1972) "Sound Change and Markedness Theory: On the History of the German Consonant System." In *Linguistic Change and Generative Theory*, R. P. Stockwell and Ronald Macauley (eds.), 230–74. Bloomington: Indiana University Press.

Verrier, Paul (1909) *Essai sur les principles de la métrique anglaise*. Paris: Libraire Universitaire.

Viel, Michel (1984) *La notion 'marque' chez Trubetzkoy et Jakobson*. Paris: Didier.

Waugh, Linda (1976a) *Roman Jakobson's Science of Language*. Lisse, Netherlands: Peter de Ridder.

Waugh, Linda (1976b) "The Semantics and Paradigmatics of Word Order," *Language* 52.1, 82–107.

Waugh, Linda (1982) "Marked and Unmarked: A Choice Between Unequals in Semiotic Structure," *Semiotica* 38, 299–318.

Waugh, Linda, and Monique Monville-Burston (1990) "Introduction: The Life, Work, and Influence of Roman Jakobson." In Roman Jakobson, *On Language*, 1–45. Cambridge: Harvard University Press.

Weinberg, Amy (1990) "Markedness Versus Maturation: The Case of Subject-Auxiliary Inversion," *Language Acquisition* 1.2, 165–94.

Weinreich, Uriel (1966) "Explorations in Semantic Theory." In *Current Trends in Linguistics 3*, T. Sebeok (ed.), 395–479. The Hague: Mouton.

Wexler, Kenneth (1981) "Some Issues in the Theory of Learnability." In *The Logical Problem of Language Acquisition*, C. L. Baker and J. McCarthy (eds.), 30–51. Cambridge: MIT Press.

Wexler, Kenneth, and Y.-C. Chien (1988) "The Acquisition of Binding Principles." Paper presented at the 11th meeting of the Generative Linguists of the Old World Colloquium, Budapest, Hungary.

Wexler, Kenneth, and Peter Culicover (1980) *Formal Principles of Language Acquisition.* Cambridge: MIT Press.

White, Lydia (1982) *Grammatical Theory and Language Acquisition.* Dordrecht: Foris.

White, Lydia (1985) "The Acquisition of Parameterized Grammars," *Second Language Acquisition Research* 1, 1–17.

White, Lydia (1986) "Markedness and Parameter Setting: Some Implications for a Theory of Adult Second Language Acquisition." In *Markedness*, F. Eckman, E. Moravcsik, and J. Wirth (eds.), 309–27. New York: Plenum.

White, Lydia (1987) "Markedness and Second Language Acquisition: The Question of Transfer," *Studies in Second Language Acquisition* 9, 261–86.

White, Lydia (1989a) "The Adjacency Condition in Second Language Acquisition: Do L2 Learners Observe the Subset Principle?" In *Linguistic Perspectives on Second Language Acquisition*, S. Gass and J. Schachter (eds.), 134–58. Cambridge: Cambridge University Press.

White, Lydia (1989b) *Universal Grammar and Second Language Acquisition.* Amsterdam & Philadelphia: John Benjamins.

Wierzbicka, Anna (1980) *The Case for Surface Case.* Ann Arbor, Mich.: Karoma.

Williams, Edwin (1981) "Language Acquisition, Markedness, and Phrase Structure." In *Language Acquisition and Linguistic Theory*, S. Tavakolian (ed.), 8–34. Cambridge: MIT Press.

Witkowski, Stanley R., and Cecil H. Brown (1983) "Marking Reversal and Cultural Importance," *Language* 59.3, 569–82.

Woisetschlaeger, Erich F. (1985) *A Semantic Theory of the English Auxiliary System.* New York: Garland.

Zipf, George K. (1935) *The Psycho-biology of Language.* Boston: Houghton-Mifflin.

Zipf, George K. (1949) *Human Behavior and the Principle of Least Effort.* Cambridge, Mass.: Addison-Wesley.

Zobl, Helmut (1983) "Markedness and the Projection Problem," *Language Learning* 33: 293–313.

Zobl, Helmut (1988) "Configurationality and the Subset Principle." In *Learnability and Second Languages: A Book of Readings*, J. Pankhurst, M. Sharwood Smith, and P. Van Buren (eds.), 116–31. Dordrecht: Foris.

Zwicky, Arnold (1978) "On Markedness in Morphology," *Die Sprache* 24, 129–43.

Index